Behind the White House Curtain

A Senior Journalist's Story of Covering the President— and Why It Matters

Steven L Herman

THE KENT STATE UNIVERSITY PRESS

Kent, Ohio

© 2024 by Steven L Herman
All rights reserved
Library of Congress Catalog Number 2023053295
ISBN 978-1-60635-477-3
Published in the United States of America

LIBRARY OF CONGRESS CATALOGING-IN-PUBLICATION DATA

Names: Herman, Steven L, author.
Title: Behind the White House curtain : a senior journalist's story of covering the president—and why it matters / Steven L Herman.
Description: Kent, Ohio : The Kent State University Press, 2024. | Includes bibliographical references and index.
Identifiers: LCCN 2023053295 | ISBN 9781606354773 (hardback) | ISBN 9781631015410 (epub) | ISBN 9781631015427 (pdf)
Subjects: LCSH: Presidents—Press coverage—United States. | Press and politics—United States. | Voice of America (Organization) | Herman, Steven L | Journalists—United States—Biography.
Classification: LCC JK554 .H47 2024 | DDC 327.73001/4--dc23/eng/20240109
LC record available at https://lccn.loc.gov/2023053295

28 27 26 25 24   5 4 3 2 1

For Yangchen

CONTENTS

Foreword *by Scott McClellan* · ix

List of Abbreviations · xi

Introduction · 1

Chapter 1 · 5

Chapter 2 · 13

Chapter 3 · 20

Chapter 4 · 23

Chapter 5 · 27

Chapter 6 · 35

Chapter 7 · 38

Chapter 8 · 42

Chapter 9 · 45

Chapter 10 · 50

Chapter 11 · 57

Chapter 12 · 59

Chapter 13 · 64

Chapter 14 · 81

Chapter 15 · 85

Chapter 16 · 89

Chapter 17 · 95

Chapter 18 · 97

Chapter 19 · 101

Chapter 20 · 105

Chapter 21 · 137

Chapter 22 · 139

Chapter 23 · 145

Chapter 24 · 148

Chapter 25 · 156

Chapter 26 · 161

Chapter 27 · 165

Chapter 28 · 173

Chapter 29 · 178

Chapter 30 · 184

Chapter 31 · 190

Chapter 32 · 196

Epilogue · 201

Acknowledgments · 209

Selected Bibliography · 212

Index · 224

About the Author · 236

FOREWORD

Steve Herman and I worked in the White House at different times, under different political climates, and from different vantage points. What we share is a dedication to the truth and a conviction in the crucial role of a free press to a healthy democracy.

We both left the White House with a deep appreciation for the hardworking correspondents in the White House press corps and their devotion to reporting the news and holding the president and administration accountable for their decisions, actions, and policies. As Herman shares, the role of a White House correspondent is oftentimes far less glamorous and much more laborious than one might surmise but nonetheless critical to scrutinizing the president and keeping the public informed in an age of misinformation and disinformation.

In *Behind the White House Curtain,* readers get a unique and rich perspective on the White House and the tumultuous presidency of Donald J. Trump from a veteran journalist and gifted storyteller. Herman's writing is shaped by decades of experience dealing with government officials and reporting from the front lines, including natural disasters, combat zones, and the 2011 nuclear reactor meltdown in Fukushima, Japan. His keen historical insights are nicely interwoven into the manuscript for additional context. Aspiring journalists, those seeking a career in politics or government, concerned citizens, and anyone interested in learning more about the presidency and White House will be well served by reading this informative and engaging memoir.

The Trump presidency and all its norm-busting chaos is something I never could have envisioned becoming reality. Covering it as a White House correspondent had to have been mind-boggling. For the Voice of America, Steve Herman, and his colleagues, it went beyond that. VOA has and continues to be a trusted source of news for a weekly audience of more than 300 million worldwide thanks to the objective, fact-based, and reliable reporting of its journalists. Herman vividly recounts the period late in the forty-fifth president's term when the Trump administration—in a brazen abuse of power—sought to dismantle VOA and turn it into a promotional arm of the president and his policies. If Herman and his colleagues had not stood firm and fought back or if Trump had been reelected, it is chilling to contemplate what might have happened.

What we can be grateful for is Steve Herman sharing his experiences in the same way he has covered the news for so many years—with objectivity, a shrewd ability to uncover the facts, and a knack for telling the story in a way we can all be better informed and more knowledgeable about what is happening and why it matters.

Scott McClellan
White House Press Secretary, 2003 to 2006

ABBREVIATIONS

ABC	American Broadcasting Company
AEC	Atomic Energy Commission
AFP	Agence France Presse
AP	Associated Press
BBC	British Broadcasting Corporation
BBG	Broadcasting Board of Governors (now USAGM)
CBS	Columbia Broadcasting System
CIA	Central Intelligence Agency
CNN	Cable News Network
CPAP	Continuous positive airway pressure machine
C-SPAN	Cable-Satellite Public Affairs Network
DBIDS	Defense Biometrics Identification System
DMZ	Demilitarized Zone (of the Korean Peninsula)
FBI	Federal Bureau of Investigation
FDR	Franklin Delano Roosevelt
G-7	Group of Seven nations of the large advanced economies
GAP	Government Accountability Project
GOP	Grand Old Party (Republican Party)
IHOP	International House of Pancakes
MSNBC	(originally Microsoft National Broadcasting Company)
MTV	Music Television channel
NAFTA	North Atlantic Free Trade Agreement
NATO	North Atlantic Treaty Organization
NBC	National Broadcasting Company
NHK	Nippon Hōsō Kyōkai (Japan Broadcasting Corporation)
NORC	National Opinion Research Center
NPR	National Public Radio
OANN	One America News Network
OIG	Office of Inspector General

OSC	Office of Special Counsel
OWI	Office of War Information
POTUS	President of the United States
PPD	Presidential Protective Division of the US Secret Service
QSL	Acknowledging receipt of an amateur radio contact
RAF	Royal Air Force (of the United Kingdom)
RFA	Radio Free Asia
RFE/RL	Radio Free Europe/Radio Liberty
SCIF	Sensitive Compartmented Information Facility
SD	Secure Digital flash memory card format
TEPCO	Tokyo Electric Power Company
UP	United Press
UPI	United Press International
USAGM	US Agency for Global Media
VOA	Voice of America
WHCA	White House Correspondents' Association
WHNPA	White House News Photographers Association
XLR	A type of circular plug-and-socket connector for audio devices

INTRODUCTION

Washington, in the District of Columbia, is divided into quadrants. Power and influence reside almost exclusively in one of the city's four quarters—the Northwest. That is the suffix of the street addresses for the White House, the State Department, many of the lobbying firms and top-tier think tanks, plus the tony townhouses of Georgetown. The US Capitol building, on the eastern side of the National Mall, is the center of the federal district from which the quadrants radiate, while the Supreme Court takes the address of 1 First Street Northeast, directly across the street from the Capitol. Gentrification has seeped into the three other quadrants, but most social functions of the elite still occur in Northwest where the first question, as soon as you get a cocktail in hand and greet a fellow attendee, will be: "So, what do you do?" Merely replying "I am a journalist"—which might elicit excitement in Dayton or Dallas—does not satisfy curiosity nor adequately denote one's place in the Beltway pecking order. The area is home to thousands of media personnel, many covering a specific industry or topic, from aviation legislation to zoological management.

There is a battalion of reporters on Capitol Hill, including a dwindling number from local and regional newspapers and broadcasters, keeping tabs on the 535 members of Congress. Many other journalists focus on a particular government agency, such as the Department of Agriculture. And then there is the elite corps covering the president.

"I'm a White House correspondent" in response to the inevitable question invariably invites from all but fellow White House correspondents the follow-up question: "What's it like?" This book offers a glimpse inside the corridors of American executive branch power, but not as someone privy to its deepest secrets nor as a denizen with decades on the beat. It delves into some formative experiences spanning six decades as a broadcast journalist that helped me avoid losing my wits when facing a president in adverse reporting conditions or confronting inevitable equipment failure. Whether covering America's nuclear weapons testing program as a rookie reporter in Nevada or numerous disasters and coups overseas as a more experienced foreign correspondent, all these experiences solidified skepticism, especially of what government officials uttered.

There are also intriguing side trips in this book's chapters, including presidents on the golf course and how they respond when asked about aliens.

In later chapters, there is discussion of the saga during the Trump administration when the president and his officials suddenly turned their attention to the Voice of America and our parent organization, the US Agency for Global Media. This was a tumultuous experience for me and my colleagues, uncomfortably thrusting us into the headlines. Most journalists prefer to report the news, not *be* the news.

The Voice of America is a unique American and media institution, which began in the early days of World War Two. Our first broadcast languages were German and then Japanese, to counter Axis propaganda on shortwave radio in an era before global TV news and the internet. VOA is probably the only news operation in the world mandated to be objective. This is enshrined in Public Law 94-350, passed by the US Congress in 1976. Most relevant is Section 503, which notes that the long-range interests of the United States are served by communicating directly with the peoples of the world and to be effective, the Voice of America must win the attention and respect of its audiences:

> These principles will therefore govern Voice of America (VOA) broadcasts:
> 1. VOA will serve as a consistently reliable and authoritative source of news. VOA news will be accurate, objective, and comprehensive.
> 2. VOA will represent America, not any single segment of American society, and will therefore present a balanced and comprehensive projection of significant American thought and institutions.
> 3. VOA will present the policies of the United States clearly and effectively, and will also present responsible discussions and opinion on these policies. (Public Law 94-350)

This language is taken seriously by every VOA reporter, producer, editor, and manager with whom I've interacted since my initial professional relationship with the organization in the early 1990s, when I was based in Tokyo.

During the final months of the Trump administration, VOA's firewall—separating government officials and our own upper management from our newsrooms—was licked by intense flames. Fortunately, we enjoyed judicial and generally bipartisan legislative support to uphold our journalistic independence. None of us desired to be drawn into a political battle, forced to become whistle-blowers, or take calls from other journalists about what was happening inside our own media organization.

The noncommercial, nonprofit Voice of America is a government-funded media operation and its staff a mix of civil servants, foreign service officers (under our own agency, not the State Department), and contractors. VOA also utilizes experienced freelancer reporters around the world, who also endure hardship and sometimes put their lives on the line to bring our audiences firsthand accounts of political upheaval, civil conflict, and disasters. VOA is not a propaganda outlet, and any clear-eyed review of the hundreds of broadcasts, correspondent reports, and online dispatches it produces daily clearly demonstrate objectivity and the highest journalistic standards.

No news organization is perfect. VOA journalists strive to continually improve while, yes, complaining not too infrequently about a shortage of personnel and resources with a heavy burden of work, as is the situation in many commercial newsrooms.

Among the audiences foremost in mind for this book are journalism students and others contemplating a career in this profession. Those looking for nonpartisan insight into the routine of a typical, but by no means celebrity journalist, who for four and a half years reported for duty daily at the most famous address in America, will also hopefully find this volume worthy of their time.

Journalism is a big tent in what many may view as a public circus. Some in the tent are advocates for an issue or a political party or have a philosophical agenda. Some of these journalists also report from the White House. How they cover a presidency is very different than my approach as a reporter tasked with explaining, as objectively as possible, America's story to the rest of the world. After the events of recent years in Washington in which modern journalism seemed to be confronting an existential threat, I concluded it was important to delve into how I did my job as a journalist at the White House to counter some unfounded assumptions about the media, including VOA, from across the political spectrum.

After working for 54 months inside the perimeter of the official office/residence of the president of the United States, I never lost my awe and reverence for the White House. I did remind myself when I entered the northwest gate that cooks, electricians, and janitors also work there every day. I realize, however, that even being a gardener at the White House is not employment at a routine job site and that the accounts of anyone toiling on the property is a subject others find fascinating. Yet another reason to write about the duties and responsibilities of a reporter at the White House and how I got there.

1

An initial revelation for those assigned to cover the Executive Mansion at 1600 Pennsylvania Avenue Northwest is some reporters do not work inside the White House and even fewer have a coveted "hard pass" (a badge allowing daily entry without having to show additional identification). Only a smaller subset of White House correspondents routinely enters the Oval Office or travels on *Air Force One*.

I was fortunate to become part of the innermost sanctum shortly after Donald J. Trump's inauguration as the forty-fifth president of the United States despite my relative lack of experience reporting on American politics. In early 2017, Peter Heinlein and I arrived at the White House for VOA as the Washington lineup of correspondents was shuffled by our editors. Both Pete and I were veteran foreign correspondents who had spent most of our careers overseas. I had just completed a short stint as VOA's senior diplomatic correspondent, extensively traveling overseas with Secretary of State John Kerry and one trip to Mexico with his Trump-appointed successor, Rex Tillerson.

A joke circulated that Pete and I had been selected for our new beat because we both had extensive experience with autocrats in fragile democracies. Our previous overseas postings required frequent travel, bringing us face-to-face with dictators, despots, and dubious democrats. Now we were reporting the world's most consequential political news from a small, dank basement booth.

Throughout many presidential administrations, reporters assigned to the West Wing ground level or below complained of being treated like mushrooms—kept in the dark and fed manure.

One of our predecessors in our cramped VOA booth, Philomena Jurey, who covered Presidents Richard Nixon, Gerald Ford, Jimmy Carter, and Ronald Reagan, titled her autobiography *A Basement Seat to History.*

The author in VOA's White House basement booth.

Others have compared their plight to prisoners in cramped, overcrowded quarters.

"Most people think the White House beat is glamorous. It isn't," recalled former VOA White House correspondent Paula Wolfson, whom I interviewed for a story that doubled as part of my own on-the-job tutorial.

"It can be a boring grind in a little booth that can feel stifling at times," Wolfson added, telling me something I had already discovered. Wolfson said that despite the mostly obstructed view, the reporters "are an eyewitness to history and the job is what you make of it."

Once cleared through the northwest gate, the authorized roaming territory for White House correspondents is quite limited with infrequent exceptions. Journalists can meander unescorted through the two narrow floors encompassing the press briefing room. Down one floor, the basement booths and desks are where VOA and a dozen or so other news outlets maintain their White House bureaus.

The only outdoor space not off limits to the journalist sits between the Palm Room doors and the winding driveway from the West Wing entrance to an area of the North Lawn. That is where TV reporters' stand-up positions are located. It is known as "Pebble Beach" (covered with gravel until 2003, when Pennsylvania fieldstone was installed and subsequently supplemented with wood chips).

Presidential departures and arrivals via the *Marine One* helicopter are generally open to media members holding White House passes and credentials. That allows escorted trips to the South Lawn, which doubles as a landing pad for the presidential helicopter. (Pro tip: Try to avoid referring to rotary aircraft as "choppers" within earshot of military helicopter pilots.)

The South Lawn arrivals and departures are an opportunity for reporters to shout questions at the president, who can feign hearing difficulties due to the noisy aircraft engines. There may also be glimpses of the president entering or exiting the Oval Office as he prepares to board or disembarks *Marine One.* We watch behind ropes and Secret Service agents—it is for the president to approach us. When the media gathers on the South Lawn driveway for the president's return on *Marine One,* the journalists have to decide whether to gather on the portico end, which leads to an entrance to the residence, or the side closest to the Oval Office. If it is a late evening, it is assumed the president will head for the residence. But if the president chooses to walk toward the other end where the media has clustered, there will be a 20-yard dash by reporters, videographers lugging TV cameras on tripods, and still photographers who had been perched on ladders. One afternoon, someone racing to the other side as I also began to pivot sideswiped my digital recorder, causing batteries to spill out and the SD card to eject. Fortunately, the president did not stop to take questions that time.

No more than a small preselected pack of journalists ever assembles in the Oval Office. This group is known as the pool, which shares its video, audio, photos, or notes with other nonattendees who toil for the other outlets on the rotating list of pooling duty. Their reports are quickly sent via email to hundreds of media recipients. The summarizations and short quotes contained in those pool reports can determine which sound bite is extracted by the television and radio networks that could be the story of the day. Few producers of these news programs have the luxury of minutes to scroll independently through the entire feed to determine the most important thing the president said. Frequently they are young, low-level staffers willing to defer to the more experienced reporters inside the White House to determine among the dozens of minutes of presidential video and audio what is the most newsworthy. Some partisan channels are merely seeking zingers as red meat for their base, depending on which party is in power in pursuit of audience retention to raise ratings. As poolers, we are mindful of these often-competing interests as we quickly dispatch our reports.

The Voice of America is assigned in-town pool duty at least a couple of times per month. That means standing by long hours waiting for something (or nothing) to happen and then hearing a squawk over the loudspeakers to quickly assemble at the Palm Room doors, adjacent to the residence wing.

"Nobody is keen on pool duty," explained Wolfson, who covered the White House from 1988 to 1992 and again from 2001 to 2009. "You have to make sure your equipment is ready to record at all times. . . . And never forget to take a good book." These days, books have been replaced with distracted scrolling through one's social media feeds.

Although pool duty is mostly mundane, it is, according to Wolfson, "a necessary evil—ask anyone who was covering the White House when Reagan was shot" in 1981 outside the Washington Hilton Hotel.

The poolers also have frequent access to the president, even if it is seeing him at a distance, which makes it difficult for staff to conceal a health crisis. Reporters and photographers who see the president nearly every day may be the first, outside of family and close aides, to notice that something has changed. In late June 2023, the journalists noticed indentation marks on both sides of President Joe Biden's face. The resulting closeup photos and queries to the West Wing led to the White House press office issuing a statement that the president had begun using a CPAP machine for sleep apnea. Biden was known to have the disorder but that, at the age of 80, the leader of the free world was now strapping a mask to his face to help him sleep was a revelation and may not have been voluntarily disclosed if reporters had not had such close and regular access to the president. Albeit a minor health issue, it helped to shed light on a condition that affects 30 million people in the United States. This is a part of the unique role the media play in American democracy, something envied by our colleagues in countries where there are less transparent traditions.

The most familiar scene involving reporters and the White House is the briefing by the press secretary, which for political junkies became must-see TV in the Trump era.

In previous administrations, the tradition had been to call first on a front-row senior wire service reporter (the Associated Press nowadays, United Press International in decades past) whose policy-oriented questions would help craft or derail the administration's news cycle for that day. The White House Correspondents' Association controls the press room seating, but the White House determines which individuals receive credentials to enter and line the aisles.

The Biden administration, in 2023, moved to tighten criteria for the coveted "hard pass," which grants regular access to part of the White House grounds. The new rules require "accreditation by a press gallery in the either the U.S. Senate, U.S. House of Representatives or Supreme Court." Hard-pass holders must also be employed full-time "with an organization whose principal business is news dissemination," although there are exceptions for aptly qualified freelancers, and willingness "to submit to any necessary investigations by the U.S. Secret Service." The stricter rules culled some fringe figures whose connection to actual reporting was suspect—those some in the White House press corps derisively referred to as "tourists." It also targeted veterans such as Fred Lucas of the conservative online website Daily Signal, who had been covering the White House since 1979. His outlet is funded and operated by the Heritage Foundation think tank, which is highly critical of the Biden administration's policies. First Amendment lawyer Ted Boutrous Jr. termed the new rules "unduly vague," noting his successful legal defense of hard-pass holders suspended by the Trump administration, which attempted to "attack and punish aggressive journalism or unpopular viewpoints and shield the White House from rigorous journalistic scrutiny."

VOA has had a full-time presence in the White House media corps and the radio pool for decades. It is currently assigned a briefing room fourth-row seat (which was between the National Journal and Fox News Radio for most of my assignment there).

The correspondents' association every year or so reviews the seating chart—the frequency of attendance and perceived clout of a news organization determines who moves forward, backward, or sideways. Some outlets share a seat, rotating their turn sitting for the briefings. Having a seat in the room is an advantage. Biden Press Secretary Karine Jean-Pierre in 2023 stated she preferred not to call on those standing in the aisles, meaning nearly all questions would be taken from those in the seats.

President Trump's first press secretary, Sean Spicer, who held the job for seven months, gave less priority, much to the chagrin of the major media outlets, to the wires and TV network journalists, instead pointing his index finger over them to other reporters, including those not assigned seats and standing on the sidelines, figuratively giving a middle finger to the first-row elites. Spicer sometimes entertained questions from mystery figures so obscure a Google search for their bylines yielded no results. Each briefing required three to five hours of preparation by the White House press office, and the press secretary needs to be up-to-the-minute on a president's thinking, Spicer told me.

Press secretaries must "double, triple, in quadruple, check everything that you're going to say and do because it's going to go through that level of scrutiny," said Spicer, who regularly faced skepticism about what he presented from the podium. Spicer had an ignominious debut when, under pressure from the new president, at a hastily arranged briefing the day after Trump was sworn in, he declared those in attendance had composed "the largest audience to witness an inauguration, period." The evidence of the size of the crowd did not corroborate his account.

"There were unequivocally times I made mistakes," acknowledged Spicer, who insisted in our interview he never told a lie at the lectern, nor did Trump ever ask him not to tell the truth. Daily televised press briefings, Spicer told me after his departure from the White House, are not a necessity. "Figure out a way to mix them in," so they don't devolve into "media circuses where it's been a yell fest, where it's been an opportunity for someone to get up and showboat."

Spicer's successor, Sarah Huckabee Sanders, decided to take a more scattered approach to the room, although during her tenure the frequency and length of briefings began to shrink. Months could go by without one and dust accumulated on the lectern. By the time Sanders headed back home to Arkansas (to prepare for a successful run for governor), the third Trump press secretary, Stephanie Grisham, totally avoided the briefing room. That didn't prevent her from writing a tell-all book. *I'll Take Your Questions Now* is an ironic title since she never did on the White House podium. Grisham, however, served the White House press well when, at the Korean DMZ, she scuffled with North Korean guards to ensure the traveling pool had access to the historical encounter between Trump and Kim Jong Un.

In the early days of the Trump administration some of the reporters who asked questions at the briefings were not in the room. They were the rotating recipients of the innovative Skype seats—their video images beamed in behind the press secretary, preselected from across the country. Those in the virtual seats were invariably friendly questioners from local radio and television stations.

In the Trump White House, exchanges with those in the nonvirtual seats frequently turned into a test of wills. Spicer, who had done no favors to his credibility with his inaugural crowd boast, found himself on the defensive when called on to explain the president's controversial tweets. He had no reluctance to turn the tables on the media, slamming journalists and accusing them of "deliberately false reporting."

The reporters and Spicer quickly became material for parody, most notably on NBC's *Saturday Night Live* with actress Melissa McCarthy portraying an unhinged Spicer ramming reporters with the lectern. The real-life Spicer, when one briefing grew tense, in a metamoment, quipped, "Don't make me make the podium move."

Behind the scenes in the press room, it was less jocular. Tempers frayed over the White House's decision to credential commentators from far-right online websites, including those accused of supporting white nationalism and trafficking in conspiracies. One such figure, who was later fired from his outlet for appearing on a podcast hosted by a prominent white nationalist, commented publicly that he was in the press room to dig for dirt on the established White House correspondents.

The grizzled standard-bearers of the mainstream media in the front row rolled their eyes and muttered curses when Spicer pointed to the back of the room and called on the so-called floaters—usually young Trump cheerleaders who would throw questions at Spicer with all the hardness of a beach ball.

For the president's supporters, the media's criticism fell on deaf ears. Many of them were already critical of the mainstream press, so journalists' complaints were taken as evidence the administration was following through on Trump's attacks on the "dishonest" media.

By comparison, the Biden-era briefings became boring. That appeared to be a deliberate effort by the Democrats in the West Wing (some of them returning from the Barack Obama presidency) to revert to a sense of normalcy and stricter media discipline, which had frustrated numerous journalists during the tenure of the forty-fifth president.

Jen Psaki brought to the Brady Room podium her experience as a State Department press secretary, and she was clearly more comfortable and adept with replying to reporters than her Trump-era predecessors. Conservative media portrayed the lack of fireworks as evidence of a too cozy relationship between a left-leaning American media and the Biden administration. Psaki did get tough questions and provocative queries, notably from front-row correspondent Peter Doocy of the conservative Fox News cable television channel.

When Karine Jean-Pierre succeeded Psaki, who left to take an on-air job at MSNBC, a cable TV news and commentary channel on the liberal side of the American political spectrum, the briefings became even more sedentary.

Jean-Pierre preferred to stick to talking points and was less likely to ad-lib as Psaki would do occasionally, which had provided for compelling sound bites on radio and television newscasts. Jean-Pierre quickly received support on the podium from John Kirby, a former US Navy admiral who had excelled previously in the briefing rooms at the State Department and the Pentagon. Kirby was brought in regularly to field national security and geopolitical questions, subjects in which he has mastery and Jean-Pierre scant experience.

"It's still my podium. There's been a misunderstanding," Jean-Pierre told one reporter who asked her how she would be sharing the platform with Kirby.

The Trump-era soap opera in the briefing room placed some White House correspondents in the spotlight, despite an effort by a majority of journalists to keep it beamed on the president and his supporting cast.

There is a never-ending struggle among the press corps to avoid being cultivated like mushrooms and kept in the dark by politicians and their press aides. The subterranean journalists in the West Wing basement seek to follow the words of former US Supreme Court Justice Louis Brandeis: "Sunlight is said to be the best of disinfectants." So, we pester, persist, and plead. Reporters might query—either in person, by text, or phone call—the West Wing press officers. We follow up or look for an alternative source of the information we desire. And sometimes we beg.

Working inside the White House as a reporter and frequently traveling with the president, I sought to provide accurate, objective, and comprehensive reporting on the presidency. No one at VOA has ever told me I must report something or tried to halt coverage of a story. Nor has anyone attempted to spin my news stories in a partisan direction, reflecting the same standards I experienced as a newsman at the venerable Associated Press. The pressures to twist a story a certain way or kill one, however, would eventually come from Trump administration officials. And that is something every reporter covering the US government has had to confront since George Washington took office.

2

I am wired—in more ways than one—caffeine in the bloodstream and various cables snaking across my torso. A digital audio recorder (usually a Marantz, Tascam, or Zoom brand) is strapped around my neck. Poised to record—the unit's flashing red light indicates I only need to push one button to take it out of pause mode.

Standing silently with a group of a dozen journalists, videographers, photographers, and audio technicians under a colonnade, I check the battery level for the third time in five minutes, even though I loaded the machine with a quartet of lithium AA batteries right before hearing the loudspeaker announcement for the White House media pool to gather at the press room doors.

Snaking out of one side of the recorder is a coiled cable with reliable XLR connectors on both ends. The top side is attached to the bottom of an aluminum pole that I can extend nearly 10 feet like a giant fishing rod. Inside the pole is more cabling connected to the bottom of a German-made Sennheiser MKH-416 shotgun microphone, which is nestled in a special blimp-shaped plastic mount covered with faux fur to dampen vibrations and cut wind noise. Also attached to the recording unit is a pair of high-quality headphones (Grado Labs indoors or the more rugged Sony cans outdoors for inclement weather) that will let me hear exactly what I am about to record—the voice of the president of the United States.

The wrangler—a young White House press office assistant barely out of college but now empowered to corral a herd of seasoned journalists—adopts a schoolmarm's tone to again admonish us not to stampede when seconds from now we burst through the doors into the Oval Office.

"Photographers first!" she says, repeating the protocol for the procession and perhaps reminding herself. We all know that in the Oval Office or other White House rooms the shooters get the front view, while outside for *Marine One* helicopter departures and arrivals, it is the radio and TV microphone holders who get priority, squatting on the pavement directly in front of the TV camera tripods and the dozens of reporters behind them.

Most of us have done this a hundred times. For some of the grizzled veterans, who have covered six or seven presidencies, thousands.

By comparison, on the White House beat for only a couple of years, I'm still a newbie and thus subject to light hazing—mainly being jostled to knock me out of position—or warnings to not let my cables get tangled with others. The still photographers will always hiss about the boom microphones creeping into their viewfinders, although sometimes they'll shoot a wide shot to include the scrum, including the TV cameras and audio equipment.

I try to stay focused on my sole mission: Record the best-quality audio of the president's voice (along with anyone else he asks to speak). A dozen domestic and international radio networks depend on me to have a clear imprint of every word the commander of the free world utters. That entails maneuvering the boom pole holding my microphone as close as I can to presidential lips, but far enough away to avoid the equipment appearing in close-up photographic and video shots. If the microphone is too far away from the president, then his voice can be obliterated by the sound of clicking camera shutters and other room noise.

We're on the move, finally.

I have carefully controlled my daily intake of caffeine (a morning pot of strong black tea from Sikkim) for pool-duty days to find that sweet spot between requisite alertness and shaky hands. I need to be playing my top game in the next 15 seconds in case anything goes amiss.

An audio connector or my earphones could come unplugged as I get bumped by others. This can easily happen when foreign journalists in the pool accompany their leader to meet the US president. Certain nationalities have worse reputations than others.

I need to ensure the recorder doesn't accidentally stop recording and the levels are neither too low (generating hiss) or overmodulated (creating distortion that cannot be fixed in the editing process).

On this day we all squeeze through the double doors efficiently and I find a spot alongside the press secretary and right behind the first lady, who is seated on a sofa. As I get bumped, I firmly grip the bottom of my boom pole to ensure it does not make physical contact with any of the VIPs.

When the size of the pool doubles to accommodate a foreign contingent accompanying their leader into the Oval Office, the visitors unskilled in the ballet of pool reporting among nineteenth-century furniture can literally upend things. This occurred, for example, in July 2017, when South Korean journalists covering President Moon Jae-in were brought in with the American pool. A couch was bumped, jostling a lamp deftly caught by Keith Schiller, Trump's longtime personal bodyguard (who is a footnote to history as the White House official the president dispatched to the Federal Bureau of Investigation to hand deliver the letter firing Director James Comey).

"Easy, fellas! Hey, fellas! Fellas, easy," Trump exclaimed as Schiller intercepted the table lamp. "Wow. You guys are getting worse."

Trump then turned to Moon, explaining, "It's actually a very friendly press, don't let that get to you. Although we just lost a table."

The American poolers, usually well behaved, did not like being blamed for a commotion caused by the foreigners.

"That shit was nuts," complained a member of the US pool.

"That guy was assaulting me," moaned another, referring to a South Korean photographer.

As I had been based for three years in Seoul, Korea, I knew videographers and photojournalists there have a reputation for being assertive and lacking in decorum in pursuit of the shot.

Every time I entered the Oval Office, I discreetly tried to ensure I was in a safe position and then slowly and gently extend the fishing pole to get close enough to the president's mouth but out of camera shot. Whenever I placed any piece of equipment too close to the president, I'd get a dirty look or even a nudge from a Secret Service agent of the elite Presidential Protective Division. During these events, everyone in the room performs their part. The journalists remain quiet until the president and his guest conclude their remarks. The first lady and others on the sofa will keep smiles on their faces with strategic slight nods.

The only sounds, until the end of the more formal remarks, are the voice of the president (and then his guests when called upon to speak) and the incessant clicking of the shutters of the Nikon and Canon (and, recently, Sony) professional cameras.

We might be in the Oval Office for 45 seconds or 45 minutes. It's all up to the commander-in-chief. Some presidents prefer our presence only for a grin-and-grab (handshakes). Others are loquacious. Trump was a marathon talker, crafting his messaging with bombast and grievances that appealed to the white, working-class voters who elected him.

While one of my hands keeps the boom in position, in my other palm is a smartphone. I snap a few photographs and immediately email them to the radio pool email list with a short summary of anything of great importance said. I then tweet the same information. It's a delicate digital juggling act I had taken some pains to master.

The president concludes his brief remarks and turns his gaze to the media gang. A half dozen of us begin to ask questions. The president sorts out one to answer. He has his favorite questioners—all presidents do—but eventually all the reporters, including me, are able to ask something.

In the Oval Office, decorum usually prevails and the tone and wording of the questions are respectful. It's more of a free-for-all on the South Lawn, where any journalist with White House credentials tries to shout over the din of helicopter engine noise.

Through trial and error, I found when competing with my colleagues for the forty-fifth president's attention—indoors or outside—I had the best shot of winning a reply if my question contained no more than seven words. Trump's patience with questioners was extremely limited and a better question is concise, regardless of the president.

The presidential response could result in a headline, other times merely a sentence in a very long transcript that perhaps would be noteworthy as a footnote to some future historian researching an arcane subject. When he was taking questions inside the White House, Trump would cross his arms, usually a signal he was calling an end to the session. Additional questions were asked, but the wrangler shouted over them, "Thank you, press!" Her voice would ride over the first few words of the president's subsequent reply, much to the chagrin of those of us recording the broadcast audio.

I always knew Trump was really finished answering questions when his tongue jutted between his teeth on the *th* digraph as he said, "thank you."

"Let's go, press," the wrangler would repeatedly and loudly implore. If we lingered to ensure we were still in position to record any additional comments, a presidential assistant would extend a palm to our upper arms to nudge us to back out of the room.

I always kept the recorder on and the business end of the microphone facing the president until I had completely left the room. One time in Riyadh, during a one-on-one meeting on the sidelines of a summit, Trump made a surprise remark about the Egyptian president's shoes, which I did not hear until later on playback when one of the photographers mentioned the footwear fixation.

"Love your shoes. Boy, those shoes. Man," Trump had said to Abdel Fattah al-Sisi, admiring the Egyptian's shiny black boots.

As I cautiously backed out of the Oval Office, trying not to bump anybody or anything, I was composing my next message to the radio pool to impart the gist of what had been said and to let them know I would upload the audio as soon as possible to our shared internet cloud.

Due to technical problems or a different recording position, the TV audio might be distorted, muffled, or too faint. Then networks rely on our radio feed—but usually the TV crews do a spectacular job.

One notable time the TV pool failed to capture usable audio was an impromptu appearance before the microphones at Mar-a-Lago on the evening of April 6, 2017. The Chinese president, Xi Jinping, had barely departed Trump's private club and we expected any moment to be given the signal for a partial lid, meaning the end of the day for the poolers as there would be no further appearances or external movement by the president. Instead, we were instructed to line up outside one of the oceanfront club's entrances and stand by, although the pool was not informed why. During our hiatus we were then told Trump would be making a statement. After a long wait, we were rushed into a conference room, where the president quickly appeared. There was no time to set up our equipment and test the audio levels. In a near panic, I slammed one end of my XLR cable into the audio distribution box and blindly hit the record button. I didn't have a spare second to put on my headphones before Trump began speaking.

"My fellow Americans, on Tuesday, Syrian dictator Bashar al-Assad launched a horrible chemical weapons attack on innocent civilians," began Trump. He explained he had "ordered a targeted military strike on the airfield in Syria from where the chemical attack was launched."

It was major news—the first use of military force by Trump. We would later learn the 59 cruise missiles began exploding on the Syrian airfield as Trump and Xi were having dessert. The American leader informed his Chinese counterpart of the air strikes he had ordered as Xi, according to Trump, was enjoying "the most beautiful piece of chocolate cake that you've ever seen."

I had assumed Trump's announcement had been carried live on TV. It had not. First word of it came from the radio and print pool reports, but I did not find out that was the case until about an hour later. I had uploaded the audio to the shared cloud server immediately for all of the radio networks, also unaware there had been a recording mistake with the TV pool audio. It was my audio that would be used by all the TV networks. This was a lesson that reinforced our critical role as radio pooler, no matter the hour or the location.

Another time the role of the radio pooler is critical is the so-called gaggles with the president, press secretary, or members of the Cabinet on *Air Force One,* as no videotaping is permitted and our audio is the only broadcast-quality recording of what gets said.

Only when I had uploaded the audio for all the networks to download, under the rules of pool reporting, was I permitted to do individual reporting for my employer. That compelled me to race to get the pool audio out as many radio networks would want to use it on their next hourly newscasts or even break into regular programming if something of tremendous importance has been uttered.

Once back in the press area, I gallop down the stairs to our White House basement two-person booth, where I pull the SD card from the recorder and insert it into the slot on the side of my MacBook. I pull up a simple audio-editing program (Audacity or Adobe Audition) and perform a brief operation to snip the extraneous sounds and normalize the peak level to –1.0 db. This takes a few seconds and then I log into the NPR-hosted cloud server to upload the session and notify all the networks that the MP3 file is there. Most of the time the exercise can be completed before the recorded TV pool video plays out to the broadcast networks. It is not really a competition, but even a couple of minutes can mean the difference for a radio newscast team in New York or London having the desired sound bite in time for its next news bulletin.

Sometimes, especially during a news conference, when I knew the president knew we were live and the whole world was watching, I would violate my seven-word rule and be tenacious when he would veer off topic. An example of this was during a hastily arranged news conference at the World Economic Forum in Davos, Switzerland, in January 2020, when I was called on:

Herman: Yes, Mr. President. You were the keynote speaker here, but you shared some of the spotlight with a Scandinavian teenager: Greta Thunberg—
Trump: Oh, that's very nice.

Herman: —who you had said needs to work on her anger. She had some very harsh words about—

Trump: I didn't say "anger." I said "anger management."

Herman: "Anger management." Yes, sir. She had some very strong words here that the United States and other industrialized countries need to do more. Do you still feel that you're doing enough? You talk about clean air—

Trump: How old is she?

Herman: She's—

Multiple reporters: Seventeen.

Herman: Seventeen now. Yes.

Trump: Oh. That's good.

Herman: But what is your response to her—

Trump: She beat me out on *Time* magazine. [*Laughter*]

Herman: But did you hear from other world leaders and business leaders who said that they think that she has a message that you should listen to?

Trump: No, I didn't, actually. But I would have loved to have seen her speak. I did not.

Fortunately, the subsequent reporter whom Trump called on in hopes of changing the topic stuck with the theme I raised and asked him if he still thought climate change was a hoax.

"No, not at all. I think what is—I think aspects of it are. I think that some people are—they put it at a level that is, you know, unrealistic, to a point you can't live your lives," Trump replied.

It was a typical Trump contradictory response, which, if dissected, could result in reporting that the president declared climate change is not a hoax or that Trump criticized environmentalists for overhyping climate change to the point it was unbearable. Without airing the full quote, his remarks would lack context. Over the course of his presidency, Trump's actions—rather than his words—clearly indicated he sided more with the fossil fuel industry than the environmentalists.

3

Working for a reputable noncommercial broadcaster, the emphasis is on accuracy over speed. Theoretically, that is a basic tenet of journalism. But for those who chase not only stories but ratings, competitive pressures influence the process. For wire-service reporters, particularly those with Bloomberg or Reuters, beating the competition by a mere second is important. It sounds ridiculous, but fortunes can be at stake for commodities market players and hedge fund managers who are poised to press a button to trade stunning quantities of foreign currency, Brent crude oil, or pork bellies futures based on what the president may have uttered about a trade deal with China.

Some of the wire-service reporters during our encounters with the president have a cell phone in each hand—one streaming the audio back in real time to their newsroom and the other writing bulletins. But pool reporters may miss something of importance while we're busy typing out what was said seconds ago or mishear a critical word, so listening to the full audio file may result in a harvest of additional news nuggets.

The print pool reporters will also dispatch some quotes as the official White House transcript might not be issued until hours later or the subsequent day.

It is a competitive environment, but among the reporters in the pool there is camaraderie and cooperation. We all need each other's help at some point. A print pooler might want to hear the radio reporter's playback to verify a garbled quote. The photographers might ask another pooler for the name of an unfamiliar guest alongside the president that they need to send along with their pictures. The videographers stay silent and depend on the reporters to ask informed questions that will elicit newsworthy answers that will get their work favorable placement on the top newscasts. And then there is the social media component. Not every reporter or photographer has an online presence, but most do. Some are better known on Twitter for their timely tweets than in their more traditional media.

A lot of news breaks on social media, especially from the White House, and a dozen correspondents within seconds of each other might post the same basic information but each with a unique perspective. Some are opinionated; some are witty. Some spend excessive time and energy battling bots and trolls.

My news organization does not permit me to opine, and any attempt at humor online would likely be too subtle for my intended overseas audiences, composed of nonnative speakers of English, thus I stick to the facts while providing a bit of color. When Elon Musk took over Twitter and the future of the platform looked unclear, I also began posting on Mastodon, as well as post.news, where engagement with followers quickly became as good or better than Twitter. That proved to be a prudent decision when, along with several other journalists, I was permanently suspended from Twitter (an event discussed later in this book). I subsequently established accounts on other platforms, including BlueSky, Forth, Spoutible, and Substack's Notes and Threads, in anticipation one would gain critical mass.

Regardless of which online service I'm posting to, I am always on the lookout for something a bit off-kilter.

One time during the Trump administration, there was a sinkhole on the White House North Lawn, outside the press entrance. It enlarged after a period of intense rain in May 2018. I decided to tweet a photo of it. Much to my astonishment, it quickly went viral. Newspapers and broadcasters around the world picked it up. Within hours, dozens of other reporters spilled out of the press room to also tweet pictures of it. They had also walked by the hole for days, but I was the first to find it "tweetworthy," if not particularly newsworthy.

As the sinkhole became a meme, the National Park Service, which is tasked with tending to the grounds of the White House, found it prudent to place a board over the sinkhole until the depression could be filled. That, of course, set off a new round of tweets by me and others about an actual White House cover-up.

After the sinkhole I became more astute, and what I previously considered mundane with scant news value was now a potentially popular tweet. One chilly day in January 2019, it was video of *Marine One* with the president on board coming in for a winter landing and snow-blowing us. Some speculated that the president had ordered the pilot to pelt us, but that was not true.

Also in January 2019, I noticed a large bucket (something resembling an industrial-sized plastic trash receptacle) on display for several days in the window of the White House family kitchen. I tweeted several photos of that. Some conspiracy theorists became excited, seeing the big bin as akin to a flowerpot in the window that spies use to signal each other. Again, the placement was innocuous and occurred amid a government shutdown, so someone had likely forgotten it was there during a time the White House was understaffed. It goes to show when there is no news, White House reporters are compelled to find even the most innocuous irregularity and try to turn it into news.

4

At the pinnacle of the White House media pecking order are not the multimillionaire television anchors or marquee commentators (they're rarely on site). Some TV correspondents of the three traditional US terrestrial networks (ABC, CBS, and NBC) and the two biggest cable news channels (CNN and Fox) do rank highly as their outlets have front-row seats in the press briefing room. But unless briefings occur regularly, that prime territory is not of much value.

Rank is also arguably determined by regular access to the president, and in most modern presidencies that comes primarily from pool duty. Among the radio and TV networks, the pool assignments rotate among broadcasters. The major wire services, however, have permanent spots for both their correspondents and photographers. Those reporters get the most opportunities to be in the room with the president and question him.

The wires themselves—which have squadrons of scribes on the major beats in the Beltway—rotate their personnel in the White House pool. But it is these super-capable reporters, be they a Zeke Miller of AP, Jennifer Jacobs of Bloomberg, or Steve Holland of Reuters—names with relatively low celebrity wattage—who generate the most questions that result in presidential headlines.

Another alpha figure of the White House media is the dean of the photographers' corps, Pulitzer Prize recipient Doug Mills of the *New York Times,* formerly with both UPI and AP. Novices assigned to the pool quickly learn the consequences of getting between the lens of the North Carolina native and any president.

On the night of February 5, 2019, we were in the Capitol for Trump's second State of the Union address, which was delayed to early February after a record-long partial government shutdown resulting from a feud between the president and House Speaker Nancy Pelosi. Mills found himself with a clear shot of the two and captured a photo of her mockingly applauding Trump with outstretched arms that was worth more than 1,000 words on their rivalry.

"Oh yes that clap took me back to the teen years," explained the congresswoman's daughter, Christine Pelosi, on Twitter. "She knows. And she knows that you know. And frankly she's disappointed that you thought this would work. But here's a clap."

Mills downplayed his ability to capture that perfect second out of Trump's 82-minute address.

"Being the pool photographer on the floor is so exciting because it's one of the few places in D.C. that we see on TV all the time, but photographers are only allowed on the floor for this one evening," explained Mills in an Instagram post. "Every Washington icon is in attendance and the light is beautiful. It's really hard not to make a (great) photo in that room."

Another powerful media component on campus (and that's how insiders refer to the White House grounds—"campus") is the cadre of terrestrial and cable network television producers. Akin to football linebackers, they are usually not household names; they don't often earn on-air credit or bylines as do the wire service reporters, but TV producers do the heavy lifting for their networks and are well respected by their peers.

On long trips, the TV correspondents have periods of downtime, although it's a grueling day when on the other side of the world fending off jet lag for middle-of-the-night live shots, which is prime time back home. The producers, however, work around the clock handling the logistics between the network control rooms and their traveling crews, supervising the hiring of local fixers, and ensuring the egos of those in front of the camera are not bruised. On these road trips, be they to Columbus or Cairo, everyone is under stress—the accompanying Cabinet members, the White House press staff, the Secret Service agents, and the traveling press. All make their best effort to get along.

The traveling press is given a general schedule, parts of which are to be used for planning only and not publicly revealed in advance, but trips rarely go precisely as planned.

For those not in the pool, on the overseas trips, there can be long periods where there is not much to report. A traveling White House press filing center is where they camp. In the room are American flags, a podium, and another raised platform in the rear for the TV cameras in case of an ad hoc briefing, but the president almost never comes into this room (which is frequently in a different hotel than where he is staying) and the majority of journalists who have traveled abroad to cover the trip will not see the president in person.

A portable production center for the TV pool is also set up in the center. Most sit at preassigned spots at long tables waiting for news to come in from the poolers. Wi-Fi with decent speed is supplied and an ethernet connection and an old-fashioned landline telephone can be ordered in advance, for which the news organizations pay handsomely. An AT&T technician is on-site to assist.

Buffet meals are provided in an adjacent room. The quality of the food varies by the country and host hotel. Many of the journalists will eat two or three meals per day here—not leaving the filing center and the hotel except for the rides to and from the airport.

Depending on the time difference with the home editors and deadlines, some of the press corps will get to enjoy the local cuisine and an adult beverage, but jet lag and an early start the following day usually mean it is not a late night out.

Occasionally on long and important trips the White House will invite some of the reporters for an off-the-record bull session in a hotel bar. This is a chance for a chat—although not for attribution—with members of the president's Cabinet, perhaps his chief of staff, the White House press secretary, and members of the National Security Council. The correspondents pay for their own drinks, and ethics rules preclude the government officials from accepting free drinks from the reporters. Although officials may use these sessions to try to sway the direction of stories, they rarely result in news headlines. Few of those invited dare not show for fear they might miss something significant that may be uttered amid stiff cocktails.

Despite his frequent attacks on the news media, Trump was one of the most prolific presidents in speaking off the record to the traveling press pool, although this was also a tradition to a lesser degree during the eight years of the Barack Obama presidency. Trump, however, did not log the marathon hours Lyndon Johnson clocked on *Air Force One* speaking off the record to the traveling press.

Under the rules of such engagements, we cannot reveal what the president says during such discussions—"off the record" is different than "background" when comments can be attributed to either "someone familiar with the president's thinking" or a "high-level White House official."

In the United Kingdom, there is a level of "deep background" conversations with government officials that results in the contorted phrase: "The BBC understands . . ." It is heard less in recent years after a BBC executive in 2017 emailed his underlings to tell them to stop using the phrase on air because it sounded "slightly pompous."

Only a few reporters will turn down opportunities to hear a US president chat off the cuff. What I have found most valuable from such not-for-attribution discussions—be they with the president or another top official—is comparing their public persona with their semiprivate selves. They are still going to be on guard to some degree, realizing they can only say so much, even in confidence, to journalists. With Trump these encounters allowed me to reject the alarm expressed by his most vociferous critics that the president was mentally unbalanced to the extent he had no self-control over what he said and did. It was clear, based on what I heard from Trump on the record, on background, and off the record—and how his staff (speaking on background) revealed his demeanor and language when he chewed them out—he was clearly able to adjust his words to the audience, setting, and the moment. In other words, Trump was able to precisely calibrate his language for the audience on hand. When no reporters are around, he speaks much more loosely and curses, as former White House officials have graphically detailed in their books. This was also evident from the *Access Hollywood* recording when reality TV star Trump in 2005 did not realize that, although off camera, the wireless microphones he and show host Billy Bush were wearing inside a bus were transmitting audio and their conversation recorded.

During my time traveling with Secretary of State John Kerry there was a stark contrast between his manner of speaking on the record and off. Kerry, who had been the Democrats' presidential nominee in 2004, can swear like a sailor (he indeed had been a naval officer).

Presidents—a notorious example being Lyndon Johnson—do not fully abandon profanity after swearing the oath of office. Apart from Sunday School teacher Jimmy Carter, all recent presidents have liberally let four-letter words fly when provoked. Carter, however, during the 1976 presidential campaign famously told writer Norman Mailer, "I don't care if people say fuck." The offending word was rendered as a dash in the published *New York Times Magazine* interview, with the newspaper explaining "he actually said the famous four-letter word that the *Times* has not printed in the 125 years of its publishing life."

5

The ultimate privilege of traveling with the president is flying on *Air Force One*. After dozens of trips on the big bird, however, I can attest it is a mixed blessing.

Those designated as poolers for the flights find their own way to Joint Base Andrews in Camp Springs, Maryland, a 12-mile drive from the White House. The president usually makes the trip in minutes on *Marine One*, escorted by two other Marine Corps helicopters. But if there is a weather call, then a motorcade, which includes a pair of press vans, is hastily arranged. The journalists who will fly on the plane are to report hours prior to takeoff at the base. They are welcome to drive their own vehicles onto the grounds of the military facility. There is also free parking convenient to the terminal for the duration of the trip—be it half a day or two weeks. When journalists arrive on base, they create their own escorted motorcade with hazard lights blinking but, unlike the presidential motorcade, observe all traffic signals and stop signs.

As a frequent traveling pooler, I was issued a Defense Biometrics Identification System (DBIDS) card to show at the guard post, allowing me to drive directly to the terminal. Subsequent to the perfunctory flashing of credentials to get onto the base, there is a more rigorous screening after the press corps enters the terminal. Like at a civilian airport, our bags pass through a scanner and we walk through a metal detector. There is a second screening for our bags and bodies.

The Secret Service's PPD calls out the dogs. One canine, actually, who sniffs all the media's equipment, which we line up on the floor for an olfactory inspection. After the dog has left, the journalists are "wanded." A PPD agent uses a handheld metal detector as we stretch out our arms and hold our wallets and cell phones.

There is usually a brief waiting period before we are escorted on foot to the tarmac. I snap a photo of the plane on my cell phone and email

Preparing to board Air Force One at Joint Base Andrews in Maryland as the White House traveling press pool reporter.

it to the pool. I make sure that the tail number of the aircraft is visible. This ensures that the media knows which *Air Force One* the president will be on.

Any fixed-wing US Air Force aircraft the president is flying on is *Air Force One,* which is an aviation radio call sign. The vice president's plane is *Air Force Two.* If the president's spouse is flying solo, that plane is *Executive One Foxtrot.*

The aircraft type and call sign occasionally are newsworthy. On October 17, 2018, First Lady Melania Trump's plane was forced to return to Andrews because of smoke in the cabin. There was initial confusion as to what type of aircraft she was on as none of the reporters on board had sent out that information prior to takeoff. That's why I suggested to other radio poolers when they have travel duty to always note the plane's tail number.

The two big planes best known as *Air Force One*—with tail numbers 28000 and 29000—are highly modified Boeing 747-200Bs. The Air

Force designates these planes as VC-25As. Fully fueled, they each weigh 833,000 pounds at takeoff. It costs taxpayers $200,000 an hour to operate the big planes. For the shorter flights, a modified Boeing 757-200 is used (designated by the Air Force as a C-32). In all, there are four of these planes operated by the 1st Airlift Squadron of Andrews's 89th Airlift Wing.

The final step of the boarding process for the press occurs at the back stairs. A member of the US Air Force ticks our names on a list, checking it against our presented identification. And with that we climb the steps, turn left, and find our assigned seat on which is usually placed a card with our surname.

As the radio pooler I was in the press cabin's third-row aisle seat, next to the Associated Press photographer, who had the window seat. The photographers will have an uneventful trip as they are permitted to take pictures in the plane only when there is a news conference, which TV can also tape.

Most of the time the media events, be they with the president, members of his Cabinet, other VIPs, or the press secretary, are either off the record (nothing can be used), on background (only attributed to a "senior White House official"), or an on-the-record "gaggle."

During a gaggle we can record audio (but not video), meaning that the radio pooler's recording is precious. It sounds straightforward, but there can be confusion. Some presidents have generally eschewed speaking to reporters on the plane. Some prefer to keep it off the record and let their hair down, so to speak. (Lyndon Johnson was known for his coarse language, which could have never been used verbatim in the media of his time.) Trump frequently caused momentary panic for press aides and confusion among journalists when coaxed by a persuasive reporter to transform a not-for-publication comment into paragraphs that were releasable. Unless I was specifically prohibited on the plane, I kept a microphone near the president and a device recording the audio.

Occasionally a bored photographer notices something unusual out the window as occurred on one return into Andrews when we spotted another military aircraft buzzing alarmingly close to *Air Force One*. Before I could blink, the still photographers had clicked their motor drives, capturing the other plane zooming by.

Another big difference between a commercial flight and *Air Force One* is the departure procedure. After we board, most of us quickly get back off the plane. We perch under the wing to watch the president arrive via *Marine One* or motorcade and try to lure him over for an impromptu question-and-answer session.

For most presidents, most of the time, it's a quick boarding with a salute to the Air Force personnel and a ceremonial wave at the top of the front steps. But from time to time there are remarks under the wing to the waiting poolers before he boards.

Once the president steps inside, we quickly head back up the rear stairs. For the pool this is a very intense next few minutes if the president has spoken. I rush to upload the audio with a quick file transfer to my computer, using a cell phone signal for the upload to the internet. The photographers send their pictures of the president, and the print and wire poolers file a quick report. This all works when we are on the modified 747s. But the newer, smaller planes are a virtual Faraday cage and we have no cell phone service inside. On those aircraft I huddle at the top of the stairs to beam material in the last few seconds before we are forced inside so the doors can be closed.

When the president is in his seat, the plane will quickly start rolling and we must be in our seats as well, although the flight attendants rarely check for unbuckled belts and seat positions unlike what every commercial flyer experiences. After takeoff there is no self-introduction from the pilot and no friendly chitchat about our flight path or the weather.

Somewhat reflective of the more disciplined style of Vice President Mike Pence, every time I flew with him on *Air Force Two* there was the airline-style pretakeoff inspection by the stewards. Pence's *Air Force Two* was "dry"—that is, no liquor served. Trump, also a teetotaler, did not ban booze on *Air Force One.*

One modern rule is strictly enforced on both the president's and vice president's planes: No smoking.

Until the Reagan administration, passengers on *Air Force One* received complimentary cigarettes and were free to light up.

The cigarettes have given way to boxes of presidential M&Ms. One legacy remains from those carcinogenic flights: presidential matchbooks.

We are allowed to use our cell phones during takeoff, but we lose all the signal bars quickly as the jet ascends. Reporters use this brief window of time at low altitude to send a "wheels up" message to their respective pools, noting the precise moment the aircraft lifts from the runway.

This will be needed to calculate our total flight time, another bit of data for which news organizations rely on the poolers. *Air Force One* tends to complete flights faster than a commercial jet taking the same route, in part because it gets priority from air traffic controllers for landing. There is speculation the extensively modified 747-200Bs have secret top speeds and altitudes. US Air Force Col. (Ret.) Mark Tillman, who was piloting *Air Force One* on September 11, 2001, has spoken of how the plane's F-16 escorts asked him to slow down because he was pushing the sound barrier and the fighter jets were burning too much fuel trying to keep pace.

The VC-25As are not designed to sustain supersonic flight and cannot violate the laws of aerodynamics. The only way any plane designated as *Air Force One* will set a speed record beyond Colonel Tillman's feat is if a sitting president straps into a seat of an F-15 or another supersonic aircraft of this branch of the US military (as the call sign of the plane would then be *Air Force One*).

The typical *Air Force One* (again referring to the usual ride, the VC-25) can fly higher than the typical cruising altitude of commercial jets (which usually stay below 38,000 feet). The listed ceiling for the presidential aircraft is 45,000 feet. This might be prudent over potentially hostile territory where flying higher would perhaps make it harder for missiles to shoot it down but make it easier to be seen on radar. And should there be such a threat, the plane is equipped with countermeasures not available to your Delta Airlines cockpit crew—radar receivers warning of hostile rockets, chaff and flares to distract those incoming threats, and even lasers meant to blind missiles.

Air Force One also has specialized communications equipment—hardened to withstand bursts from nuclear detonations, which can cripple typical radios.

There have been significant telecommunications systems upgrades to the planes since September 11, 2001, when confusion prevented the president from quickly getting precise details of the al-Qaeda attack.

Air Force One contains an operating room for medical emergencies and a self-contained baggage loader. There are likely gizmos inside and attached to the jet of which we are not aware. Despite what has been depicted in Hollywood movies, the planes do not have a secret escape pod, according to the Air Force. The three decks of the VC-25 encompass about 4,000 square feet of internal space. And the president has his own office, bed, toilet, and shower.

Another unique and publicly known item on the presidential VC-25, with a fuel capacity of 53,611 gallons, is a refueling probe on the nose of the plane. There is no indication *Air Force One* has taken a midair JP-8 fuel refill but should this be required during a national emergency, it is believed that with the number of crew typically on board, the plane could stay aloft for five to six days.

This capability, however, might not exist in the next generation of planes Boeing builds to be flown as *Air Force One,* as the White House has nixed the refueling capability despite the objection of some members of Congress.

At one point the replacement project seemed in total jeopardy.

"Cancel order!" President Trump tweeted in early December 2016, complaining that the estimated cost of $4 billion for two new planes was "out of control."

The contract for the modified two 747-8 jets called for the aircraft to be ready for service by 2024. A bit of headline irony here: the actual aircraft selected by Boeing to undergo the modification were originally built for Transaero, a Russian airline that went bust in 2015 before it could take delivery of its new jets, which were found to have structural cracks in aluminum components.

In late 2022, Boeing revealed its losses connected to modifying the pair of planes were approaching $2 billion, blaming supply chain delays, technical challenges, and a lack of workers at its facility in San Antonio, Texas, with the requisite clearances for the high-security project.

Until the new planes go into service, the president is stuck primarily flying on vintage 1986 airframes. In the press cabin the blue leather seats remind me of economy-plus or old-style business class on US domestic flights. The width and pitch of the seats are wider than in commercial economy, but they do not fully recline.

The entertainment options are sparse in comparison to the typical cross-country airline flight. There are a dozen audio channels with music ranging from "Big Country" to jazz and the audio track for the movie shown on small screens at the front of the cabin. If it is a weekend and a golf tournament is under way, the television will be tuned to that—no surprise as many presidents are avid golfers. On a weekday flight a movie may be on the screen and, of course, the commander-in-chief can order whatever he wants shown in his cabin. The journalists can select the TV channel on up front (likely whatever the president is watching) or a movie of our choice. The choice is usually that of the photographers on board who are big on the modern classics, such as *Jaws* (which I tend to watch without headphones—the 1975 thriller is much more entertaining that way).

Journalists usually have no access to the onboard internet. The traveling press pool can ask to use a phone line to file urgent material should the president or another member of his traveling party make a major announcement. This is known as a "wire call" and it rarely occurs. There is a strict call order list with the wires at the top and the lowly radio pooler the last one able to place a call.

The first time I was on board for a wire call there was some uncertainty among the wire reporters whether radio gets a turn. I assured them we do—although at the bottom of the list. The wire call procedure requires some instruction. The caller must dial the plane's operator and give one US telephone number to ring. A few minutes later the operator calls back with the surprised party on the line. The reporter must securely press two buttons on the side of the phone to speak while dictating a short report. I had not warned my newsroom that day of a possible urgent call. Fortunately, one of our newsroom's most experienced editors, Barry Newhouse, took the call and knew what to do.

Placing such collect calls from *Air Force One* are said to be very costly. I have never learned the amount because no one from VOA ever tracked me down to inquire about a mysterious phone bill as they did about the exorbitant charges for sandwiches and chips at one of Trump's country clubs.

The media members on the plane are always eager to get a good in-flight meal, not knowing when we will next have time to eat. There are always snacks and fruit free for the taking, as well as served set meals from the fully stocked rear galley.

The Air Force stewards—who perform the role of flight attendants—are not in military uniform in case they need to give safety orders to someone who might outrank them. The women wear mid-length black skirts while the men are dressed in black slacks, white shirts, and black vests with a Velcro presidential seal. They also have a gold-colored rectangular tag pinned to their outerwear displaying their name but no rank.

Even a takeout-style cup of coffee is served with distinction—emblazoned with the presidential seal on top of a paper napkin with the logo and the words "Aboard the Presidential Aircraft." Meals come on a plastic tray with the presidential seal, as do the Pickard fine china plates (made in America since 1893), which have a gold trim spelling out "Air Force One." No plastic utensils here—we get a full set of dinnerware. Beverages, including water, are served in glasses displaying the presidential seal. It is a smooth ride, usually, with some of the world's best pilots in the cockpit, who do their best to ensure the safety and comfort of the president. But it can get bumpy.

On one flight on tail number 28000, we ran into a serious pocket of turbulent air, knocking Press Secretary Sean Spicer and several reporters off balance. No one was injured and once back on his feet, Spicer continued the session without hesitation.

Most *Air Force One* flights are domestic in destination, frequently involving a return to Joint Base Andrews the same day. Presidents, of course, do sometimes travel overseas. For those international trips there is usually a refueling stop—ideally at a US military base. When we went from the Group of Seven meeting in Canada to the first summit with Kim Jong Un in Singapore, the plane departed the Canadian Forces Base at Bagotville in Quebec with a gas stop at 3 A.M. local time at the Souda Bay military base on the Greek island of Crete. Most of us disembarked for a middle-of-the-night off-the-record informal chat with a senior administration official under the port-side wing of the plane during the refueling.

Extended time on *Air Force One* is grueling for officials, the crew, and journalists, who find themselves working during the flight. For example, the trip from Canada to Singapore exceeded 17 hours. The president has the luxury to snooze fully horizontal in his private cabin, wake up refreshed, and begin a full day on arrival as he did on the flight from North America to Asia. The rest of us, who also need to hit the ground running, try to find a way to get some time napping in flight. For the journalists this is challenging since no one wants to sleep through an unplanned visit to our cabin from the president, a Cabinet member, or the press secretary. Although no one can say for certainty what the president will do in flight, I try to ascertain from one of the press officials on board whether the president is going to leave us alone.

Embarrassing incidents for the media (and others) on board *Air Force One* have occurred in the lavatories, with phones accidentally dropped into the toilets. The bathroom amenities are excellent—on par with commercial business class. There are soaps, antibacterial gels, skin lotions, toothpaste and toothbrushes, razors, plush recyclable hand towels, and mouthwash. No one wants to have bad breath when face-to-face with the president.

6

Many US presidents, since World War Two, have taken their first trip abroad to a neighboring nation or a critical ally to demonstrate closeness of bilateral ties. For Dwight Eisenhower, Gerald Ford, Ronald Reagan, and George W. Bush, it was Mexico (although Eisenhower went to South Korea as president-elect). The initial international trips of John F. Kennedy, Lyndon Johnson, George H. W. Bush, Bill Clinton, and Barack Obama were north to Canada. Richard Nixon went on a tour of Europe five weeks after his inauguration. America's key transatlantic ally, the United Kingdom, was Jimmy Carter's premier trip outside the borders of the United States, as it was for Joe Biden.

Donald Trump, in keeping with the nontraditional nature of his presidency, remarkably chose Saudi Arabia despite his campaign rhetoric to impose a "Muslim ban" on travel to the United States. The kingdom, of course, was a key geostrategic player due to its location in the volatile Middle East and power and wealth derived from oil. Critics noted Trump's long-standing ties to Saudis as sources of loans and other means to money, going back to 1991, when on the verge of bankruptcy, the New York City real estate investor sold his yacht at a significant discount to Saudi billionaire Prince Alwaleed bin-Talal.

During that initial week overseas Trump would also go to Jerusalem, Bethlehem, Rome, Vatican City, a NATO summit in Brussels, and a G-7 leaders' meeting in Sicily. I was there for all of it—a marathon of travel and reportage that put significant stress on the White House press and staff, Secret Service agents, and our hosts.

There were highlights (the president, a black yarmulke atop his golden coiffure, tucking a note inside the Western Wall per Jewish custom) and lowlights (Trump shoving aside Prime Minister Dŭsko Marković of Montenegro to get to the front of the pack for the NATO leaders' group

35

photo). However, two images from the first stop will likely outlast memories of the other destinations. The first was a smiling Trump, clad in suit and blue-and-white tie, waggling a saber in the Saudi capital while he bobbed to the drumming alongside men in traditional dress during a ceremonial sword dance. The second indelible image was the pose with Melania at his side, facing the Egyptian president and Saudi king as they all laid hands on a mysterious, glowing orb. At both these events, I was hovering near the president, out of camera view, simultaneously recording audio as the radio pool reporter, furiously dispatching descriptions to the pool chain and Twitter, and trying to snap a few pictures to capture the incongruity of what the sound and written words could not fully convey. We also witnessed Trump entering the Royal Court as bagpipes played to receive a gold medal, the Collar of Abdulaziz Al Saud, the kingdom's highest civilian honor, from King Salman.

I had flown to Riyadh on the White House press charter plane from Joint Base Andrews with a refueling stop at Hahn airport in Germany. Already jet-lagged and barely conscious, I got almost no sleep the first night in Saudi Arabia attempting to track down my luggage, which had gone to the other hotel, where most of the White House journalists were staying. I was assigned to the Ritz Carlton (not yet known as the world's most luxurious torture chamber), where the pool reporters were lodged. Such baggage boondoggles are common on presidential trips for those rotating in and out of the pool daily (as is the case with those assigned radio duty).

I have scant memory of the sleep-deprived three-day stay in the Saudi capital as pool reporting meant working from early morning until late at night. My heroes of the trip were the Bangladeshi waiters of the hotel's Italian restaurant who agreed to keep the restaurant open past 11 P.M. so a few of the famished and very weary White House journalists could finally eat a meal. We tipped them handsomely and wished we could have awarded them the Collar of Abdulaziz Al Saud.

I left Riyadh in one of the press vans near the rear of the presidential motorcade to the airport, our nervous local driver's right foot hard on the accelerator pedal attempting to keep pace with the speeding high-powered vehicles. Nothing seems more hazardous in our line of work than riding in motorcades when speeds approach 90 miles per hour with vehicle bumpers inches apart. Typing pool reports on my laptop or cell phone was a necessary distraction. The *Air Force One* flight that day would be historic—the first known nonstop journey from Saudi

Arabia to Israel. (Joe Biden, in 2022, made history flying in the other direction, and soon after commercial flights between the two countries with no diplomatic relations commenced.)

The Israelis, not wanting to be outdone by the Saudis, put on a welcome at Ben Gurion International Airport that Trump would brag about throughout his term. Prime Minister Benjamin Netanyahu ordered all his Cabinet ministers to attend. There were red carpets and multiple military honor guards. A photo I snapped of the pomp highlights the ham radio W7VOA "QSL" card I exchange with amateur radio operators around the world with whom I've made contact on the shortwave bands.

Something occurred on the tarmac in a fraction of a second and is what most of the world will remember of the arrival. With wife Melania on his left, the president reached out his hand for the first lady to take. Instead, she flicked her wrist to swat it away, a scene that went viral and launched a million-meme march across the internet, increasing speculation about the state of Trump's third marriage. The first lady's press secretary, Stephanie Grisham (later to become White House press secretary), would recall the slap was more akin to a game than a spat—the president "often tried to hold her hand or messed with her hands on purpose in front of the camera to irritate her" and in this particular instance Melania rebuffed him, considering it was "against protocol to hold hands at such a formal ceremony."

7

During the coronavirus pandemic, the James Brady Press Briefing Room in the White House experienced a mutation. Most of the 49 seats sat empty during news conferences. The briefings were never conducted by the press secretary—but by the president himself. Trump did not use the room to talk with reporters until COVID-19 reached pandemic proportions, although he had been loquacious with the pool reporters in the Oval Office and other venues, including during overseas trips.

For the first three years of the Trump administration, my VOA colleagues and I took turns in our assigned seat in the fourth row for briefings by the press secretary or other officials. The first wave of culling due to social distancing left every other seat unoccupied and sent us to the back of the room in a seat shared with PBS. The second wave left two occupied seats in each of the seven rows. VOA was usually in the room only when we took our turn as the radio pool reporter.

Some networks dropped out of the rotation entirely for fear of infection, so VOA volunteered as often as possible, even though that meant sitting closer to wandering photographers and other people than the six feet (approximately two meters) recommended by the Centers for Disease Control and Prevention.

Getting into the room and within questioning range of the president— either for the pool sprays or the briefings—required passing two temperature checks, one at the northwest gate and the other inside the West Wing. Paul Farhi, media reporter at the *Washington Post,* asked me what it was like to transition from the routine to the risky.

Navigating the West Wing, I replied, had become "like trying to avoid triggering an invisible delayed-action land mine." Farhi's article mentioned I had covered natural disasters, worked in combat zones, and traveled to Fukushima, Japan, in 2011 to report on the nuclear reactor meltdown. I said I had never felt as much apprehension about getting to a story as riding the Metro to the White House over the past week.

I no longer rode the Metro, the mass-transit rail system in the Washington, DC, region. Service had been severely reduced. For a couple of weeks, I drove from Northern Virginia to downtown DC until the parking garages began to pull down their shutters at 6 P.M. I began using a ride-share service and, like many people unclear on the real risks from the virus, hoped a car handle didn't contain the virus or that the driver wouldn't sneeze.

A few correspondents and photographers began wearing masks by April 2020. None of those on the podium, standing far less than six feet apart, did.

Chanel Rion, a journalist with the right-wing One America News Network, defied the social distancing diktat of the White House Correspondents' Association, which controls the seating, and stood in the back of the briefing room. She contended she was a guest of the press secretary. Trump repeatedly called on her for questions. The WHCA removed OANN from the seating rotation as punishment, but Rion was undeterred. Trump knew well who she was. There was a photograph of the president's hands on her bare shoulders at the Mar-a-Lago Christmas party in 2019.

The president was less familiar with some of the other reporters in the room. "Who are you with?" he would often ask reporters, usually those who were African American or of Asian descent. He asked that question one day to my VOA colleague Patsy Widakuswara, days after she had spoken with him during a gaggle on an *Air Force One* flight.

"Boy, amazing," he replied to her when she identified herself as a Voice of America correspondent.

Patsy then asked her question again about whether he would waive visa restrictions for immigrant doctors amid the pandemic.

Trump ignored her repeated query, saying, "Okay. Who else please?"

The COVID briefings could drag on for more than two hours. On a few days when the weather was nice, they were moved outside to the Rose Garden. The briefings started with President Trump, Vice President Pence, and two prominent physicians—Anthony Fauci and Deborah Birx—in supporting roles. The meeting was officially the White House Coronavirus Task Force briefing. Trump referred to them as news conferences, but COVID-19 was the key topic. Some of what Trump said as president and as someone without public health credentials was potentially harmful if anyone took him literally. Trump riffed about injecting bleach as a possible treatment, hitting the body with "very powerful light," and contending 99 percent of COVID-19 cases were nothing to worry about.

The president touted an antimalarial drug, hydroxychloroquine, as a COVID-19 treatment. A man in Arizona died after he ingested a similar-named aquarium fish medication, chloroquine phosphate.

"We saw his press conference," the deceased man's wife told *NBC News.* She explained they had the fish drug on a shelf because she had previously had koi (ornamental carp) and because "we were afraid of getting sick," they mixed it with some liquid and quickly became very ill.

"Everybody around the president lives in fear of contradicting the president. On his worse comments, they say he was just kidding or being sarcastic, but they will never say he's wrong. The problem is he is wrong most of the time," Joe Lockhart, a White House press secretary in the Clinton administration, responded when I asked for his comment on why Trump's outlandish musings on responses to the pandemic went unchallenged at the time by administration officials.

Based on Trump's whims or reporters' questions, comments from the president during these coronavirus briefings also included oil prices, Joe Biden's mental state, the million-dollar base salary of the head of the Tennessee Valley Authority, criticism of VOA and other broadcasters, and a possible pardon for the "Tiger King," the protagonist of a Netflix crime documentary.

When an opportunity arose from my briefing room seat, I tried to get Trump to answer questions about the pandemic. It could be a frustrating experience.

At one session I asked Trump about states collectively taking matters into their own hands on deciding when to reopen, a move that undermined his directives and touched on the issue of federalism echoing the intense debates between Thomas Jefferson and Alexander Hamilton in the early days of the republic (although I didn't add that historical context to my question as Trump certainly would have cut me off). As it was, he began replying while I was still in mid-sentence, having decided he needed to hear nothing further. His answer summed up his simple, vague, and somewhat contradictory philosophical approach to the presidency, which would cause him no shortage of legal grief after his term in office.

"The president of the United States has the authority to do what the president has the authority to do, which is very powerful. The president of the United States calls the shots. If we weren't here for the states, you would have had a problem in this country like you've never seen before. We were here to back them up and we more than backed them up. We did a job that nobody ever thought was possible. It's a decision for the president of the United States. That being said, we're going to work with the states."

Trump continued his convoluted explanation that it was "like a microchip. They're pinpointed. We have local government that hopefully will do a good job. And if they don't do a good job, I'd step in so fast. They can't do anything without the approval of the president of the United States."

Imagine having to report that succinctly and simply so that it could be understood in more than 45 languages. That was my job.

On days when VOA didn't have a seat in the briefing room, I covered these COVID events from a newly configured studio located in the small library room of my rambler home in a historic hamlet halfway between the White House and George Washington's Mount Vernon. Later in the pandemic as the US death toll headed toward one million, I moved farther south to a secluded peninsula in Virginia.

I was not the first person desiring to put more distance between myself and the nation's capital during an epidemic. In centuries past, Washington, DC, had to contend with smallpox epidemics. Yellow fever was a worry until the end of the nineteenth century. Malaria was once so endemic in the city built on a coastal floodplain that congressmen used it as an excuse for missing meetings. In 1881, more than 100 Washingtonians died of the mosquito-borne disease. The Spanish flu a century ago claimed 3,000 Washingtonians. About one in five residents of the District of Columbia became infected with the coronavirus and at least 1,400 died, but that is considered by health authorities to likely be a significant undercount because the number includes only those whose coronavirus infections were confirmed by molecular laboratory tests.

History frequently repeats itself in Washington, and epidemics are no exception.

8

Reporters who frequently asked questions of President Trump honed techniques to try to extract effective answers from him. It was a skill more critical as the United States and the world confronted the coronavirus pandemic.

"I just think it's a nasty question," the president responded in March 2020 to Yamiche Alcindor of *PBS Newshour* when she asked about denying responsibility for disbanding the White House pandemic office.

CNN White House Correspondent Jim Acosta queried Trump during a meeting with bankers in the Cabinet Room: "What do you say to Americans who are concerned that you're not taking this seriously enough and that some of your statements don't match what your health experts are saying?"

"That's CNN. Fake news," the president responded. No further questions were entertained that day.

Trump was the critic-in-chief when it came to assessing journalists' questions, a tradition dating back to the early twentieth century when President Theodore Roosevelt was interviewed (albeit off the record) by reporters in the morning while his barber shaved him.

Trump often was the one wielding the rhetorical razor—frequently cutting off reporters before they could complete a full sentence. His instant retorts could be sharp. "What a stupid question," he would sometimes reply.

Trump once told Alcindor, a native of Miami born to parents from Haiti, "That is such a racist question."

Trump did make himself more accessible to journalists than most presidents. His predecessor, Barack Obama, had called on reporters from a prepared list. But Trump maintained tight control over which questions to field, the length of the interactions, and which voices were prominent.

"Ask a multi-part question and it's important in your first few words to get his attention and get an answer," noted *National Journal* White House Correspondent George Condon, who has questioned ten presidents. That proved difficult with this president. Trump is "going to cut you off and he's going to seize on the beginning of your preamble," said Condon.

Probing follow-up questions to challenge the US president when he misstated or distorted facts rarely got completed. Trump would halt the questioner or immediately attack the reporter or his or her news organization, rather than offer any evidence to back up his assertions.

Members of the White House press corps would frequently shout questions at the president over the roar of helicopter engines on the White House South Lawn. Condon told me he learned a key lesson from covering President Ronald Reagan. "And it's true for every president—a simple, short question is always the most effective."

Former CNN Senior White House Correspondent Charles Bierbauer also recalled Reagan avoiding answering questions yelled by reporters amid the helicopters. "Pro-Reagan crowds in the Rose Garden or on South Lawn would hoot and chastise us" for shouting questions at the president, Bierbauer told me when I rang him to jog his memory. "So, you shout over each other to get the president's attention. You risk being ignored, dismissed or disparaged."

Bierbauer, who became a distinguished professor and dean emeritus at the University of South Carolina, observed that White House reporters covering Trump had to "look for the slightest edge," situating themselves where Trump was most likely to see and hear them, "knowing the buzzwords that work."

The chaotic and noisy situations are also opportunities the president can play to his advantage.

"He is, after all, the conductor; you are the bleating bassoons," said Bierbauer.

"He can pick and choose which questions he wants," agreed Noah Bierman, White House reporter for the *Los Angeles Times*. Rarely could the television audience hear the question. "So, if you ask a very challenging question that might put him in a bad light, he can answer it any way he wants. And the public may not know that it was actually a very difficult and challenging question."

Unlike some of his predecessors, Trump frequently took questions at the end of the "pool sprays"—the quick visits to the Oval Office, Cabinet

Room, or Roosevelt Room for the limited pool of journalists who share what we gather with other news outlets.

These events traditionally showed the public the visuals of routine office meetings: a handshake and brief, anodyne comments made by the president and a visiting head of state, or the start of a Cabinet meeting with grim-faced officials seated around a table. Trump, however, turned these events into media spectacles, often lasting more than an hour with extensive unscripted commentary, as well as numerous questions taken from reporters.

Trump could compliment a reporter's question, even if it is unremarkable—something that would also distract the questioner.

"That's the best question you ever asked," Trump once replied to me in the Oval Office, when I queried whether he had yet congratulated the new British prime minister, Boris Johnson.

I reminded him I had asked the question earlier and he had said no. The president explained he had, minutes before, been on the phone with Johnson right before we had walked in. A small piece of news resulted from repeating my question, which did not happen with most of the questions put to Trump when he was president. He gave extended exclusive interviews to certain media outlets, including Fox News, seen as a cheerleader for his administration compared to other US cable news channels more critical of him.

Greta Van Susteren, now with the Newsmax cable channel, had extensive experience interviewing Trump for decades before he became president. Known for her nonconfrontational style, she suggested the best question to a president "begins with 'why' and you just let them talk. You get a lot more information that way."

Trump gave Van Susteren two interviews during overseas presidential trips (in Singapore and Argentina) for her weekly VOA television program. Van Susteren, who has been interviewing presidents since George H. W. Bush, lamented the frequent acrimony between reporters and Trump, later telling me it went "so far off the rails on both sides," noting "all presidents are always gaming us in the media." She added, however, it remains the job of the journalists "to scrutinize the people in power."

Bierman agreed. "I think it is important that we, as reporters, remind the public that our primary job is to question authority, no matter who it is and to ask tough questions," he said. "It might seem at times like we're being rude or pushy, but we're there as their proxies and we need to make all the people we cover accountable and sometimes uncomfortable."

9

Despite never visiting Washington as a child, I was a 1960s kid who had a picture chart on my Cincinnati bedroom wall listing all the US presidents in chronological order, which I tried to memorize. Few of my classmates had ever heard of Franklin Pierce or Chester Arthur. They couldn't cite the shortest stint in office for a president (the 31 days of William Henry Harrison) or knew who was the heaviest (William Howard Taft, a rotund 350 pounds near the end of his presidency). I was partial to Big Bill—his family name was plastered all around Cincinnati. Taft Theatre, Taft Museum, Taft Broadcasting, Taft High School (named after his son, a US senator). A few decades later I would meet President Taft's great-grandson, Ohio Governor Robert Taft.

Seven US presidents were Buckeyes by birth and an eighth, Harrison, had represented Ohio in both chambers of Congress. It wasn't that I went around the playground spewing presidential statistics—I wasn't that weird. But I was an American and an Ohioan. And from an early age I was interested in the way the world worked and came to realize I had been born in an era when one nation—mine—had achieved power unparalleled in history. But there were hints from Walter Cronkite on the *CBS Evening News* that we were not omnipotent. The television coverage of the Vietnam War did not resemble the heroism of World War Two. And when I asked elders about the Korean War, which ended in a stalemate a half-dozen years before my birth, I got little clarity but discerned it was something very different from the World War Two glorified in my textbooks.

The tone of the songs on the radio switched quickly, moving from the Drifters' chipper references to carousels and amusement park foods in mid-1964 to more ominous somethings in Buffalo Springfield's "For What It's Worth" at the very end of 1966.

I was a late Eisenhower-era baby but had no memory of him as president; however, he tops my list for the Americana memorabilia I collect despite the former army general having defeated Senator Robert Taft of Ohio for the Republican nomination in 1952.

Eisenhower's successor, John Fitzgerald Kennedy, was the charismatic image beamed into the black-and-white television in our living room as I went from crawling to walking. The broadcast of his funeral is one of my earliest memories. I was too young to have comprehended the enormity of the tragedy, but I can recall the marathon programming with its lack of the familiar laundry detergent commercials, the somber mood, and the remarkable sight of 300,000 people lining the route from the White House to the Capitol to watch a horse-drawn caisson carrying Kennedy's flag-draped coffin. Only years later during secondary school would I fully comprehend what Kennedy's election had meant to many Americans—it was possible for someone other than a Protestant to be president.

For young Americans well into the twenty-first century, who clearly see discrimination against people of color and nonnative English speakers, it is probably difficult to fathom that well into the previous century, those of Irish and Catholic descent were considered an inferior class. When Kennedy ran for president in 1960, detractors declared a Catholic in the White House would take his orders from Pope John XXIII.

Pundits pointed to the presidential candidacy of an earlier Catholic Democrat—New York Governor Al Smith in 1928—whose campaign had been crushed by religious bigotry. For Kennedy's campaign to be deemed viable, he needed a victory against Hubert Humphrey in West Virginia, which was the least Catholic state in the Union. Usually overlooked in primary seasons, Kennedy lavished attention on the impoverished state. His two brothers, as well as his wife, also visited, including trips to coalfield country. Humphrey made a terrible mistake during a joint appearance at a Mercer County event, saying he was happy to be in Virginia. The crowd corrected him, but Humphrey (later vice president under Lyndon Johnson) plowed on. Kennedy, next up, made no such mistake, telling the crowd he was delighted to be in West Virginia. Kennedy would capture nearly 61 percent of the vote in the state's primary, forcing Humphrey out of the race.

A quarter of a century later I lived in West Virginia, working as a staff reporter for the Associated Press, traversing 44 of the state's 55 counties. One day at a roadside market, I realized the lingering power of JFK. One booth sold velvet paintings. Only three historical figures were featured: Jesus Christ, Elvis Presley, and John F. Kennedy.

It was Kennedy's successor—thrust into the presidency by assassination—Lyndon Johnson, who first impressed upon me the awesome responsibility and power of a president. Johnson could send a fleet of planes to bomb faraway lands. But he also dispatched soldiers to Alabama to protect people who wanted to peacefully march for what the TV reporters called "civil rights." Sometimes the demonstrations were not so civil. The outrage became even more difficult for a white kid north of the Mason-Dixon Line to comprehend when rioters smashed and looted businesses in the Avondale neighborhood of Cincinnati, where my paternal grandfather ran a secondhand merchandise store.

Watching the drama-filled nightly newscasts while doing my homework, I became fascinated with Johnson at the White House and wondered how he made important decisions.

As an eight-year-old in Ohio, I made my move to get involved in politics in 1968. Riding my bicycle in our middle-class Roselawn neighborhood, inhabited mostly by a mix of second-generation Italian Catholics and Ashkenazi Jews, I handed out campaign buttons and bumper stickers for the state's Republican attorney general, Bill Saxbe, making a bid for US senator.

Saxbe was victorious. Mission accomplished. I had no ideological affinity with the tobacco-chewing Saxbe whom, of course, I had not met. But it was *fun* to have some direct involvement, albeit at the lowest level possible, with an adult political campaign. Saxbe later spent a year as attorney general of the United States at the end of the tumultuous Nixon presidency (and some months into the Ford administration)—an appointment made by Nixon despite Saxbe's criticism of the president. Saxbe was subsequently appointed by Ford to become ambassador to India, where decades later I would be based as a VOA bureau chief.

The first US senator from Ohio I would ever meet was former astronaut John Glenn, who was elected to succeed Saxbe (although Howard Metzenbaum had been appointed to fill Saxbe's seat when he became attorney general). My burgeoning interest in civics was among more typical boyhood passions, ranging from numismatics to baseball. But even among these hobbies the presidents appeared. They were on the coins I collected (always checking change for that elusive 1944 steel penny with Abe Lincoln on the obverse). And presidents got to throw out that ceremonial first pitch on opening day of the Major League Baseball season, where the first game was usually held in Cincinnati, a tribute to the Reds being the oldest professional team. Taft started the tradition in 1910, tossing out a ball to Washington Senators pitcher Walter Johnson to the delight of the 14,000 fans. The event nearly turned into disaster when a foul ball off the bat of Philadelphia Athletics slugger Frank Baker hit Secretary of State and former congressman Charles Bennett in the head. A dazed Bennett waved to the silenced crowd and the game continued.

The first US president I saw in the flesh was at a baseball game—Richard Nixon at the All-Star Game in Riverfront Stadium in Cincinnati on July 14, 1970. Nixon stayed for the entire game, which lasted 12 innings, longer than my family endured as my mother insisted on leaving before the end of the regulation nine innings to beat the traffic out of the parking lot, meaning we missed one of the most controversial moments in baseball history when my hometown hero, Pete Rose, plowed into catcher Ray Fosse to score the game-winning run for the National League.

I had missed the climax of one of the most exciting All-Star Games, but I had seen a president with my myopic eyes—he was a distant blur in the crowd of nearly 52,000. My political development at that stage was also still nascent. I supported the president (all of them in succession) because, in that era in my family, that was synonymous with patriotism. My father was not an ideologue and would cast his vote for whom he regarded as the better man (they were always men back then), regardless of party. Only in later decades would my family become politically polarized as has happened across the country.

My father and the newscasts reminded me that the "Silent Majority" supported Nixon, although since the 1968 campaign it was abundantly clear that a lot of young people did not, but they were dismissed as dope-smoking hippies in my household. I did not understand why Johnson would not run for reelection.

"I shall not seek and I will not accept the nomination of my party as your President," I watched Johnson announce on March 31, 1968, citing the "division in the American house." I knew he was the most powerful man in America, and it was incomprehensible how he could give it all up just like that. Reflecting on this after Watergate and Nixon's resignation some years later, it seemed like a bad decision by Johnson. Some historians indicate the real reason he decided not to run in 1968 was his fragile physical and mental health. Johnson, in retirement in Texas, had a replica Oval Office built, out of which he worked, and ordered a custom-built Lincoln Continental black "presidential" limousine with a television and radio-telephone in the backseat. Both are on display at the Lyndon Baines Johnson Presidential Library in Austin.

Gerald Ford gave the impression of being a nice enough guy, but some adults around me could not forgive him for pardoning Nixon. And he was parodied by Chevy Chase as a bumbler whose brains had been scrambled by a college football injury.

In 1975, a year before Ford's failed attempt to transition from unelected to elected president, I watched a speech in Las Vegas by a Democrat who would be among the 17 or so to run for his party's nomination. As I shook hands and exchanged a few words with the politician, the relatively obscure candidate struck me as a down-to-earth fellow who lacked the charisma or fervor to become president. How wrong I was. Jimmy Carter would win his party's nomination and defeat the sitting president the following year.

In recent years, when asked who I think is going to emerge the victor for presidential contests, be they primaries or general elections, I tell them how wrong I was during my initial attempts to handicap such races.

I interviewed Carter twice in his postpresidential career as a humanitarian. I didn't have the heart to recount how I sold him short after our initial encounter.

10

A benefit to beginning my journalism career as a teenager in Las Vegas in the late 1970s was although it was a relatively small media market at the time, everybody who was anybody came through town at least once a year. The casinos lured millions of visitors annually, and the gambling-infused hospitality led to an infrastructure for hosting major trade shows and conventions. Those events attracted celebrity guest speakers from the president on down. At one such industry gathering, a cluster of local reporters assembled for an interaction with George H. W. Bush, then vice president. I cannot recall what question I asked him or whether his reply merited inclusion in our local newscast. But such media opportunities allowed us to fill in on the spot for the networks who would not send a crew unless it was known the event would be of national significance.

My radio mentor, Bill Buckmaster (subsequently a longtime public TV news anchorman and radio talk show host in Tucson, Arizona), taught me the technique of "dialing for dollars." Our bit of news voiced around a snippet of audiotape could be fed through the phone lines to various radio networks. Back then these "wraps" could each net us $20 to $40 and if successful in feeding several networks a couple of times a week, it amounted to a respectable supplement to our meager salaries.

Hearing my voice hours later on the CBS or NBC hourly radio newscasts was a thrill, and I suspect that when I began "stringing" for the broadcast, few in the audience had any idea that the reporter on the scene in Las Vegas was a teenager.

The side work helped build my confidence at a young age that I could perform at the network level. Some in the industry noticed and would remember my Las Vegas reporting decades later. I never fantasized about becoming a White House correspondent. It wasn't imaginable. If I was very lucky, I said to myself, I could dream of being a radio field reporter in a larger nearby market—such as Phoenix. Perhaps I would one day work at KNX, the highly rated all-news radio station in Los Angeles. I thought I might, as a tourist, eventually peer through the gate of the White House from Pennsylvania Avenue, but I didn't harbor any dream of working inside that building.

My career path began in seventh grade at Fremont Junior High School in Las Vegas. Seventh graders were allowed to take one elective, and I struggled to choose. There were few options—including industrial arts for the boys and home economics for the girls (it was a different era)—and I contemplated selecting the boys' class, colloquially known as "shop." My mother, rightly concerned about me handling sharp tools (I showed no potential as the handyman type despite my father's skill as an electrician), suggested the safer journalism elective, saying, "You're a good writer." That was a revelation to me as my mother rarely uttered compliments. I wasn't sure what "journalism" was, and when it was explained I would be able to work on the school newspaper, I was intrigued.

Florence Beebe, a patient woman in her early 60s, taught special education, typing, and journalism. The journalism students sat in the typing classroom once a week. In later years, when I began working full-time in newsrooms, I realized typing had been the most valuable skill acquired from middle school as I watched two-fingered typists struggle with keyboards. Mrs. Beebe's most critical contribution was letting me write while correcting grammar, improving my style, and instilling the fundamentals of journalism: Who, what, where, when, and why. The work as a reporter and editor on school newspapers felt natural, fun, and rewarding over a five-year period—more so than math, science, or any of the attempted extracurricular activities (most unsuccessfully the Valley High School track and field team, for which I was never chosen to compete and ended up listed in the yearbook team photo as "unidentified").

Las Vegas in the late 1970s outpunched its weight class as a regular dateline for big news stories, at least those that could generate headlines beyond Nevada. The fodder was provided by celebrities, colorful politicians, hotel disasters, as well as mobsters and resulting bodies in the desert and other intriguing homicides. This gave fledging journalists the opportunity to cover stories more commonly experienced at the national level, to learn and make rookie mistakes that would make me a savvier reporter when I found myself, decades later, reporting from Lima, Kathmandu, or the White House.

Besides the organized-crime skullduggery, the celebrity performers on the Las Vegas Strip, boozy conventions, and shady politics, the expansive desert yielded more than murder victims. To the north of the city was the Nevada Test Site. A sprawling 1,355 square-mile federal reservation larger than the state of Rhode Island, it was best known for testing nuclear weapons. Before my family had moved to Nevada in 1971, aboveground tests had been set off on a regular basis (there were more than 100 of them), becoming a tourist attraction in Las Vegas as visitors could see the mushroom clouds rising from the north.

One of my first investigative series of reports focused on the health effects of those who lived downwind from these atmospheric blasts. It was evident that Atomic Energy Commission (or AEC, a predecessor to the Department of Energy) officials would wait until the winds were not blowing toward Los Angeles to explode their bombs. The radiation clouds headed toward less populated and less influential communities. It was an early lesson in what we now would call environmental justice as the federal government sought to downplay the severity of the fallout. In the late 1970s some of those in the affected communities gathered and analyzed data linking high rates of diseases, such as acute myeloid leukemia, to the weapons tests. Subsistence farms and ranches had suffered exposure, and locals had consumed contaminated beef, milk, and vegetables. From 1951 to 1962 the radiation that went into the atmosphere from those tests was equivalent to 20 times the amount released during the 1986 Chernobyl nuclear accident in Ukraine.

The single-worst episode, little known even now to the American public, occurred on May 19, 1953, part of what was Operation Upshot-Knothole, testing a new and more efficient hollow-core nuclear bomb design. The blast created more fallout than had been anticipated. Carried by the strong early morning winds, the radiation blanketed the town of St. George in Utah, which was inhabited by about 4,500 people, most of them Mormons.

"Dirty Harry," as the bomb test came to be known, had a yield of 32 kilotons and was responsible for half of the total radiation the public within a 300-mile radius of the test site was exposed to during the entirety of testing in Nevada. The radiation levels maxed out Geiger counters in the Utah town, but almost no one was advised to take shelter. Schoolchildren were out on a playground an hour after the radiation had settled. The AEC, amid growing concern, issued an emergency film to try to convince the public they were not in danger.

The AEC, however, did not take preventive measures for future tests, such as warning those downwind to stay indoors immediately following a detonation or not to consume local vegetables or milk for a period of time, although some government health experts knew this should have been recommended.

A postscript to the "Dirty Harry" test: A year later, a major Hollywood movie was filmed for several weeks outside of St. George on soil contaminated by the fallout from that test and nearly a dozen others that had been conducted in 1952. The film, titled *The Conqueror,* coproduced by Howard Hughes, starred John Wayne and focused on a thirteenth-century war between Genghis Khan and Tartars. It is considered one of the worst movies of the 1950s. Wayne, a heavy cigarette smoker, would die of stomach cancer at the age of 72. Nearly half of the cast and crew of 220 would develop cancer by 1980, and 46 were dead of the disease by that time.

As I would find out, subsequently covering a federal trial about another nuclear test, it is difficult to definitively conclude any individual exposure is responsible for a cancer case decades later, but when the epidemiological statistics indicate an anomaly, it should raise concern among journalists and public health officials.

Federal officials continued to resist taking responsibility for cancer deaths from the atomic tests when I began dealing with them decades later, an early lesson in obfuscation with legal and lethal consequences.

By the time I began my journalism career, the nuclear tests had gone underground. The last atmospheric US nuclear test had been conducted on November 4, 1962.

The middle-of-the-road music format radio station where I worked for several years, KORK AM, had a three-person news team, something of a rarity these days except at a few major-market all-news radio stations. Bill Buckmaster and his team (including Jackie Glass, who would become a district court and syndicated TV judge) took reporting seriously, and it was an excellent training ground where I was given considerable responsibility for field reporting, as well as producing and anchoring newscasts. Every time there was a nuclear detonation at the Nevada Test Site, the US Department of Energy would provide a live audio feed for local radio stations to warn residents and tourists about imminent tremors, the effects of which were magnified in the upper reaches of the expanding number of high-rise hotels and casinos on the Las Vegas Strip.

From one of those underground tests, on May 10, 1978, I learned to be skeptical regarding what government officials might claim. The nuclear test was code-named Transom, and the weapon was buried at 2,100 feet. The test—part of the Energy Department's Operation Cresset, which consisted of 16 announced and seven secret detonations in the Nevada desert—was expected to have a yield of 20 to 150 kilotons, powerful enough to shake buildings in Las Vegas. KORK and other radio stations aired the countdown seconds before 8 A.M. Energy Department spokesman David Jackson then described dust rising from ground zero and a few seconds later, feeling the rocking motion at the command post.

At our radio station, Buckmaster's news team swung into action to gather reaction, including from the Top of the Strip restaurant's legendary maître d' August Nogar at the Dunes Hotel & Casino. He was always flustered by the atomic blasts. Nogar would reliably tell us how the seismic swaying made him nauseous. His flamboyant commentary made for somewhat hilarious sound bites, which Buckmaster, for years, had supplied to various radio networks in the United States and around the world, earning a modest outcome income—part of our "dialing for dollars" side gig. On that day the Dunes maître d' was uncharacteristically calm, intoning he certainly did not detect any movement atop the 24-story tower. Neither could we find anyone else who experienced a shaking sensation. This was unprecedented. Based on this reporting of an apparent nonevent, the Energy Department spokesman was compelled to belatedly admit the nuclear test was a dud, and he had been dutifully reading off a script, not describing in the countdown broadcast what he had actually seen and felt (which was nothing). "National security precautions," he said, prevented him from explaining why Transom had failed to detonate.

This was an early and important tutorial as a journalist that government agencies and public officials sometimes lie. And it was a revelation that helped me build healthy skepticism when government officials told me and other reporters to believe their words and statements, not other evidence we had gathered. This is now referred to as *gaslighting,* a term taken from a 1944 movie, starring Charles Boyer and Ingrid Bergman, in which the male protagonist repeatedly tells his wife she is imagining things that are actually happening—including the dimming of the home's gaslights—convincing her she has gone insane.

A far more serious incident at the Nevada Test Site had occurred some years before the faked dud test. This was the 1970 Baneberry incident— prior to the start of my journalism career. Nearly a decade later, the ramifications of that flawed nuclear test played out in a federal courtroom in Las Vegas, and the case would continue through the appeals process until 1996.

The 41-day Baneberry trial in 1979 was the first big courtroom case I covered extensively. The experience, while no substitute for a proper legal education, did provide a solid grounding in the rules of evidence and on-the-job training about how to quickly transform highly technical testimony into understandable daily news reports for a nonscientific audience.

Baneberry is a poisonous desert fruit, an ironic code name that government scientists surely regretted shortly after sunrise at Yucca Flat on December 18, 1970, when something unplanned occurred 900 feet below the desert surface, 65 miles northwest of Las Vegas. The nuclear device, like all others the United States and the Soviet Union detonated since 1963 when an atmospheric test ban had gone into effect, was supposed to contain its radioactive force underground. The blast, less than the equivalent of 20,000 tons of TNT, disturbed an adjacent pocket of water, creating a 100-yard-long surface crack, sending a toxic cloud 8,000 feet aboveground. About 900 Nevada Test Site employees were in the area, including two Wackenhut security guards, Harley Roberts and William Nunamaker. Both would die four years later of acute myeloid leukemia after being among the 86 test site workers exposed to the radioactive fallout.

The guards' widows sued the federal government, with Judge Roger Foley determining those responsible for the test blast had been negligent. Foley's ruling would eventually be reversed on appeal, with a three-judge panel in San Francisco determining the widows did not have enough proof their husbands had been harmed by the radiation exposure. The case, which the KORK news team also covered for the national radio networks, prompted congressional investigations that led to the enactment of the 1990 Radiation Exposure Compensation Act.

In June 2022, President Biden signed into law an extension of the 2020 termination of the trust fund to pay successful claims filed in connection with work in uranium mines and processing the radioactive ore (for which the government has agreed to pay compensation of $100,000). Those found to be what the government characterizes as "onsite participants" of atmospheric nuclear weapons tests may be eligible for a onetime payment of $75,000. Civilians who lived downwind from the

Nevada Test Site are eligible for a onetime lump sum compensation of $50,000 on condition they "establish a subsequent diagnosis of a specified compensable disease," which are certain types of cancer, according to the US Department of Justice.

The conclusions of legal cases stemming from test detonations of atomic weapons or nuclear accidents can linger for years or decades, just like the radioactive isotopes those incidents allowed to escape containment.

11

There were other mysterious activities at the Nevada Test Site when I reported about it during the late 1970s. A rancher had his land seized by the US government in the interest of national security. We couldn't get a straight answer as to why or even which federal agency was responsible. The property was near something called Area 51. For most of the twentieth century it was a closely guarded secret, known to few who did not work there or have a very high government clearance.

Groom Lake, a salt flat, is at the core of this highly classified facility. I was among the few journalists in Las Vegas who became intensely curious about the desert lake in the late 1970s. We were told it was run by the military or the CIA, depending on what source one was speaking with. It did not take a lot of digging to determine this is where spy planes were tested, modified, and flown, including the U-2 and the SR-71. There were whispers of far more exotic aircraft, supposedly using extraterrestrial technology. I was never able to make a definitive conclusion about such claimed alien influence. There was no credible firsthand witness willing to go on the record.

One reporter, George Knapp, whom I had worked with at the Las Vegas PBS television station, KLVX, became an award-winning investigative reporter at the CBS affiliate, KLAS-TV, developing a decades-long cottage industry reporting on the supposed alien connection to Area 51. Decades later, he is still trying to solve the mysteries. Knapp is a frequent host of the syndicated radio show *Coast to Coast AM,* which focuses on the paranormal.

Some US presidential candidates promised to make public the government secrets about unidentified aerial phenomenon and tell us if there has been contact with aliens visiting Earth. Trump acknowledged being briefed on the topic, saying, "we're watching for extraterrestrials," and alternatively stating he didn't particularly believe people who claimed to have seen UFOs while he also wondered out loud if they're real. In an interview with his son, Donald Trump Jr., the president hinted he knew more about the 1947 Roswell incident (which I also investigated), stating, "I won't talk to you about what I know about it, but it's very interesting."

When the FBI seized highly classified documents Trump had taken home with him to Florida after his presidency, I wondered whether any of them were about aliens.

Other former presidents have been equally reticent to reveal what they know. Having been informed of something that potentially could disrupt the social order, did some presidents vow to never make the knowledge public?

Barack Obama, on a late-night talk show, said he had asked about aliens after taking office and was told the US government was not keeping aliens in a lab, as has been long speculated. Obama did state what is obvious to most who have an interest in the subject—there are objects in the sky that move in an unexplainable manner. Obama's fellow Democrat, Bill Clinton, was also known to have a significant interest in the phenomena and on a visit to Northern Ireland in 1996 stated, "If the United States Air Force did recover alien bodies, they didn't tell me about it, either, and I want to know." George W. Bush, asked on a late-night TV talk show about what he knew about aliens, said he would not reveal anything he had been told on the topic as president, even to his daughter, who was curious to know.

Other twentieth-century presidents had an interest in the mystery, including Jimmy Carter, who revealed having his own close encounter and vowed never to ridicule anyone claiming to have seen a UFO. During the 1976 presidential campaign (which is when I first met him), Carter promised, if elected, he would release "every piece of information" on the subject. After his victory, however, Carter reversed himself, saying public disclosure might have "defense implications" and pose a threat to national security.

The one US president who probably knew a great deal was Harry Truman. He was the commander-in-chief in July 1947, when something unusual occurred in Lincoln County, New Mexico.

Decades later I would visit there and interview some of those who claimed to have observed what happened.

12

By the late 1990s, Roswell, New Mexico, had turned its UFO legacy into a tourist industry. As busloads of visitors, some from as far away as Japan, disembarked in the sleepy desert town, dozens of pairs of walnut eyes observe them from alien-illustrated billboards and windows of Roswell's fast-food joints, gift shops, and motels.

The tourists' main stop was the ambitiously named International UFO Museum and Research Center. Inside, historical displays, documents, and photographs were on display alongside tacky UFO-themed art. While the museum may have converted few skeptics, conversations with some of those who were in the Roswell area in the summer of 1947, a couple of years into the Truman presidency, had me giving the tale more credence.

Nearly all Roswell's witnesses had kept the story to themselves for about half a century, fearing ridicule, remembering secrecy oaths they had signed or threats from military officers.

Walter Haut, age 76 at the time I met him in 1999, was perhaps the UFO museum's best exhibit. One of the few survivors at the core of the story, he paced the corridors of the Main Street attraction he helped create. As a member of the elite 509th Composite Bomb Group, at the time the world's only atomic air force, which had dropped the August 1945 warheads on Hiroshima and Nagasaki, Haut spent the early postwar era as Roswell Army Air Field's public information officer. On July 8, 1947, he was ordered by the commanding officer to issue an unprecedented press release stating the military had recovered a crashed flying saucer.

By that time, flying saucers or flying discs had been in the headlines for days. (The acronym UFO for unidentified flying object was decades away. During World War Two, pilots had referred to the mysterious aircraft as foo fighters.) The Roswell incident was not an isolated one. During the previous two weeks there had been flying saucer sightings in nearly every one of the 48 states.

Within hours of 1st Lt. Haut's noontime press release, the story was on the Associated Press and United Press wires and the front pages of western US afternoon newspapers. Later that day, high brass from outside New Mexico issued a new explanation that, in essence, said, Never mind; it's only a balloon.

Many who were there that day said the subsequent announcement was a cover story and Colonel William Blanchard's order to Haut to distribute the flying saucer press release was the truth.

Haut, who died six years after I met him, told me, "Very definitely no," Blanchard did not make a mistake.

"I'm sure Blanchard saw parts of the material," he insisted 52 years after the event.

The debris, scattered over a remote ranch 85 miles northwest of Roswell, was spotted by foreman Mac Brazell on horseback on July 3. The rancher was inspecting his spread after an intense thunderstorm the night before. He picked up some of the baffling material and rode to see his closest neighbors, the Proctors, eight miles away.

"Now I'd say it looked like plastic. But back then we didn't have plastic," said Loretta Proctor, who was 85 when I spoke with her during my New Mexico visit.

Proctor, who died in 2013 at the age of 98, said the material was tannish-brown with a purplish section, containing what she described as figures and while extremely flexible, it couldn't be burned or broken, even with hardy ranch tools.

Proctor, a mother of eight who drove a school bus over dirt roads for nearly 20 years, bristled in response to skeptics' retorts that Brazell, her family, and others who handled the material were confused or naive country bumpkins. She pointed out the US military "has told at least three different stories" about what crashed next to her ranch.

The Pentagon's latest version has been the balloon story, calling it part of a secret project, code-named Mogul, which was attempting to conduct acoustic monitoring of expected Soviet nuclear blasts. The military said the purported alien bodies recovered were test pilot crash dummies. Independent investigations determined a large quantity of debris was flown out of Roswell Army Air Field in multiple cargo aircraft and could not have been from a balloon, as such tests with dummies were not carried out until 1952.

President Truman told others that while he did not give serious thought to UFO reports, he did ask to be briefed quarterly about significant sightings, according to the late Major General Robert B. Landry, who served as the president's Air Force aide between 1948 and 1953.

"The report was to be made orally by me unless it was considered by intelligence to be so serious or alarming as to warrant a more detailed report in writing. During the four-and-one-half years in office there, all reports were made orally," said Landry in an addendum to his 1974 oral history for the Truman Library. "Nothing of substance considered credible or threatening to the country was ever received from intelligence."

Glenn Dennis, a young mortician in Roswell in 1947, however, provided me with tantalizing recollections that suggested alien bodies might have been found in New Mexico. He said he received several phone calls on July 8 from the military base asking strange questions about acquiring child-size caskets and how to preserve tissue in a body that had been out in the sun for a few days. Later that day, transporting a slightly injured enlisted man back to the base hospital, Dennis recalled he saw strange debris in a slightly ajar door in the rear of a field ambulance and an unprecedented level of security inside the base hospital. He spotted a friend, whom he described as a deeply religious nurse, in a corridor holding a towel to her face.

"She screamed at me, 'Glenn, get out as fast as you can!'" Dennis recounted. Moments later, he was threatened by an army captain, who told him not to start rumors and if he mentioned what had happened, "somebody will be picking your bones out of the sand."

The puzzled and frightened mortician was escorted off the base. The following day, at lunch, the nurse revealed she had been summoned to take dictation, in a makeshift autopsy theater, that began with the words "crash bag, two small mutilated bodies." Dennis said the convent-educated medical professional was nearly in shock as she sketched a four-fingered alien with a face remarkably similar to the big-eyed, slit-mouthed creature that decades later became ubiquitous on T-shirts, key chains, and coffee cups. Dennis said when he tried to ring her back at the base later that afternoon, she had vanished. Later in the week he was told she was no longer assigned to the base and never heard from her again.

"She asked me to take a secret oath never to reveal her name," said Dennis, 73 when I spoke with him. "So I never did."

Dennis died in 2015.

I have spoken with thousands of people during my half century as a journalist and believe I have developed a decent ability to detect when an interviewee is evasive, exaggerating, or lying. Haut, Brazell, and Dennis came across as forthright as any individuals I have interviewed.

At the so-called Corona crash site, between the Gallo and Hasperos canyons, northeast of the Capitan Mountains, nuclear physicist Stanton Friedman surveyed the suspected debris field where combing of the remote terrain by UFO researchers over years had not unearthed a shred of evidence. Friedman was greatly responsible for creating the Roswell UFO mania, interviewing key witnesses to the incident that may have been fully unveiled for only a few hours on the afternoon of July 8, 1947. He called it a "cosmic Watergate" cover-up, referring to the break-in of a building that led to President Nixon's downfall.

Friedman, who died in 2019, did not hesitate to debunk elements of the now mythical story, which had made him perhaps the most credible scientist investigating the event. He pieced together a theory that on the night of July 2, a pair of sister craft most likely collided in midair. The cause, he said he believed, was a bolt of lightning or interference from powerful radar transmissions beamed across southern New Mexico in preparation for a scheduled V-2 rocket test at the White Sands Missile Range. I did not find the explanation satisfactory, envisaging such advanced life-forms would certainly have the aerodynamic technology to avoid midair collisions due to natural or human events.

"If we could get the *Washington Post* or the *New York Times* to spend one-tenth as much as the time as they did on Monica [Lewinsky], we would blow it to smithereens," Friedman told me, referencing the sex scandal that led to President Clinton's impeachment.

The physicist criticized mainstream media for not interviewing the witnesses and always accepting the Air Force's explanation, which he contended did not hold up under journalistic or scientific scrutiny. He asserted that documentation uncovered in the 1990s should convince most skeptics that what fell near Roswell was most certainly something far more secret and exotic than a balloon.

Private investigators during the 1990s interviewed numerous witnesses, who claimed they or relatives near Magdalena, New Mexico, 120 miles west of Roswell, in early July 1947 saw a nearly intact craft lodged in the side of an arroyo. The witnesses recalled observing dead, dying, and one relatively uninjured alien at the site being removed by US troops, who forcefully escorted away passersby, including a group of summer school archaeology students from New Mexico State University.

Friedman, who said he had worked on US government secret nuclear projects, contended his independent research proved "a few people in government have known since 1947" that Earth was being visited by extraterrestrials. He was frustrated by those, including me, who insisted the UFO investigators had not produced a smoking gun. There was one intriguing piece of evidence, perhaps not a smoking gun, that may have been staring skeptics in the face for decades. Digital enhancement in 1999, a few months before I showed up in Roswell, of an AP photograph from the *Ft. Worth Star-Telegram* edition of July 8, 1947, showed General Roger Ramey, commander of the 8th Air Force, and Colonel Thomas Jefferson DuBose posing at Ft. Worth Army Air Field next to pieces of a radar reflector from a weather balloon as part of the hastily issued cover story. In the general's hand is what appears to be a telegram, previously unreadable. Various experts examining it decades later pieced together unencrypted phrases from the teletype print they stated refer to "Roswell NMEX," "victims," "emergency powers," "weather balloons," "story," and a "disk."

Skeptics say some of those words are probably biased interpretations (people seeing what they want to see) and the telegram could have been a news dispatch, rather than a military message.

According to the library of the University of Texas at Arlington, there is a $10,000 reward offered by a private individual for the "first person or group/lab that can provide a definitive read of the Ramey memo." (Email rameymemo@gmail.com if you believe you are successful). "No one has collected the reward," according to Kevin Randle, a member of the library's research team about the memo.

"We did a complete new scan of the [photograph's] negative just before COVID but that didn't reveal any new details," said Randle, a retired military officer and author of books about UFOs and the Roswell incident, whom I contacted in 2023.

Another member of the research team, Brenda McClurkin, who was the head of the library's special collections and archives, concurred. "Regardless of all the advances in technology the mystery still prevails," she told me.

For the believers, the photograph could be a key piece of the puzzle to resolve whether we are alone in the universe.

13

The visit to the purported UFO crash-landing site and the interviews with the elderly witnesses in the New Mexico desert occurred during a break in my 16 years in Japan, where I worked as a foreign correspondent, a radio newscaster, and a media executive—sometimes all three simultaneously. Eventually, due to working in excess of 90 hours every week and missing the thrill of firsthand reporting, I decided to return exclusively to journalism, even if it meant giving up a higher salary, as well as the perks and business-class seats of corporate work.

In the 1990s I began working as a freelance reporter in Tokyo for a half-dozen broadcast networks of the United States, Canada, Germany, and elsewhere. The life of a stringer is financially unpredictable, dependent on the flow of hard news and one's success in pitching feature stories to distracted editors in different time zones. Collecting payments sometimes took months of pleading via email and hectoring network accountants on international phone calls. When Voice of America bureau chief positions became vacant in Johannesburg and New Delhi, which offered a stable income, a reliable payday, a pension plan, and job security, I applied for both with the encouragement of VOA editors and got the gig in India.

After roaming about South Asia for three and a half years (2007–10), including trips to Afghanistan to cover the war and visits to Sri Lanka to report from the front lines on the army's vanquishing of the Tamil Tigers, I moved to Seoul as VOA's Northeast Asia bureau chief. There I split my time between covering the Korean peninsula and Japan, which meant having two cell phones.

One afternoon in Seoul, my Japanese mobile phone blew up. The device's automated earthquake alarm ringing incessantly. I had a Pavlovian response of momentary fear whenever the two-chime "ding ding" sounds gave minimal advance warning the ground is about to shake. It could forebode a gentle tremor or a shaking so violent everything came crashing down.

The Japanese earthquake phone app renders warning of tremors anywhere in the island nation above a certain threshold. But at 2:46 P.M. on Friday, March 11, 2011, the alarm had never erupted quite in this manner—alert after alert with numbers defying credence. As my heart pounded, I hesitated to relay the data on Twitter; my first reaction was this was a false alarm or a test of the early warning system suffering a runaway malfunction.

Japanese scientists had long sought to forecast tremors for the world's most seismically active country. But predicting quakes—based on everything from changes in the level of static on FM radios to observing the behavior of fish—had repeatedly failed. The best method developed so far can warn of quakes only seconds before they begin to potentially cause damage. This is based on the motion of relatively speedy (up to 8.5 miles per hour) seismic P-waves, largely imperceptible to humans, which move faster in the Earth's interior than the potentially destructive S-waves (crawling as slowly as 0.6 mph).

On that late winter afternoon, on full alert at my desk in the VOA regional bureau in Seoul, I received an automated warning in less than nine seconds, sent to my cell phone at the speed of light. This had to be a mistake, I repeated to myself. The initial mapping showed maximum-level Shindo 7 shaking in the city of Kurihama in Miyagi Prefecture, Japan.

The Shindo scale indicates the severity of shaking at specific locations, different from the logarithmic Richter readings, which indicate the magnitude of a quake directly above its point of origin. Regardless of the Richter measurements, the Shindo scale indicates the potential for damage at a specific place, and due to Japan's pervasive seismic-monitoring system (more than 4,000 stations nationwide) linked to computers, the Shindo reading is available to first responders, the media, and the public many seconds—or even minutes—before the intensity on the Richter scale is estimated.

A Shindo 7, according to the Japan Meteorological Agency, indicates "most or all residences collapse or receive severe damage, no matter how earthquake-resistant they are."

A quick check of several online seismographs in Japan displayed similar numbers on the Shindo scale. Seconds later the preliminary Richter readings appeared on these same websites: M7.9 and at a relatively shallow depth of 6.2 miles.

I then issued the first tweet of what would be more than 1,500 I would send that month about the disaster: "Major quake in Japan," immediately followed by another: "Tsunami warning."

After centuries of being dragged down by the Pacific Plate, the edge of the Eurasian Plate sprang up with a force few beings alive, from fish to primates, had ever experienced.

I had lived in Tokyo for many years, experiencing my share of seismic jolts, swaying to Shindo 4s and M6.0+ tremors. On the upper floors of high-rise buildings, the larger quakes cause Japanese officer workers, unfazed by the frequent gentle swaying of towers, to lose their cool and offer glimpses of suppressed alarm on normally stoic faces.

During the March 11 quake, in Tokyo skyscrapers there was no pretense of remaining calm. Many people dove under their desks after releasing themselves from the initial paralyzing panic amid violent rocking. The swaying continued for minutes.

Two minutes after my pair of initial tweets, I followed with: "This is a big one in Japan capable of causing many casualties." A couple of hours later I would tweet: "This is the disaster Japan has feared for decades."

I avoid hyperbole on air or on social media. But based on my experience with earthquakes, I was highly confident that what I tweeted was not an exaggeration, recalling my reporting from Kobe in January 1995 after the M6.9 quake, which had been Japan's deadliest and costliest tremor to that point. Sixteen years later another calamity was unfolding.

Tuning in to NHK, Japan's quasi-official broadcaster, via satellite TV, within a few minutes of the quake (which would turn out to be much stronger than initially feared) the screen displayed a map of the country's northeastern coast with a blinking line of red—indicating a tsunami warning. Up to six meters (about 19.7 feet) high on the Pacific coast was the initial forecast. I had never heard such urgent concern in the voice of an NHK announcer typically known for restraint that would have made Walter Cronkite envious.

In Seoul, 750 miles west of the quake's epicenter off the coast of northeast Japan, I did not feel the quake, separated by the sea between the Korean peninsula and the main Japanese island of Honshu. (The upgraded M9.0 reassessment would not be issued until two days later.)

In the closing minutes of trading, the Tokyo Stock Exchange's benchmark Nikkei index tumbled 180 points, and the Japanese currency, the yen, began to drop on world markets. The natural disaster, its worst elements yet to hit the coast, had already cost Japan billions of dollars.

Live feeds from stationary cameras NHK had installed across Japan for such a day gave a glimpse of the terror. The remote-controlled camera system documented a lethal tsunami unprecedented in Japan in modern times enveloping numerous coastal towns. The actual peak of the tsunami in some communities would later be estimated to have been more than 130 feet high.

The earthquake deformed the seafloor, 80 miles offshore from Sendai, generating the tsunami, which gained momentum as it moved toward the main Japanese island of Honshu. After pummeling the beaches of the Tohoku region, it carried trucks, buildings, and—invisible to the stunned live television audience—thousands of people. Moments later the wave reversed course, dispatching bodies and jumbled debris out to sea—most gone forever but some flotsam would eventually wash up on beaches in Hawaii and California months and years later.

By the time I arrived at Incheon airport, outside Seoul, all remaining flights to Japan had left or been canceled. But within 24 hours of the tsunami's impact, I managed to find a flight to Fukushima Prefecture via Osaka.

I had selected that destination based on utility—it was the last airport still open near the devastated coast. The closest major commercial airport to the Tohoku coast, Sendai, had already been submerged by the tsunami.

As the few passengers at Osaka airport heading for Fukushima boarded the flight, a US television network producer, who had flown there from Beijing, paused at the gate as she was about to hand her boarding pass to the agent. She openly expressed concern that she had never had children and feared her ovaries might be cooked in Fukushima. Ignoring maternal instinct, she boarded the jet.

There had been vague information, at this point, of trouble at Fukushima Nuclear Power Plant 1, run by Tokyo Electric Power Company (TEPCO). We did know that a small amount of vapor had been deliberately vented at two of the damaged reactors to relieve pressure in the units. But no one was aware that the Rector 1 core had already melted and fallen to the bottom of the reactor pressure vessel. We had no concrete reason to believe it was not safe to land in Fukushima. I also surmised that unless there was a Chernobyl-level meltdown, any radiation we would be exposed to dozens of miles from the plant would be tolerable.

Overall, the bottom line for me as a correspondent is to get as close as possible, with minimal risk, to the scene of breaking news. I would be puzzled days later to learn that French news organizations were not only forbidding their reporters from going to northeastern Japan but were relocating them from Tokyo to Osaka, the opposite direction from the disaster. Even more befuddling was Japan's major news organizations, famous for pouring huge assets onto the scene of any big story, appeared to give Fukushima a pass, relying on the exhausted reporters and producers in their small bureaus in Fukushima and Koriyama.

Japan's mass media would rely for days, weeks, and months on government statements and TEPCO handouts, clearly failing to engage in independent reporting, which was absolutely crucial at the time. Even when Japan's "nuclear village" was suffering its worst-ever crisis, the nexus of overlapping interests among the country's atomic energy industry, its government, and the mainstream media remained intact. The restrained reporting could be excused as a way to avoid panic, but I was distressed that little attention was paid to particular nuggets of data, such as the official twice-a-day radiation readings for cities and towns in Fukushima Prefecture.

My experience covering US nuclear testing in Nevada, during which I schooled myself in rudimentary nuclear physics and learned not to solely depend on government-issued messages, now had me on guard in Japan.

While the Fukushima readings were not of a level to spark immediate health concerns (such as the figures showing 20 μSv [microsieverts] per hour at Iitate village a week after the quake struck), they were significant, demonstrating radiation had drifted from the plant to the northwest. Fukushima City also had been recording elevated readings. By comparison, TEPCO acknowledged at that time that some of the workers at Fukushima-1 had already been exposed to more than 100 mSv (note that milli is 1,000 times micro) of radiation, a dose that if absorbed in an instant was considered to elevate one's risk for cancer.

The international media, despite intense interest in the story, had little concrete information concerning the crippled nuclear plant. The citizens of towns closest to Fukushima-1 had evacuated their homes. There were grainy long-distance video feeds—via Japan's networks—of white smoke rising from the plant. But no one provided context.

While Japan's domestic news coverage mitigated serious concerns, the foreign media—which with rare exception did not have reporters on the ground in Fukushima much less expertise in the subject—gave the world the impression of an apocalypse.

Talking about sieverts and beta particles apparently was considered too technical to explain to lay audiences. In studios in New York and London, the experts who received the most airtime were those espousing doomsday scenarios. Few producers bothered to vet the credentials of these self-proclaimed experts. As long as someone was a physicist or a medical doctor, they could get on air despite their obvious biases. However, TEPCO and other members of the nuclear industry suffered rapidly deteriorating credibility.

Before the end of the week, I was able to speak on the telephone with a source—a respected senior figure in Japan's nuclear power industry—who speculated that two or three of the Fukushima reactors had probably suffered complete meltdowns. But he would not go on the record. I needed a second source to confirm this before making the bombshell information public via Twitter or on the VOA airwaves. I rang Taro Kono, whom I trusted, an opposition party lawmaker and son of a former foreign minister. (Kono would later serve as foreign minister and defense minister under Prime Minister Shinzo Abe.) I informed Kono what the source had told me and asked whether he had learned anything similar. He sounded surprised by what I told him and replied no such information had filtered to him through his government and industry connections. I could not find a second source and thus held onto the astounding information.

The Japanese prime minister, Naoto Kan, would later contend the government never withheld any information from the public but that "accurate information never reached me."

Roaming around Fukushima, speaking with those who had escaped both the tsunami and the radiation plume, I was unaware at the time of how the story was playing internationally. Working beyond 24 hours consecutively with hardly a break for a meal, I went on air live countless times and sent out hundreds of tweets, doing my best to report what I saw and heard and relaying the scant data being issued by local authorities, the central government, and TEPCO.

It was impossible to sleep for more than short bursts. When my phones stopped ringing, the hotel violently shook from the hundreds of aftershocks. I felt compelled to check the magnitude of the larger ones and confirm that a new tsunami warning had not been issued. In the initial 72-hour period after the M9.0 tremor, more than 250 quakes of magnitude 5 or higher were recorded—an average of one every 17 minutes. At least 45 of those were above magnitude 6, and three exceeded magnitude 7.

NPR's Doualy Xaykaothao was across the hall from me in our quake-damaged budget hotel. We kept the doors to our rooms open all night so we could communicate verbally and as a precaution not to get trapped in our rooms should a significant tremor bring down the walls or ceiling. I told Doualy not to worry unless items began to slide off tables. This hardly assuaged her. She had never experienced an earthquake, and my nonchalant attitude to the significant and frequent aftershocks had her likely thinking I was an idiot who threw too much caution to the wind. I also downplayed the risks to our health from the elevated radiation readings being tabulated several times a day by local authorities.

My only serious concern was that with commerce gradually grinding to a halt, even in undamaged parts of Fukushima Prefecture, we could find ourselves stranded without a way out or adequate food. With transportation routes destroyed or disrupted, the precious reserves of supplies that survived the natural disaster quickly disappeared. Even when the roads were patched, many truck drivers were fearful of venturing too close to the crippled nuclear power plant.

We were based in a location supposedly a safe distance away from the leaking reactors and steaming fuel rods, but radiation levels in Fukushima Prefecture's two biggest cities registered significantly above normal. Each passing day, fewer and fewer restaurants and stores opened. Those still operating had fewer items for sale. Some eateries offered specials—such as the fermented bean curd curry I had for lunch, or the $18 "Disaster Sushi Set," which became dinner every other day. I chased the fish with a few cups of yet abundant *sake* (rice wine) after particularly stressful reporting days. Some meals had become merely *onigiri*, rice rolled into a ball and wrapped in seaweed. A couple of those at midday, washed down with a typical Japanese "energy drink" (a dose of vitamins in a healthy liquid jolt of caffeine and nicotine), sustained me until late in the evening. Unlike the stereotypical journalist, I'm neither a coffee drinker nor cigarette smoker, so a one-bottle dose of the two drugs gave me a desperately needed boost.

Most hotels in Fukushima Prefecture were not fully functioning—some might have electricity but no running water. Others have water but no power. Others were deemed dangerous and would not take guests due to structural damage.

Our hotel in Koriyama, the Route-Inn, showed minor quake damage to the pavement. In the lobby was a certificate attesting to the building's earthquake building standards.

The vending machines in the hotel and elsewhere in Koriyama quickly emptied. Maid service stopped. Only a skeleton staff remained. Those at the front desk spent much of their time answering phone calls and telling the walk-ins, including the newly homeless, evacuees, and journalists, that there are no more rooms at the inn. Yet, the hotel stood practically empty. Every day, we were asked politely when we intended to leave. The front desk staff appeared anxious to shut down but reluctant to demand we check out. I knew that in a less hospitable country we likely would have been kicked out. Without a hotel we would be totally reliant on the kindness of strangers or might have had to seek refuge in overcrowded refugee centers, which we had visited to interview the displaced.

With no gasoline available and after the mass exodus of evacuees from the 20-kilometer safety zone around the nuclear power plant, there were fewer vehicles on the roads each day. It was still possible to get a taxi. They were fueled by liquid propane gas, and drivers assured us that reserves in the storage tanks, at least in Koriyama, remained adequate.

In Sendai, a three-hour drive to the north, vegetable prices doubled after the tsunami destroyed a chunk of the Miyagi Prefecture capital. That said, there did not seem to be the pervasive price gouging one would expect after such a calamity. Merchants may have traditionally ranked near the bottom of Japan's social hierarchy (below the samurai and farmers) but trying to make extra money in times of adversity is considered unseemly and un-Japanese.

The traditional Japanese stoicism was on full display. There was a touch of bitterness in a few voices and some subtle signs of frustration but no show of anger. Everyone seemed to take in stride the dwindling supplies of goods and services. I speculated that this part of Japan would soon see what followed in the dark days immediately after the county's defeat in World War Two: a thriving black market in scarce and rationed goods.

A few people were willing to voice the darkest fear—what the scientists and government officials contended was impossible—a meltdown with one or more reactors going critical, spewing dangerous levels of radiation across the Tohoku region.

Sipping his sake and eating his Disaster Sushi Set, a local construction planning company president reminded me that many modern Japanese descend from the samurai warriors, shown in the twentieth century in the spirit of the kamikaze pilots who were willing, without complaint, to meet their fate. The bearded, smiling Takeshi Munakata said he believed in Japan and Japanese technology to pull the nation through the triple tragedy, but if "I die, OK. No problem."

We continued ingesting our libation and raising toasts to stoicism.

Prime Minister Kan, speaking during a nationally broadcast news conference, informed the Japanese people that all information was being shared with them about a situation he acknowledged was "very grave." His only reassuring words, without providing specifics, were that "quite soon" the whole situation would be under control.

We now know that might take 50 years.

The US State Department, on March 17, strongly urged "U.S. citizens to defer travel to Japan at this time and those in Japan should consider departing." American diplomats later confided there was significant frustration with the Japanese government amid a perception by US government experts that the situation at Fukushima could spin out of control because of a lack of a concrete response by the Japanese. The somber advisories issued by embassies prompted thousands of foreigners in Japan, known as *gaijin* in the Japanese language, to become "fly-jin."

While Japanese officials reiterated there was no reason to flee the country because of the crippled nuclear plant, store shelves emptied and in Tokyo many businesses, including restaurants, were closed within a week after the initial event. In Koriyama eight days after the natural disaster struck, long lines snaked for more than a kilometer outside several gasoline stands, where drivers were told they could purchase only a limited amount of fuel, usually 10 liters. By that time, there were hundreds of thousands of survivors living in paralyzed communities while thousands of others had moved to makeshift shelters.

I struggled to explain the situation regarding the nuclear power complex. It could not be adequately summarized in a sound bite or a paragraph, which was what those interviewing me around the world were looking for. Compared to the Three Mile Island 1979 partial-core meltdown incident in Pennsylvania, it was obviously worse. But nearly all experts concurred at the time that the plant design and current circumstances meant we would not see a catastrophic meltdown at Fukushima on par with that in 1986 at Chernobyl in Ukraine, history's worst power plant accident.

Fukushima-1 was 40 years old, although some of its six reactors were newer. During the March 11 quake, the reactors did what they were designed to do in such a large seismic event—safely shut down. What failed in the entire design was adequate property protection to prevent a huge tsunami from destroying the power lines feeding the system to keep the fuel rods cooled. The backup generators, placed too closely to the shore, were also swamped.

It remains hotly debated whether the earthquake itself caused critical damage to the plant. TEPCO continues to adamantly deny that. What we knew, based on information from the Japanese government and TEPCO at the time, was sobering: Reactor No. 1, where operations were suspended after the quake, suffered a cooling failure and a partial core melting. It vented vapor. The building housing the reactor had been damaged on March 12 by an apparent hydrogen explosion and the roof was blown off. Seawater was pumped in, meaning the reactor could never again be used.

Reactor No. 2's operations were also suspended after the quake. It also had a cooling failure and seawater was pumped in, destroying the reactor. The fuel rods were fully exposed temporarily, vapor was vented, and the building was damaged by the blast at reactor No. 3 on March 14. An explosion was heard near the suppression pool of the containment vessel on March 15, raising fears the containment vessel housing the reactor fuel had been cracked. Since the outer building had not blown off, water could not be sprayed in from the outside.

Reactor No. 3 was fueled by MOX (containing highly toxic plutonium), giving the greatest cause for concern in the days following the tsunami. Its operation was suspended after the quake. But it also suffered a cooling failure. A partial melting of the core was feared. Vapor had vented. Seawater was initially pumped in, meaning that—as was the case with reactors 1 and 2—it could never be used again to produce electricity. Additionally, the building damaged on March 14 by an apparent hydrogen explosion had high levels of radiation the following day, and a plume of smoke was observed March 16, presumably from the spent-fuel storage pool. Seawater was dumped over the pool by helicopters on March 17, but much of it appeared to be dispersed by the wind.

Reactor No. 4 was initially deemed the second-most serious situation. It was under maintenance when the quake struck, and its fresh fuel rods (much more dangerous than the spent rods in other reactor buildings) were all safely submerged at the time to keep them cool. However, the temperature in the storage pool reached 183 degrees Fahrenheit on March 14. There was a fire the following day, likely caused by a hydrogen explosion at the pool. A fire was also observed at the building housing the reactor. A renewed nuclear chain reaction was feared after the pool water level dropped. Only the skeleton of the building survived the fire.

Reactors 5 and 6 were also undergoing maintenance when the quake struck. Water temperature in their spent-fuel storage pools increased to about 147 degrees Fahrenheit on March 17, but the reactors were cooled and of less concern compared to the others.

The emergency workers on the site could remain at the plant for only brief periods and could not get too close to the damaged reactors and spent-fuel ponds, so it was impossible to quickly ascertain the full extent of damage and the level of the pools after several days of spraying water. The best clues came from radiation monitoring, both on and off site. Those were the numbers I watched closely. But finding timely and accurate data was not easy.

I was among those near the atomic power facility on March 15 when an estimated 10 million becquerels per hour of radioactive substances spewed from the three crippled reactors. For days, several foreign correspondents considered foolhardy and millions of people in Japan with no choice absorbed significantly higher doses of radiation than we normally would have been exposed to.

Few of us, in or near the hot zone, were equipped with dosimeters.

After spending a week in Fukushima Prefecture close to the crippled plant, it seemed prudent to see how much clicking my own body would register while reporting from a radiation-screening checkpoint.

Modern Geiger counters actually don't click. As is the case with so many other devices, they have mostly gone digital. But they still measure radiation exposure in "clicks per minute."

Arriving at the Koriyama Municipal Gymnasium was akin to walking on to the set of a science fiction movie. Men clad head to toe in white anticontamination suits calmly guided visitors through the gauntlet. Other "space men" unloaded boxes full of white masks. Japanese, young and old, displayed no emotion as a mysterious device rendered their radioactive fate.

When my turn came, the needle on the analogy meter began to jump as the man in the space suit scanned my torso. I knew not to become immediately alarmed. Decades before, I had taken an online cram course in radiation. That education and my experience reporting about radiation led me to conclude it was unlikely I had suffered more exposure than I would on a transpacific flight—or, at the very worst, a chest X-ray. When the Geiger counter descended to my feet, I looked at the meter and my heart jumped. The reading pinned the needle.

I noticed a subtle look of surprise in the technician's eyes. He switched the meter to a higher scale and intoned that perhaps I should wash my footwear, a battered 20-year-old pair of Danner boots.

"What is the reading?" I asked in Japanese with the same nervous voice one might use seeking the results of a biopsy.

"3,000 cpm [counts per minute]," he replied. CPM is a comparatively crude measurement to determine radiation exposure, calculating the number of atoms in a certain quantity of radioactive material that are detected to have decayed in one minute. Anything above 100 is considered a concern. I asked what the typical reading in Koriyama was for a test subject prior to the radiation leakage from any of the six troubled reactors at the Fukushima-1 plant. The technician replied that it would have been 300 to 600 cpm. He explained it was likely my boots had picked up the radiation from material falling from the sky in the rain and snow during the past couple of days. By comparison, the reading on my torso peaked around 1,500 cpm.

I was assured that the current readings, even on my boots, were nothing alarming. But Doualy, my NPR colleague, received a verdict of a 10,000 cpm reading on her shoes.

As we moved toward the exit, a pair of white-suited men handed both of us a yellow card. While this is not a good sign in soccer, I was assured that the paper certifying we had undergone radiation screening was an "all-clear" document. It would allow us entry to one of the shelters now home to more than 200,000 evacuees from the core of the Fukushima hot zone. If I had needed medical attention, based on my scan, I would have been given a green card and presumably escorted to a decontamination center. We saw ambulances on standby outside the complex.

So far, the authorities said, only a handful of people apart from nuclear-plant workers had generated more than brief concern, and they were merely advised to wash their hands and face.

Guidance to perform a simple sanitary task did little to assuage millions of people, and not only those in Japan. As the Twitterverse was permeated by alarmist tweets and links to web pages with scant scientific credence, even people in other countries wondered if they should remain indoors or pop iodine tablets. Koreans and Chinese worried that fish and vegetables—in particular those from Japan—might be a health hazard. Skepticism about the veracity of the scant and opaque information

VOA's Steve Herman reports
from the outskirts of
Fukushima, Japan after the
2011 earthquake.

Steve Herman @
@W7VOA
Big big aftershock in Fukushima now!

Steve Herman @
@W7VOA
When reporting in that environment, no time to reflect, get emotional, etc. Similar to cop or firefighter. #VOAsaachail

Steve Herman @
@W7VOA
Most people from other countries would be amazed by how calmly and orderly Japanese have handled the tragedy. #VOAsaachail

PRESS

You can find the latest VOA
reporting under #VOAalert
Follow Herman's tweets
at @W7VOA

Steve Herman's reporting from the Fukushima disaster, including his breaking news tweets, is part of an exhibit of the public tour of VOA's headquarters in Washington.

released by TEPCO and the Japanese government allowed panic to fill the void.

When I realized that I had been brushing my teeth with Koriyama tap water now certainly containing a significantly elevated level of iodine-131, an isotope with a half-life of eight days, I called one of my ham radio buddies in California who used to live in Japan. He was also a veteran internal medicine physician.

"Don't worry about it," Dr. Paul Ryack assured me. "At your age, by the time you develop thyroid cancer—and that's a very small chance—you'd be dead of something else anyway."

Ironically, a popular treatment for thyroid cancer is radioactive iodine.

The only moment on that assignment when I thought covering the disaster could cost me my life was when I stood a couple of miles inland on what had been Sendai farmland, now barren except for scant debris left in the wake of the outgoing tsunami a few days earlier. An NHK radio announcer implored people, such as myself, to rush as far inland as possible. An offshore aftershock had prompted a tsunami warning, and I was standing in the impact zone. A lone patrol car spotted me. The policeman said I could stay where I was but not to approach any closer to the shore. A few minutes later the Japan Meteorological Agency seismologists declared no tsunami had been spotted. The alert was declared a false alarm and the massive rescue efforts along Japan's northeast coast by military troops and police officers resumed. Helicopters surveyed the damage and searched for survivors along the coast. Thousands were found. Thousands were dead.

The prefectural capital, Sendai, suffered a double whammy. The damage from the earthquake, by then declared the largest one ever experienced in modern Japan, paled in comparison to that caused by the subsequent tsunami.

At Sendai's main port, hundreds of cars and trucks were destroyed in every imaginable way. Some were flattened. Others compressed horizontally to a fraction of their size. Some faced each other as if they were involved in a violent head-on collision. Other vehicles were piled one atop another.

As black smoke continued to billow from several buildings at the port, Japanese soldiers walked through the acres of mud and rubble looking for bodies. The scene also attracted the curious, snapping photographs and peering inside the crumpled cars and trucks. Others riding bicycles could be seen loading unscathed boxes of facial tissues and packages of toilet paper, which strangely littered the port.

Many people faced scarcities of daily necessities, spending much of their waking hours waiting in lines. It was a situation younger Japanese had never encountered and only have heard about from their parents and grandparents who survived adversity during and after World War Two.

The killer waves reached three kilometers inland in Sendai, leveling buildings and trees. Half of the city's 1 million people had no electricity in their homes. Hundreds of thousands of residences and businesses were without water. Although downtown Sendai suffered some quake damage, it still looked like a modern Japanese city, protected by its relative elevation. A limited amount of commerce continued to supply the stunned population with necessities.

Keiko Tanaka, six months pregnant, walked with her mother along a street in central Sendai, carrying a big box loaded with spinach, lettuce, and onions. They had waited in line at a greengrocer for 30 minutes and said the price of vegetables had doubled since the earthquake, casting doubt on my belief Japanese merchants would not engage in price gouging.

Tanaka said they were trying to stock up while they could, amid rapidly dwindling commodities and warnings from authorities that a magnitude 7 aftershock would strike at any time. Not only could a significant fresh tremor generate a further destructive tsunami, it could topple the exposed cooling towers at Fukushima.

The interior of the Tanaka home was a mess because of the quake, but Mrs. Tanaka expressed feeling lucky to live in a part of the city that still had electricity and running water. Her family worried how long it would last, with scheduled rolling blackouts beginning across the country and the official predictions of big aftershocks.

Vegetable shoppers were not the only ones waiting in line. Hundreds of people could be seen patiently waiting to get into the very few clothing, hardware, and convenience stores open. For drivers, finding an open gasoline station had become nearly impossible. The wait for fuel extended for hours. Nearly all restaurants were shuttered. But in central Sendai, a branch of the Nakau beef bowl restaurant chain stayed open. It offered only one menu item—curry wheat-flour noodle soup. Every meal included a cup of free hot water.

Manager Akihiko Yamaguchi said business had been predictably brisk since the earthquake struck, knocking out most competitors. Yamaguchi vowed to remain open as long as possible to give the people of Sendai encouragement to carry on.

Residents, despite their weariness, expressed confidence Sendai would again thrive, noting the city had faced adversity before during its 400-year history. Twenty percent of Sendai was destroyed by American bombers in World War Two. It managed to rebuild, becoming the Tohoku region's economic hub. Japan had the financial resources to repair Sendai, its second rise from destruction in less than 70 years. But in neighboring Fukushima Prefecture, an agricultural rice basket, regaining consumer confidence for its crops, even though most farmland was deemed safe, became a more daunting challenge.

No one died immediately from radiation due to the reactor meltdowns, but delayed and poorly arranged evacuations of some Fukushima hospitals and other care facilities were blamed for scores of patient deaths. In those initial weeks, everyone, including most members of the media, seemed anxious to get as far away as possible from the crippled nuclear facility on the Pacific coastline.

Correspondents, as I have noted, are usually the first to race to any disaster site or combat zone, but fear of bodily harm by an invisible culprit restrained typical reportorial instincts. For some time, there was no legal reason barring us from the hot zone despite a perception to the contrary. After prudently assessing the risks, I decided to take advantage of this loophole.

Although police at lightly manned roadblocks tried to prevent any unauthorized vehicles from entering the 20-kilometer radiation exclusion zone, they had no means to legally enforce the barricades. That would soon change as authorities designated five additional municipalities as part of the "deliberate evacuation area" and announced the entire zone would be legally off-limits, even to homeowners scurrying back in to retrieve belongings.

Los Angeles Times Northeast Asia Bureau Chief John Glionna and I gained access all the way to the main gate of Fukushima-1 a month after the meltdowns. We saw not a single person outside in Futaba and Okuma, which *had* a combined population of about 18,500. The doors of some businesses remained open through which people hastily had fled. Some of the roads were impassable. The pavement in places had been split apart by the quake. A railroad overpass lay crumpled next to one road. Power poles leaned at sharp angles.

The immediate area around Fukushima-1 looked relatively unscathed. The worst damage could be seen over the hill, where a tsunami believed to have reached 45 feet in height—well above the 19-foot-high seawall— washed away backup generators to cool the plant's reactors and fuel rods. That had set off the unimagined chain reaction of one disaster after another.

John, always loquacious, had managed to convince a young Japanese fellow, who said his normal job was being the frog mascot for an area sports team, to become our driver. Our impromptu chauffeur wore a T-shirt emblazoned with the phrase "It's a Good Day to Die."

After a drive up the slope to the main gate of Fukushima-1 we were greeted by two guards outfitted in hazmat suits, helmets, and dual-intake respirator masks. Perhaps "greeted" is the wrong word.

Our attempt to ask questions was rebuffed. The only return communication was the hand signal to make a U-turn. The license plate of our vehicle was noted. It was manifestly clear we could not proceed farther and were not encouraged to loiter.

In the parking lot, I spotted a panel with one of those messages typically seen at industrial or construction sites. It was a billboard erected by the "TEPCO Fukushima-1 Nuclear Power Plant Safety Committee." The message, obviously unchanged since March 11, made what could only be read as an extremely ironic proclamation: "This month's safety slogan: Be sure to check everything and do a risk assessment. Zero disasters for this year."

Some predicted and hoped the accident would ultimately end Japan's nuclear power industry, which had met 30 percent of the nation's energy needs. Even former prime minister Junichiro Koizumi changed his position and called for zero reliance on nuclear power, saying the industry lied to him and other leaders for decades about the safety and affordability of atomic energy. Japan reversed course in 2022 after Russia invaded Ukraine, amid concern about the global oil supply in the years ahead.

The Fukushima case was a public relations disaster for the nuclear power industry, beyond the setbacks of Three Mile Island and Chernobyl. Proponents argue major accidents are rare and preventable and for a world eager to reduce greenhouse gas emissions and free itself from dependence on Russia or Saudi Arabia for gas and oil, nuclear power must be in the mix.

Japan found itself facing a huge bill for cleaning up the Fukushima disaster and paying compensation to victims. The total will eventually tally in the hundreds of billions of dollars, and the cleanup could take half a century more. Even for the world's third-largest economy, it is a staggering sum.

Was the calamity, which came perilously close to making a sizable portion of Japan uninhabitable for decades, avoidable? Should Japan's media have done a better job scrutinizing the cozy alliance between government officials and TEPCO? Japanese mainstream media itself all too often has served as a docile mouthpiece of the government. Japan, however, is not the only democracy where reporters and editors face constant pressure from bureaucrats and powerful politicians to parrot the party line. American journalists have confronted criticism and threats for their inquisitiveness from presidents and other top government officials since the early days of the republic. During the administration of Donald Trump, the gloves came off.

14

Weeks after becoming president, Donald Trump ramped up criticism of the news coverage of his administration, taking to his favorite social media platform. "The FAKE NEWS media . . . is the enemy of the American People!" he tweeted. That initial tweet name-checked the *New York Times,* CNN, and *NBC News* for his enemies list. The message was quickly deleted and replaced by an almost identical note that added two more domestic television networks: ABC and CBS. The social media attack, which was the latest in a long series of Trump broadsides against the news media, came after the president had left Washington for a visit to a Boeing aircraft plant in South Carolina.

As the president arrived at his Mar-a-Lago estate in Florida, which he referred to as the Winter White House, social media and the networks crackled with debate about the significance of Trump calling some of the country's premier journalistic outlets "enemies of the people," a phrase that goes back to ancient Rome and was used with chilling finality during the communist revolution in Russia a century ago.

"As an American diplomat, I stood up to petty tyrants who called journalists 'enemies of the people,'" tweeted Tom Malinowski, former assistant secretary of state for democracy, human rights, and labor. "Guess that's not our policy anymore."

A professor of Russian and East European studies at the University of Pennsylvania, Mitchell Orenstein, noted Trump was using "one of the most controversial phrases in Soviet history." The phrase has its roots in Latin, during the Roman Empire, but "enemies of the people" gained its most notorious associations in the twentieth century during Soviet dictator Josef Stalin's purges, which killed tens of millions of people. An "enemy of the people" in the Soviet Union was someone stigmatized by social origin or prerevolutionary profession. The label alone was akin to a terminal illness, and merely being a friend of an enemy of the people was cause for official suspicion.

"What it basically meant was a death sentence," explained Orenstein.

China's dictator, Mao Zedong, also denounced as "enemies of the people" those who criticized the Maoist policies and commands that led to the Great Famine and the death of tens of millions of Chinese.

There is no evidence Trump knew of the historic connotations of the phrase when he wrote his tweet. Pulitzer Center Senior Adviser and veteran journalist Marvin Kalb, author of a book titled *Enemy of the People,* said he believed Trump picked up the phrase from former Democratic pollster Pat Caddell, who used it during an interview on a right-wing Breitbart radio program. (Caddell also considered "Make America Great Again" the "greatest slogan of my lifetime.") Orenstein, who was teaching one of the few courses on communism at an American university when Trump became president, said that one would hope "American presidents would be educated enough to know something like that."

Congressman Ted Yoho, a Republican on the House Foreign Affairs Committee, dismissed the tweet as not particularly consequential when asked about it on CNN. The president "has got his style," Yoho, formerly a large-animal veterinarian, said. "Things will adjust."

Whether they subsequently did or not depends on one's political perspective. In a dispatch shortly after the Trump tweet, French news agency AFP noted that while many US presidents have criticized the press, "Trump's language has more clearly echoed criticism leveled by authoritarian leaders around the world."

J. M. Berger, a fellow at the International Center for Counter-Terrorism at The Hague, was among those who agreed with that characterization, calling Trump's language "radical." Some of Trump's supporters on the extremist fringe "may see language like 'enemy of the American people' as ratifying violence," Berger told VOA. The president's tweets "could also incite others who are inclined toward violence, whether because of a political ideology or mental illness," warned Berger, author of several books and studies on extremist groups' use of social media. The messenger has long been the target of hostility.

στέργει γὰρ οὐδεὶς ἄγγελον κακῶν ἐπῶν—that's Sophocles 2,400 years ago cautioning that "no one loves the bearer of bad news."

There has probably not been a single US president—except for perhaps William Henry Harrison, who wasn't in office long enough to gain negative press coverage—who has not complained about perceived media bias. Two consecutive presidents, Democrat Lyndon Johnson and Republican Richard Nixon, had particularly contentious relationships with the American media establishment. I recall the scenes from the battles in Vietnam most every day on the nightly news in the 1960s. When CBS broadcast a report in 1965 showing a US Marine using a Zippo lighter to set villagers' huts on fire, Johnson exploded and rang *CBS News* President Frank Stanton at home and raged. "Frank, this is your President, and yesterday your boys shat on the American flag." Johnson also questioned the loyalty of *CBS News* correspondent Morley Safer, who was Canadian. Johnson believed the NBC network was biased against his administration and warned he was watching it "like a hawk." Republican Nixon had an "enemies list" (Daniel Schorr—then at CBS, later with NPR—was number 17 on the top 20), and the president urged the Federal Communications Commission to not renew broadcast licenses of stations he did not like. Nixon also wanted the three TV networks to feel they were facing possible antitrust action to break them into smaller pieces. "If the threat of screwing them is going to help us more with their programming than doing it, then keep the threat," Nixon told a White House aide in an Oval Office conversation caught on tape.

A subsequent Republican with decidedly more experience before cameras and microphones, Ronald Reagan preferred not to be openly combative with the media when frustrated with news coverage, although the criticism resulted from his own gaffes. Reagan revived Franklin Roosevelt's fireside chats, taking his message directly to the American public with weekly radio addresses, and the recycled tradition held until it petered out in the administration of Donald Trump, who preferred unfiltered tweeting for immediate and frequent communication with his constituency. Reagan, an actor-turned-politician who became governor of California, the most populated state in the nation, realized reporters would spin stories that would not usually show him in a favorable light.

"You must keep on seeking the truth and I'll keep on telling it, even though you don't recognize it," he said at the White House Correspondents' Association dinner in 1982.

The truth is most correspondents who work at the White House are relentless in seeking to confirm facts, trying to obtain information ahead of colleagues and competitors, and do not have an agenda to deliberately cast the president in an unfavorable light.

Trump, however, found himself under a steady spotlight during the entirety of his presidency. This was a leader who frequently took to giving orders as the chief lighting director ahead of his appearances in the East Room as he wanted to control the direction and intensity of the beams focused on him. Outside the grounds of the White House, much to his frustration, he had limited control of how he was portrayed, except on *Fox News* where he would berate correspondents, program presenters, and executives when he was angered by particular stories.

Trump suffered from overexposure and was unflatteringly portrayed by much of the world's media. His disinterest in governing was transparent. Even those he thought were most loyal in the West Wing dished to reporters about each other and about the president. They were frustrated repeatedly because key decisions affecting domestic and geopolitical policies were frequently made by Trump in a fit of pique. Sometimes it was apparent his announcements lacked substance, a glaring example being the empty pronouncements following highly publicized meetings with Vladimir Putin and Kim Jong Un. Critics, including those in his intelligence agencies, the National Security Council, and at the Department of Defense, eventually had little hesitation airing their observations that Trump often catered to people, places, and subjects that would benefit his postpresidency hotel business rather than the long-term interests of the nation.

15

One concern for any member of the White House press pool is getting left behind the pack. Not accompanying the presidential limousine in the motorcade denotes a fundamental failure of pool duty. It can happen by not showing up at the designated call time. But one evening, through no fault of our own, the entire pool was left behind—fortunately, it wasn't on a remote airstrip in an unfriendly nation but immediately south of the White House fence.

At the 2018 National Christmas Tree–lighting event, an inexperienced aide failed to signal us to load into our vans prior to the president and first lady exiting the stage at the event at the Ellipse. They left. We were left behind with no immediate explanation. It was a serious enough anomaly that the president of the White House Correspondents' Association, Olivier Knox, immediately investigated and concluded it was a "logistical glitch," not a deliberate snub.

That did not allay all suspicion. Trump, as president-elect, left behind his de facto pool of reporters, once to go to dinner and a second time to play golf. This was the first time it had happened while he was president, and few could help wondering if it was not a coincidence. It was quickly pointed out this would not be without precedent. Trump's predecessor, Barack Obama, did it twice.

In the first instance, in April 2010, Obama left the White House for one of his daughter's soccer games two hours prior to the time the pool had been told to gather. The second occurrence was in January 2012, when the pool was notified of a change in the call time to 8:15 A.M. Unfortunately, they were informed of this at 8:16 A.M. Only one journalist, *Fox News*' Bree Tracey, was nimble enough to reverse time and dutifully informed colleagues the president and first lady had gone to a daughter's basketball game.

Trump, despite his frequent disdain for the journalists he encountered daily, once in office did not seek to evade the protective pool. We were allowed to accompany him on the rides to his properties for dinner or golf. For whatever reason, this was one fight he chose not to pick with the establishment media. The Secret Service, keeping to the tradition, also ensured poolers had their place in the motorcades, and when Trump wanted us out of sight while he dined or golfed, at least one of its agents remained with us to keep the security bubble intact until we would rejoin the motorcade for the ride back to the White House or to drop off the president at Mar-a-Lago. It was probably the more boring duty a Secret Service agent could draw, although all members of the detail are highly trained to put themselves between the president and any potential assailant.

Protecting the president of the United States involves far more than willingness to step into the path of gunfire. As part of their extensive preparation—ranging from firearms instruction to first aid—all several thousand Secret Service agents and officers also must learn how to drive. It is a course far beyond what a civilian would encounter to obtain their state driver's license.

The Secret Service training takes place at a 600-yard-long track in the state of Maryland, and it is more than the fundamentals of defensive driving. Among the techniques is the J-turn, in which the driver spins a reversing vehicle 180 degrees and quickly continues, facing forward, with brisk acceleration. For the Secret Service, this is part of what it calls "protective driving." It has one goal: "Safely get the protectee out of the area—the 'kill zone,' and to move them to a safe location as quickly and expeditiously as possible," according to Thomas Murach, Secret Service assistant to the special agent-in-charge.

Even after the completion of that five-day training, Secret Service personnel are not ready to get behind the wheel of the 20,000-pound armored presidential stretch limousine known as *Cadillac One,* or *The Beast.*

Anyone driving the president or vice president must pass a separate, advanced five-day training known as the Protective Operations Driving Course, which has about a 60 percent pass rate.

"If an agent doesn't pass the advanced course, they would continue normal duty and can try again at a later date," according to Secret Service Public Affairs Specialist Julia McMurray. "It's not a never-ending cycle of attempts and fails. They can only go a few times." Another special course—considered as challenging as limousine driving—is for the motorcycles (which roll with sidecars in better weather).

"It's heavy. It's almost like 900 pounds," explained motorcyclist and Secret Service Technical Officer Lloyd Llamas about the agency's big bikes when I visited the agency's training complex in Maryland. "And you're running with two wheels. And they make you do things that you can't imagine you could possibly do with that."

Those are not the Secret Service's only two-wheelers. Agents and officers must learn special techniques to drive bicycles. They are instructed in special techniques for all-terrain vehicles and even battery-powered golf carts. Another unique Secret Service vehicle—and the only one the president is likely to ride that is bigger than *The Beast*—is a bus known as *Ground Force One,* last seen on the road during Obama's 2012 reelection campaign. The roomy million-dollar black bus, with 500 square feet of interior space, has a twin, which was utilized by the Secret Service to drive Obama's unsuccessful general election opponent, Mitt Romney. Driving the president not only means getting behind the wheel in different types of executive transportation but also different kinds of streets. For example, different countries have various curb designs. To train properly for this, the Secret Service at its facility in Laurel, Maryland, had part of one street built with two different types for drivers of full-sized utility vehicles to learn how to properly run over the curbs.

All this drilling is meant to prevent a repeat of the Secret Service's worst moment on November 22, 1963, when President Kennedy was assassinated in Dallas by a sniper's bullet as he sat in the backseat of a Lincoln Continental open convertible. That compelled a hardening of titanium plating, as well as a permanent bulletproof roof for the car, which was used by President Johnson until 1967. Formal training for Secret Service drivers didn't begin until 1970. The training techniques have changed as the vehicles have evolved—going all the way back to the 1939 Lincoln K-Series car, which was President Franklin Roosevelt's favorite ride.

Roosevelt's 12-cylinder engine vehicle had a retractable roof, allowing the polio-stricken president to appear before crowds without leaving the car. It also was the first to be significantly modified for protection of a president, equipped with armor-plated doors, bulletproof tires, thick windows, and storage compartments for weapons of the agents who rode along standing on extrawide running boards and gripping exterior handles. "In the past, we taught what's called threshold-braking.

Or if your car didn't have anti-lock brakes, you would bring the wheels to the point they're almost locked up but not quite," explained Murach.

Some elements dealing with stability control were removed from the training as modern vehicles are more stable. And tire technology has evolved with the rubber gripping much better nowadays on slick surfaces.

The Secret Service, which is under the Department of Homeland Security, protects not only the president and vice president, their immediate family members, and former presidents and first ladies, but also visiting foreign leaders and major candidates in US presidential campaigns. Successful candidates who end up getting a ride to the White House driveway quickly find out they can get anything they want as president—except the keys to the car. When President Biden in August 2022 wanted to take the wheel for a TV program taping with comedian and car collector Jay Leno, the Secret Service had them drive their cars at its Maryland training site.

16

Perhaps no day exemplified the critical value of White House reporters traveling with the president than November 22, 1963.

John F. Kennedy decided to visit Texas, ahead of his planned reelection campaign the following year, to demonstrate unity among himself and two feuding members of his Democratic Party in the state, Governor John Connolly Jr. and Senator Ralph Yarborough. The Republican Party had been making inroads in the Lone Star State, and the 25 electoral votes of Texas would be critical to vanquishing Kennedy's expected challenger, Senator Barry Goldwater of Arizona.

On the morning of November 22, Kennedy, accompanied by First Lady Jacqueline Kennedy, took a 14-minute flight from Fort Worth to Dallas, a city considered ultraconservative and anti-Kennedy, the second-to-last stop scheduled on the trip to five Texas cities in two days.

Sid Davis was a pool reporter on *Air Force One* the evening prior on the flight from Houston to Fort Worth.

"There was some concern, not only in the press corps, but there was concern among other people about whether there could be trouble in Dallas, but trouble didn't mean assassination. Trouble meant that the crowds might not be happy with him and might boo him, might disagree with him, might not turn out," Davis recalled at the age of 95 when I interviewed him at his home in Bethesda, Maryland.

"We were stunned when we got to the airport, at Love Field, from Fort Worth that morning. The crowd at the airport was enormous, usually it would be about 1,000 people or 500 people at the airport. Most of the people would be on the motorcade route down into town," said Davis, who was the White House correspondent for Westinghouse Broadcasting.

"The president decides he wants to walk over to the fence to all the people who came to greet him at the airport. And there were thousands of people. And Jackie, for the first time that I can recall, was very pleased and very happy this is happening and walked with him holding his hand and then they went to the railing. The crowd was—behind the fence and shaking hands, walking down a quarter mile. The airport was mobbed. That was the first time we said to ourselves, the press, 'This isn't Dallas, is it?' They were so enthusiastic. A lot of young people came. They got into the limousine and now we headed into downtown Dallas, which was a couple of miles away."

John and Jackie would never make it to the Trade Mart for the president's speech to the annual meeting of the Dallas Citizens Council. The motorcade, which was to travel about 10 miles, was longer than usual.

"Every big shot in Dallas wanted to be in the motorcade with the president," Davis remembered. "So, you had a lot of extra cars. City councilmen, the police chief, the fire chief, you had all these extra cars."

Vice President Lyndon Johnson and his wife Lady Bird were in a Lincoln four-door convertible, behind a Cadillac convertible, known as *Halfback* or the *Queen Mary*, which was loaded with eight Secret Service agents sitting inside or standing on the running boards. That vehicle was immediately behind Kennedy's car, a modified 1961 Lincoln convertible, with the code name SS-100-X, which also carried the first lady, Governor Connolly (who would be wounded that day), and his wife, Nellie. Secret Service Agent Bill Greer was driving and his colleague, Roy Kellerman, in the front right seat.

Davis, presumably the last surviving journalistic witness to the pair of pivotal events that traumatic day in Dallas, was on press bus number one in the motorcade, 13 vehicles behind the dark-blue presidential limousine.

"I heard the shots. Sitting next to me was Robert Pierpoint of *CBS News*. Bob Pierpoint was a war correspondent in Korea. He jumps out of his seat and he shouts to the 40 of us on the bus: 'That's gunfire, that's not backfires of a car. That is gunfire.' He's screaming his head off at Rory Eliot, the bus driver, to catch up with the presidential limousine. The presidential car had disappeared from the motorcade," recalled Davis.

The motorcade dissolved and the press buses were among the vehicles that went to the Dallas Trade Mart, where Kennedy was supposed to deliver his speech. The crowd inside, awaiting the luncheon speech while listening to organ music, was unaware something was amiss until dozens of reporters burst into the room in frantic search of telephones.

"The president's car, after this incident took place, just shot forward in a tremendous burst and headed right for the hospital and passed the

Trade Mart completely by," Davis told Westinghouse listeners from the venue, accurately reporting a "sniper" had targeted the president.

At the Trade Mart the crowd was eventually informed that the president had been shot. Some women went limp with grief, Davis informed his audience.

"We are awaiting word from the hospital on the president's condition," Davis, on a telephone line, said on air. "Almost a complete chaos has now taken place."

Outside the venue, a police officer flagged down a 1948 Cadillac to take Davis to the hospital.

"I went immediately to the emergency room. And I was immediately thrown out of the emergency room. But I saw Mrs. Kennedy there. And I went over where she was standing and she was talking to one of the doctors. And she took a piece of the president's skull out of her suit pocket and showed it to the doctor. And she said, 'Would this be of any help?' At this point, they had not announced Kennedy's death. And the doctor said, 'No, Mrs. Kennedy, it would not be of any help.'"

Davis then heard Father Oscar Huber, a Catholic priest, say, "He's dead all right. I just gave him the last rites."

Minutes later the announcement was made in a nurses' room at the hospital by White House Deputy Press Secretary Malcolm Kilduff, his voice shaking with emotion, that Kennedy had been pronounced dead as a result of a bullet wound to the brain. Kilduff then lit a cigarette, the lighter in his hand quivering.

"At that point, all hell broke loose. And I went on the air and announced President Kennedy was dead on the basis of what Kilduff said," recalled Davis.

Going on the air again from a phone in the hospital administrator's office, Davis told listeners across the country: "We do not know whether the last rites came prior to his death." He added that Johnson had gone into seclusion and the reporters did not know where he was.

"The president was fatally injured. There was, apparently, no chance to save him" due to the accuracy of the sniper's bullet, Davis added in his broadcast. Right after that, Davis found himself drafted as an ad hoc pool reporter.

"A guy named Jiggs Fauver, a White House Press Office transportation person, said, 'You're going to be a pooler,'" recalled Davis. "You've got to get out of here and Merriman Smith [UPI] and Chuck Roberts

[*Newsweek*]. There's three of you. We have a car waiting, a police car is waiting for you outside" to rush him and the two other reporters to the airport, where *Air Force One* was parked.

"We went through the streets of Dallas, in and out of traffic. We went over front lawns, driveways, everything, racing for Love Field. They didn't want *Air Force One* to leave without us. And we got to Love Field. *Air Force One* was gearing up. Jim Swindal, the pilot, was preparing to leave. I boarded the airplane," said Davis, who, with Roberts and Smith, sprinted the last 200 yards to the aircraft.

Davis spotted a bank of telephones and he asked Kilduff if he had enough time to make a call. The press official told him to hurry. Davis could not get through to his Washington bureau, so he called UPI in New York and told them Johnson was about to become president aboard *Air Force One* on the Dallas tarmac.

"I followed Lyndon Johnson around the airplane as he met with staff," Davis said, recalling a level of access at a moment of crisis unimaginable to any White House reporter decades later.

Davis witnessed Johnson calling Robert Kennedy, the president's brother and attorney general. Johnson, still technically vice president at that moment, told the attorney general that *Air Force One* should immediately fly back to Andrews Air Force Base in Maryland. "Mrs. Kennedy agreed. She did not want the body to remain in Dallas because that would have meant an autopsy delay," according to Davis.

Robert Caro, Johnson's biographer, described an immediate transition with Lyndon Johnson. During his vice presidency, Johnson had seemed depressed, usually seen with a hangdog expression.

I told Davis what Caro had written.

"He did take charge" on board *Air Force One,* said Davis. "LBJ stepped in and said, 'We're going to take the oath in Dallas.' And then Judge Sarah Hughes, a federal judge, had been brought out to the airplane to administer the oath."

I asked Davis why he thought Johnson wanted to immediately take the oath on the plane and not wait to hold a ceremony back in Washington.

"Johnson was a very bright guy," said Davis. "He saw the problems of going back to Washington. That would take three or four hours. Then there were members of Congress who would get involved and say we're going to have a ceremony. We're gonna do this or do that. And Johnson didn't want that. Mrs. Kennedy didn't. They wanted to have the swearing-in. The only way to do that was to do it in Dallas."

Only 99 minutes had passed since Kennedy had been declared dead when Johnson, after asking for a tall glass of ice water, raised his right hand to take the oath of office with his left hand on a Bible that had been on board the plane. Johnson insisted on having the president's grieving widow stand next to him in her bloodstained dress. Davis recalled the ceremony lasted 28 seconds and was witnessed by a couple of dozen people on the plane.

"I don't think the bloodstained dress bothered him. He wanted her in the picture. He put his arm around her shoulder. And he called her at one point he called her, 'Darlin', you stand here,'" said Davis. "To not have had her in that photograph would have been terrible. And he knew that. He knew she had to be in that picture. And she, what she was thinking, was I've lost my husband. But she was willing to do all of the things Johnson was telling her to do. My judgment is she wanted to be in the picture."

Davis had a chance to fly back on the plane to Washington as one of the press poolers. It would have required him and *Newsweek*'s Roberts to flip a coin for the remaining seat.

"Should I flip him or stay here?" Davis asked his boss in Washington, Jim Snyder.

"Stay there," Snyder can be heard replying in an off-air recording of their conversation prior to Johnson taking the oath of office from a tearful Judge Hughes in the presidential compartment of the plane. "There were 40-some White House correspondents that flew out there with me. And since I was the only pooler in that little group, and I had all the story, I volunteered to stay there and give the pool report to the rest of the White House correspondents." That also meant Davis would not be able to go on the air again immediately to give his Westinghouse audience further details of one of the most tragic days in American history. Before he stepped from the plane, Davis, as the brief oath-taking concluded, saw the new president embrace Jackie Kennedy and then hugged the new first lady. Johnson then said softly, "Let's get this plane back to Washington." Nine minutes later the plane was airborne.

On the tarmac "they lifted me on the top of a trunk of a car. And I gave the pool report," Davis recalled in our interview. "I did not file my story until I gave the pool report."

Going on air to describe the ceremony, Davis concluded his report, saying that as he walked back into the airport, a man came up to him and said, "This country is sick. Maybe this will shake it up."

I asked Davis when the enormity of what he had witnessed hit him.

"Steven, you know, the White House correspondents have a reputation for the bottle," he replied. "Pan American World Airways was our favorite airline. The one thing they knew all about us was what booze we drank. And going back to Washington that night about 11 P.M., not a single one of the 50 reporters had a drink. The most unusual thing. The stewardesses turned out the lights and brought pillows so that we could sleep."

Fourteen hours after the president's death, Davis was back at the White House reporting live from inside the northwest gate, noting 13 kerosene flares had been placed around the driveway where an honor guard of Marines with polished bayonets received the cortege. Davis paraphrased the words of a Kennedy favorite, poet Robert Frost, who had died earlier that year, closing his 4 A.M. broadcast: "I have promises to keep and many miles to go before I sleep." Then Davis attempted to sign off but began to cry.

"At that time, I just broke up on air," he told me, becoming emotional in his Bethesda, Maryland, living room recalling the moment nearly 60 years ago. "I just couldn't hold it back. Now, there's an old rule in broadcasting. It says: If you're not sure, don't do it, don't say it, don't play it. And I violated every rule in the book."

17

Over the course of a presidency much of the protective pool duty in motorcades is mundane and forgettable. Frequently it involves hours of waiting in vans, libraries, or diners as presidents watch their kids participate in sports or press the flesh behind closed doors at political fundraisers.

For the White House press corps, however, there is no presidential activity less exciting than golf. Watching the president golf would be boring. But we do not even get to do that.

During the Trump presidency, the press vans in the motorcade would accompany the limousine to the entrance of his private clubs and then veer off. For a while during the start of the Trump presidency when the golfer-in-chief traveled on weekends to his course in Sterling, Virginia, we would be sent to the lounge overlooking the indoor tennis court, where we could watch country club members whacking balls. Sandwiches and refreshments were provided for which our media organizations were billed banquet rates. (After correspondents complained about the high prices, we lost access to the sandwiches and were banished from the club, having to cool our heels at a nearby pizza joint while Trump golfed.) Something I did on a lazy October Saturday in 2017 may have resulted in a decision to subsequently keep the press vans away from the club entrance. There was no indication that day's travel to Sterling would be noteworthy. But the photographers were always ready in case there was a funny sign to snap held by one of the few occasional roadside demonstrators.

As we pulled away from the club on that day onto Lowes Island Boulevard, Juli Briskman noticed her quiet bicycle ride was being interrupted by several slow-moving black vehicles.

Briskman was not happy and quickly deduced, when the motorcade overtook her, the identity of the occupant reading a newspaper in the backseat of one of the vehicles. From our vantage point, many vehicles toward the rear, we paid little notice to the lone cyclist until she extended a middle finger at the front of the motorcade. Two of the photographers sitting a row ahead of me in the van reacted instinctively. I was a fraction of a second slower and my shot of the woman's offending digit was obscured by the rearview mirror of our vehicle.

"Hey, you guys get that?" I asked the *New York Times* and AFP photographers. They replied in the affirmative. All presidential motorcades in the modern era will usually have at least one bystander making such a gesture and as we headed back to the White House, I didn't give it much thought.

That evening I checked in with one of our editors in the newsroom, Mia Bush, and asked her if any of the wires had issued a photograph of the cyclist flipping the bird at the president. VOA subscribes to three of the major international news wires: AFP, AP, and Reuters, as well as the TV and photographic services.

Mia's fast research located the AFP photo taken through the window of our van by Brendan Smialowski and she emailed it to me. I attached it to a tweet and put it on my time line, figuring it would merit, perhaps, a couple of dozen retweets and a few snarky comments, either hailing the cyclist a hero or a traitor. The tweet soon took on a life of its own. The mystery cyclist was quickly embraced as a hero of the Resistance and a villain by the Trump movement. The tweet and the mystery woman's photo were soon on cable news and caught the attention of late-night TV comedians.

On Monday morning, the cyclist identified herself and placed the image on her social media accounts. The next day, the 50-year-old marketing analyst overseeing government contracts was forced by her company to resign for posting online "obscene content."

Briskman decided not to fade quietly into obscurity. She used her newfound fame to pursue political office—not to directly challenge Trump, rather as a proxy far down the ballot and a year prior to the president's 2020 reelection race. She ran as a Democrat against the Republican incumbent for the Algonkian district seat on the Loudon County Board of Supervisors. She was elected.

A news cycle usually lasts a day. Briskman took a much longer ride.

18

Baseball fan William Howard Taft was the first president known to golf, a recreational pastime early twentieth-century politicians sought to keep from their constituents as it was considered a game for the rich. Taft's predecessor, William McKinley, enjoyed watching golfers on the course, but there is no concrete documentation of him playing a round. Taft's caddies were equipped with ropes in case they needed to extract the obese chief executive from the deep bunkers on the Myopia Hunt Club's course in Massachusetts.

Taft started a trend, although subsequent presidents did not require evacuation from the sand. Since Taft, there have been only three non-golfers in the White House: Herbert Hoover, Harry Truman, and Jimmy Carter. Theodore Roosevelt had a myriad of other distractions. Hoover considered the sport inappropriate as the nation plunged into economic recession. Truman and Carter didn't like the game.

While detractors of Trump or Biden criticized them for their perceived time on the links, it is likely no president will beat the record of Woodrow Wilson, who played at least 1,000 rounds during his time in office as a stress reliever—that is nearly one round every other day. Foul weather did not deter Wilson. It is said he had the Secret Service paint golf balls black when it snowed so he could see them.

Warren Harding was arguably the worst presidential golfer, rarely scoring below 100. During a round of golf in Vancouver, Canada, in late July 1923, Harding first displayed signs of heart failure and died days later in San Francisco.

Calvin Coolidge golfed a few times as president, preferring the sport of shooting clay pigeons. History records that when he departed the White House for good, the only item he left behind was his bag of golf clubs.

Polio, at the age of 39, put a stop to Franklin Roosevelt's game a dozen years before he entered the White House.

Dwight Eisenhower's love of golf, despite being a congenital slicer and an unreliable putter, was well known. He played 800 rounds during eight years in office and broke 80 four times at Augusta. Ike had a putting green installed on the White House South Lawn, outside the Oval Office. His love of the game is credited with doubling the number of golfers in the United States during his presidency.

Eisenhower's successor, John F. Kennedy, despite a bad back, was considered one of the most skilled presidential golfers, although he did not get much time on the course during his presidency, which was cut tragically short by assassination. Kennedy hypocritically had been among those who publicly chastised his Republican predecessor for devotion to the game.

Lyndon Johnson is said to have had no love for the links but would endure it to secure votes from senators for legislation he was pushing, including the 1964 Civil Rights Act. He was known to take as many shots as he liked, ignoring the rules, cajoling the golf balls, and swinging like he was chopping wood or trying to kill a rattlesnake.

Richard Nixon had taken up the game as vice president to try to stay in the good grace of Eisenhower. Historians note that after he finally managed to break 80, he gave it up during his troubled second term.

Scoring in the 80s was no problem for Gerald Ford, although his swing was considered erratic. He did, however, during an exhibition match at Pinehurst, North Carolina, manage to outdrive legends Arnold Palmer and Gary Player.

Ronald Reagan is not remembered much for golfing, although he had a powerful swing. One time, while playing on the famed Augusta National course in Georgia, a gunman took hostages in the pro shop and demanded to speak to the president. The man did not have a political agenda; he had been suffering a family crisis. Reagan and Secretary of State George Schultz, who had invited the president to play at the course, were driven from the club in their golfing attire. Over a two-hour period, all the hostages escaped or were set free and the armed intruder was arrested.

Bill Clinton was considered a decent golfer, although fellow players would grumble about his frequent mulligans (for the uninitiated, that's a do-over without penalty). He reinstalled the White House putting green Nixon had removed.

Both George H. and George H. W. Bush had golf in their DNA. The elder Bush's father had been a president of the US Golf Association.

George H. W. Bush was known to have golfed only 24 rounds in office, giving up the game as a gesture of support for US soldiers in Iraq and Afghanistan. This came after he received criticism for telling reporters to "watch this drive" right after making a statement on terrorism.

Barack Obama, the first left-handed presidential golfer, played about 250 rounds in office. He favored courses on military bases over the private clubs in the Washington metropolitan area.

Trump and golf were virtually synonymous before his presidency. He was an avid amateur and owner of as many as 17 courses in the United States and abroad. Trump spent more than 300 days of his presidency golfing, although he stayed away from his courses for 50 days during the 2019 government shutdown. Among sports journalists, Trump is considered a reverse sandbagger—a player who is not as skilled as his handicap says and costs himself shots on the course to ensure he keeps his vanity handicap. Some fellow players accused Trump of cheating and scoffed at his claim he could drive a ball 285 yards off the tee.

While in office, Trump did not allow the press pool to witness his play. As previously noted, after being banished from the premises of the Sterling club, the poolers and the press vans broke from the motorcade to divert to a pizza joint. When Trump played at his course in West Palm Beach, Florida, we cooled our heels in the public library and on holidays when that facility was closed, the alternative hold point was a nearby International House of Pancakes, where one morning we watched a bemused French journalist marvel at fellow diners consuming one of America's most unhealthy meals—the IHOP cheeseburger omelet with pancakes: about 2,000 calories with more than 4,500 milligrams of sodium and 45 grams of saturated fat.

The golf forays were of little value to the pool photographers, who were not permitted to witness Trump at play. Occasionally a TV news crew would get blurry, long-distance shots that would confirm Trump was indeed on the course, although the White House rarely would acknowledge on the record that the president was doing what everyone knew he was doing.

One Saturday in April 2019, the White House disseminated two official photographs of Trump golfing with radio talk show host Rush Limbaugh, a strong supporter of the president, while a third photo showed them together on the 27-hole West Palm Beach course with professional golfer Lexi Thompson. The White House Correspondents' Association president at the time, Olivier Knox, quickly sent an email to members reminding them "that using/tweeting official White House photo handouts undermines our still-photo colleagues and our principles. Please do not post them on social media or use them in your publications or broadcasts." All the images were taken by White House staff photographer Joyce Boghosian. The golf outing took place a day after the release of a special counsel's report into the 2016 Trump campaign and Russia.

"The White House typically doesn't release photos of Trump's golf partners, nor does it usually share details of each of his trips to hit the links," noted Rachel Frazin on the *Hill* website, which focuses on political coverage.

Bloomberg News, the *Hill,* VOA, and Yahoo News were among the news organizations posting some or all of the pictures on their social media accounts or websites. Individually, journalists from ABC, Bloomberg, CBS, NBC, the *New York Times,* Reuters, VOA, and the *Washington Post,* among others, also tweeted the photos, with several explaining the context. There had been tension, not only during the Trump administration, between the White House and press photographers assigned to cover the president concerning imagery access.

"A White House photo release, no matter how accurate the image, provides only one perspective—one that is carefully screened and approved," the White House News Photographers' Association complained in a July 2005 letter to Dan Bartlett, an assistant on communications for President George W. Bush.

"Eventually the Bush administration agreed to drastically reduce their usage of the handouts," according to an account of the controversy published five years later by Clint Hendler in the *Columbia Journalism Review* when the issue flared again in the Obama administration.

"The job of the official White House photographer is not to provide news photographs that have gone through layers of an approval process before being deemed fit to release. It's not enough to let only reporters in and think that you are really granting access to the press in a transparent way," complained WHNPA President Dennis Brack in a March 2010 letter to then White House Chief of Staff Rahm Emanuel.

Restricting access for photographers and forcing the news media to rely on official images to tell the story blurs the line between journalism and propaganda, and in the case of presidents, it allows them to airbrush history.

19

While Trump and the West Wing staff ignored criticism of his golfing, they would bristle at the skepticism about the president's so-called "executive time." In February 2019, an insider leaked months of Trump's private schedules.

The release of the information was a "disgraceful breach of trust," declared Madeleine Westerhout, the director of Oval Office operations. In a tweet, Westerhout said what the documents did not show "are the hundreds of calls and meetings" the president takes every day.

In December 2020, the publicly released schedule for Trump's White House activities became less specific when "the president discovered that, for the first time, my understanding, that we released a public schedule of his to the public," former White House Deputy Press Secretary Judd Deere told the House committee investigating the January 6, 2021, insurrection. "And so what became the new version of the public schedule was basically a couple of sentences about what his day would consist of rather than specific times and titles of events in an outline form."

During his tumultuous presidency, Trump usually did not make it to work in the West Wing until after 11 A.M., preferring to watch television and make phone calls from the residence. It was a routine he would repeat in the evening.

Insiders, after their departure from the Trump White House, wrote about the chaotic and unstructured decision-making process of the administration. Born into wealth, Trump had never worked for anyone except his father. He had no law degree, no MBA. He ran a private family business bearing his name and was never answerable to a board of directors or shareholders. Only other family members were to be trusted, and they had the most influence despite outsiders holding more senior titles than his children and son-in-law. For Trump, rivalries between underlings were an amusing sport. *The Apprentice* TV program he had hosted effectively continued as a reality show when Trump became president.

Trump in office gave the impression, through words and action, that there was little distinction between his personal business priorities and the interests of the United States.

Trump's second press secretary, Sarah Huckabee Sanders, had pushed back on the assessment that the schedules revealed the majority of the president's day was spent in unstructured "executive time," reinforcing the image Trump preferred to devote many hours watching news on cable television and tweeting about it. "President Trump has a different leadership style than his predecessors and the results speak for themselves," said Sanders at the time, adding that the president "spends much of his average day in scheduled meetings, events, and calls." Much to the embarrassment of the White House, the 95 pages of private Trump schedules were obtained by the Axios website and posted online.

Kellyanne Conway, counselor to the president, told reporters at the White House the following day that "whoever leaked it, doesn't know what he's doing for a net block of time." Conway explained that the version of the schedule that leaked was distributed daily to 388 people in the administration, but few had access to an even more detailed presidential agenda.

The leaked schedule showed 60 percent of the president's time since the previous November's midterm elections was set aside for him to casually meet with staff members, peruse the stack of newspapers delivered to his office, watch television, and make phone calls to officials and informal advisers.

"What's not entirely unusual are swaths of unscheduled time on the public schedule. It's true that not all of the commander-in-chief's engagements can be broadcast to the world," explained Ned Price, a special assistant to the president during the administration of former President Barack Obama and who subsequently became State Department spokesman in the Biden administration.

"What's stunning in this case is that there's nothing behind the curtain for Trump. Nothing. And the fact that they delineate 'policy time'— an hour every once in a while—speaks to the fact that the remainder of the time is taken up with *Fox News* and other favored presidential pastimes," Price told me at the time.

Sanders disputed that assessment, contending Trump's schedule allowed "for a more creative environment that has helped make him the most productive president in modern history."

What is indisputable is that different presidents have had individual management styles.

Historians note that early in his presidency, Bill Clinton was habitually late and often deviated from the planned schedule.

Obama and his predecessor, George W. Bush, were more punctual. Former administration officials say Bush's schedule was tight and planned months in advance. Obama occasionally had blocks of unscheduled time, but that usually was for preparation ahead of a big speech or major international travel. Books by former Trump administration officials indicate the forty-fifth president had a short attention span and expressed impatience in briefings about military and intelligence matters. White House officials disputed the characterization Trump was not interested in such topics or had only a superficial understanding of them. What is clear, according to news reports and those close to the president, is that he preferred succinct presentations with more visual elements than those that had been typically prepared for his predecessors. The concept of "executive time" was introduced for Trump by one of his White House chiefs of staff, John Kelly, for a president who bristled in response to being locked into a fixed schedule.

As we witnessed frequently, many of Trump's meetings and discussions as president occurred spur of the moment. This was bewildering for White House staff who had come from backgrounds in previous administrations or on Capitol Hill. They expected their environment to resemble Aaron Sorkin's television show, *The West Wing,* but without the liberal slant. Instead, they found themselves living in a Monty Python program, alternating between the skits of "Ministry of Silly Walks," the "Argument Clinic," and the "Spanish Inquisition."

Trump's third of four press secretaries, Stephanie Grisham, colorfully described it as "a clown car on fire running at full speed into a warehouse full of fireworks."

White House pool reporters would discover details about events when summoned to the Oval Office, the Roosevelt Room, or elsewhere at the White House. Often, Trump would make an announcement on Twitter, his favorite social media platform, giving insight into which issue he had suddenly prioritized. Trump tweets were also meant to distract the media and public from the latest uproar, usually the result of a previous tweet, by creating a new melee. It was the primary reason I told my editors many mornings I would not be able to inform them until mid-afternoon what would be the topic of the day's news story I would produce, as it was likely something not listed in the publicly released schedule.

20

Joining the White House press corps is surprisingly easy. It is up to the White House Press Office to decide who will be granted an appointment pass—a temporary credential that allows access to the briefing room and a break room (with espresso machines courtesy of Tom Hanks), the ability to enter the two areas where the press secretaries have their offices and attempt to pester them, and to stand outside in front of the West Wing around the north driveway. It is likely easier to get an appointment pass than to secure press credentials from the Sioux Falls Fire Department.

On any given day, many of those wearing a badge with a big "A" on it (for "Appointment") are from news outlets that most journalists have never heard of. Google searches fail to yield bylines for some of these supposed reporters or their publications. Others claim to represent industry-focused or regional publications who appear to have correspondents nowhere except at the White House. Most of them are considered a benign presence except for their crowding of the halls. It is baffling to some gainfully employed White House reporters that a handful of these interlopers, who never seem to produce any stories, sit in the briefing room day after day. Are they independently wealthy? Homeless? Being paid by a foreign government? The imagination runs wild.

Occasionally there are incidents.

A photographer working for a publication tied to a controversial Chinese spiritual movement violated protocol and handed a folder to President Trump as he walked out of the East Room following a reception. The White House should have known better as there had been an incident during a previous administration with someone from the same publication, *Epoch Times,* causing a disruption. That occurred when a reporter credentialed for the arrival of Chinese President Hu Jintao on the South Lawn shouted at George W. Bush to get Hu to stop persecuting the Falun Gong movement. She then yelled directly to the Chinese president: "Your time is over. Evil people will die early." While US presidents sometimes received questions they interpreted as insulting, at least it was never as disparaging as that.

When Trump made a rare unscheduled appearance in the White House briefing room to mention there would be an announcement soon about him and Kim Jong Un, a freelance Korean photographer lost it and began yelling with joy: "Mr. Trump, you're going to win Nobel Prize." The audio technicians were furious that the outburst covered the words of a speaking president. Ahead of a scheduled briefing, respected Fox News Radio correspondent Jon Decker objected to the presence of a right-wing conspiracy theorist in the briefing room. That prompted a subsequent false claim from the fringe blogger that Decker, a lawyer (subsequently a correspondent for Gray TV), had assaulted him. I was among the witnesses, and as was the case with a dozen other bystanders, we saw no physical contact.

At the Helsinki news conference by Trump and Russian President Vladimir Putin in July 2018, I stood to the side a few rows from the front, conveniently next to the audio distribution box to record broadcast quality sound for radio. I also live-tweeted and attached photos as we waited for the presidents to emerge from their one-on-one meeting. Suddenly there was a commotion a few rows back and I immediately began recording video on my iPhone. A security official struggled with an older bespectacled gentleman, who had been credentialed by the White House, sitting in the press seats.

"We have an incident," I quickly tweeted and attached video of the struggle that showed the individual, Sam Husseini, holding a sign reading: "Nuclear Ban Treaty." He then shouted, "I want to ask a question." Husseini did not get his wish and was ejected.

Husseini had obtained credentials as an opinion writer for the *Nation,* a venerable liberal weekly magazine based in New York City. But any cursory vetting of Husseini would have revealed his real job was as communications director of the Institute for Public Accuracy, which matches journalists with "progressive scholars and policy analysts."

Although no charges were filed against Husseini, he said he was detained by Finnish authorities at the Presidential Palace, manhandled, and cuffed on his hands and legs before being taken to a holding facility.

"They wouldn't call my family to tell them I was unharmed," complained Husseini, who likely was fortunate he pulled the publicity stunt in Helsinki and not Moscow.

White House correspondents trace their professional lineage to William "Fatty" Price, who, in 1896 at the age of 35, showed up in Washington from South Carolina and applied for a job at the *Evening Star.* The city editor gave the 300-pound journalist a tryout—go to the White House and see if you can find a story.

President Grover Cleveland had little use for newspaper reporters. He referred to them as "ghouls" and when he did speak to journalists, he had no qualms about lying to them. Price, drawing on his experience in his home state of interviewing passengers who stepped off trains passing through town, stood outside the North Portico of the White House, quizzing Cleveland's visitors as they arrived and left. The technique worked. Price was given a column in the *Evening Star,* "At the White House," which flourished in the presidencies of William McKinley, Theodore Roosevelt, and well into those of William Taft and Woodrow Wilson. Competing newspapers realized they were missing out, as during the 1898 Spanish-American War when the attention of reporters shifted from Capitol Hill to the White House. They sought to emulate Price's news-gathering innovation of talking to people, and soon there was a fledging press corps covering the Executive Mansion.

Again, it was Price who set precedent. Invited inside from the North Portico, he initially took notes by holding his writing paper up against a wall. Soon, on the second floor, a table, chairs, and writing materials were brought in for reporters, outside of a secretary's office and under the watchful eye of a doorman. There the scribes were allowed to politely make inquiries to visitors and ask the president's secretaries for scraps of information, although some aides expressed disdain for the print rabble. The press corps had finally established itself inside the White House and it has never left.

There was a major difference in the era of Fatty Price. When the president passed by the press quarters, none of the journalists asked him any questions, following decorum.

There was, from the start, a pecking order. George Cortelyou, one of the de facto press secretaries (the title was yet to be formalized), wrote and distributed news releases. They first went to those representing the three major news services before being put into the hands of the rest of the press pack. When President McKinley traveled, Cortelyou provided reporters with advance copies of the speeches (a practice that has largely gone by the wayside in recent administrations, although excerpts are provided in advance of some major presidential addresses). Stenographers were also on hand to record the president's extemporaneous remarks, a service that continues to this day. For decades the stenographers were provided by outside contractors. During the Obama administration they were brought onto the federal payroll and currently have a reputation for transcripts that are accurate, thorough, and impartial regardless of which party is in power.

During my rotations as a radio pool reporter there were several instances when the stenographer's handheld digital recorder might have missed a presidential utterance and I helped them clarify the transcript for the historical record. The stenographers do not use external microphones extended on boom poles as do radio and TV crews. I did not have any qualms about helping verify quotes in such public situations. After all, VOA's material is in the public domain and we share our audio with all of the other accredited radio networks. The transcripts ensure the president is not misquoted by the media. But sometimes it is the media that conversely ensures the official record is accurate.

Theodore Roosevelt, the vice president who succeeded McKinley when the latter was assassinated in Buffalo, New York, becoming at the age of 42 the youngest president in American history, had a more sophisticated understanding of the press—and the power of photography— and how to use it to his advantage. Roosevelt had understood the power of the press to burnish his image since his days as one of the volunteer Rough Riders of the Spanish-American War and then as governor of New York. His skills at self-promotion were vital to his meteoric rise from cavalry officer to vice president.

While Roosevelt's relationship with reporters could be contentious, he did formalize their presence inside the White House, ordering plans for the journalists to have a room included in the Executive Office Building he was having built, now known as the West Wing. The first White House press room was far from spacious—it could barely fit Fatty Price. But it did have telephones so reporters could call in their stories. Hours after McKinley's funeral, Roosevelt telephoned the bureau chiefs of United Press, Associated Press, and the *New York Sun,* inviting them for a meeting in the Cabinet Room where he promised greater access to journalists. But his promise came with a caveat—if they published something he felt was indiscreet, he would withhold further news from that reporter's outlet.

While there were daily briefings for the White House correspondents, Roosevelt was very selective about with whom he interacted. Starting in 1901, Roosevelt frequently extended invitations by telephone to a few of his favorite reporters to come listen to him while he was in the White House barber's chair getting shaved in a narrow reception room in the early afternoon. These presidential seances or "the barber's hour," as they were known, were off the record. Roosevelt would allow the journalists to use pieces of information he revealed, as long as they did not mention the source—akin to what we would now term "deep background." The president, in response to a reporter's question, would jump from his chair—not infrequently as the nervous barber brought his razor down on Roosevelt's face—and speak in an excited manner before settling briefly again for the interrupted shave to resume.

Reporters disobeyed Roosevelt's conditions for their conversations at their own peril. "If they did anything else he would not allow them near the White House or office, and he has been known to have them dismissed from their papers," wrote a former newspaper correspondent, Army Captain Archie Butt, who had become one of Roosevelt's aides. Unlike such thin-skinned predecessors as Washington and Adams, Roosevelt was known to fight back intensively against journalists he perceived as leaking, lying, or mischaracterizing his comments or actions. Any stories about his family were strictly off-limits.

Those banished were deemed to have entered the Ananias Club, named after a biblical figure who was fatally struck before St. Peter for lying to God. The young president cultivated relations with a new generation of reporters whom he referred to as the "muckrakers," investigative journalists bent on exposing corporate corruption and conditions in the big city slums.

Roosevelt's immediate successor, William Howard Taft, a rotund Cincinnati lawyer, had been cooperative with reporters while he was secretary of war and during his presidential campaign, but once elected he reduced the access the White House correspondents had enjoyed with Roosevelt. Taft said Roosevelt's "heart was generally on his sleeve and he must communicate his feelings. I find myself unable to do so."

Taft, briefly at the start of his presidency, did hold news conferences, either in his office or in the Cabinet Room and, unlike Roosevelt, provided chairs for the invited reporters, although latecomers had to stand. Most of the time reporters went looking for news elsewhere, leading to rumors ending up in print, with Butt (who had stayed on for the new administration and would perish on the *Titanic*) lamenting that Taft "did not understand the art of giving out news."

Taft did become the first American president to have his speeches distributed on phonographic recordings. During the 1908 campaign, the

Victor Talking Machine Company of Thomas Edison recorded on flat disks or wax cylinders a series of two-minute excerpts of the political speeches of Taft and Democratic Party rival William Jennings Bryan. The brevity of the recordings compelled candidates to get to the point, presaging the modern sound bite.

The new technology did not determine the outcome of the election. Bryan, a magnetic orator and a three-time presidential candidate, lost to Taft, who reluctantly agreed to make the recordings (which Bryan had already enthusiastically done). An underdog in the 1912 election, Taft was less reluctant to make recordings, which were sold nationwide.

"How foolish the American people would be to hazard the continuance of this [prosperity] by voting into power a party whose first declared principle is hostility to the policy of protection upon which our business is conducted," said Taft in one recording, predicting that putting the Democrats in power would "halt and paralyze business" by reducing tariffs.

Taft's recorded words failed to electrify the electorate.

Although a divided Republican Party had nominated the incumbent, his predecessor, Roosevelt, was upset with Taft for not continuing his progressive policies. Roosevelt bolted from the Republican Party and ran as the candidate of the Progressive Party. The split allowed Woodrow Wilson, the Democrat nominee and governor of New Jersey, to win the presidency with only 42 percent of the popular vote. But he captured a landslide total of 435 electoral votes to Roosevelt's 88 and Taft's humiliating eight. Wilson, who had previously referred to newspapermen as "contemptible spies," became the first US president to hold regularly scheduled press conferences. The initial one, on March 15, 1913, was a disappointment to the more than 100 journalists who attended. Wilson's responses to questions were polite but succinct. A week later, Wilson attempted a do-over, inviting a group of reporters to the East Room explaining that during their previous encounter, "I did not feel I had anything to say." That day the president said he did have some things to say and although a text of his remarks was distributed to the press by the White House, it was with the understanding that "this speech is not to be published."

Wilson's news conferences, conducted with dozens of reporters standing at a respectful distance from his desk, resumed with the president speaking in a low voice and giving responses that were convoluted. Wilson appeared quite reticent to respond to questions about foreign affairs, a highly charged topic at the time with revolution south of the border in Mexico and war looming in Europe.

In the middle of 1915, Wilson, who came to enjoy the press briefings as "delightful interludes in a busy day," had had enough of the formalities—abandoning the press conferences to avoid any further questions about whether the United States would be drawn into war after Germany torpedoed the *Lusitania,* in which many Americans died. In his second term, Wilson resumed holding news conferences, but the president could still not be quoted, with Wilson explaining that the discussions with him were "for the guidance of your own minds in making up your stories."

The next US president was a hit with journalists. Warren Harding, after all, was one of them. The hands-on owner, publisher, and editor of the *Marion Star* in Ohio, Harding continued to be intimately involved with his newspaper even as president. He resumed the twice-a-week news conferences Wilson had abandoned. They were informative encounters. After bowing as they entered the Oval Office, as many as 50 scribes would listen to the soft-spoken Harding describe highlights of Cabinet meetings, freely answering written questions but in keeping with tradition, he was not to be quoted directly.

Harding, on May 30, 1922, became the first US president to speak on the radio, six months after he had a wireless receiver installed in the White House. Harding had turned down numerous requests to participate in radio events, and the US Navy was hesitant about having its two primary radio stations used for expressly political purposes. It was an official event on Decoration Day (now known as Memorial Day) when the president's voice first hit the airwaves. At the dedication of the Lincoln Memorial, Harding's voice was broadcast over the navy's NAA and NOF stations. William Taft, now the chief justice of the Supreme Court, introduced Harding. The first presidential words spoken on the radio: "Mr. Chief Justice: It is a supreme satisfaction officially to accept on behalf of the government this superb monument to the savior of the republic."

The microphone was hidden in a white box stuck atop a white pole so it would blend in with the monument's white columns. The signals from the radio stations were picked up by other broadcasters and relayed across the country.

When Harding died in office the following year, bringing an end to a scandal-tainted administration, his vice president and former Massachusetts Governor Calvin Coolidge, a media-savvy, second-generation politician, ascended. With a reputation as a vice president for not speaking freely and rarely agreeing to be interviewed, he had been dubbed "Silent Cal." But as president, Coolidge would hold 520 press conferences during his 67 months in office. Questions were submitted in advance in writing, and Coolidge would choose which ones were worthy of a verbal reply. Again, he was not to be quoted directly. Early in his administration he was usually referred to as "a senior administration official" and, later on, by such phrases as "those in a position to know the mind of the president."

During Coolidge's administration, media technology evolved. Motion pictures joined the printed word and still photography in American journalism. The thirtieth president regularly appeared in newsreels, comfortably posing, sometimes in costume, in front of large boxy cameras mounted on tripods. He would be the first chief executive to appear in a talking picture newsreel. His only restriction on photography was to not have his picture taken while smoking his frequent cigars.

Coolidge, a proponent of technological advancement, understood the power of radio. He asked for help to improve his "radio manners," working on his speaking style and voice pitch, and understood that broadcasting made archaic the ostentatious nineteenth-century style of political oratory.

Coolidge was the first American leader to deliver a radio-specific address, the president's annual message to Congress (now known as the State of the Union address) on December 6, 1923, which was heard by millions of Americans, including schoolchildren in classrooms.

"Since the close of the last Congress the Nation has lost President Harding. The world knew his kindness and his humanity, his greatness and his character," began Coolidge. The quality of the transmission was so clear that Coolidge's rustling of papers as he turned pages could distinctly be heard. No longer did the American people need to depend on the White House reporters to belatedly inform them of the president's actions and words. They could finally hear it instantaneously without an interlocutor.

It was President Herbert Hoover in 1932 who assigned a secretary specifically to deal with the press. Although Hoover, as secretary of commerce, had been one of the best background sources of administration news during the Coolidge administration, he generally shunned the press corps as president and tended not to respond to even the most innocuous questions. A veteran reporter of the *Minneapolis Tribune,* George Akerson, was installed in a corner office a few steps from the president's desk and specifically detailed to handle the media. Akerson moved the

White House reporters to more spacious quarters, and photographers had their own space for the first time.

While most of what Hoover would say in response to written questions submitted 24 hours in advance during these press conferences was still on background, some responses were allowed for the first time to be directly attributed to the president and were distributed to the White House press via mimeograph (another Edison invention).

Something Hoover did not tolerate was reporters rushing for the exits to file their stories during the rare instances the president uttered something significant. Hoover also complained that reporters had no questions to submit but would then decline to reply to many of the queries they had submitted in writing. That in turn discouraged reporters from bothering to write questions. The mutual frustration caused the relationship between the press and the president to deteriorate even further following the 1929 stock market crash.

Akerson gave more access to the newsreel cameramen, much to the chagrin of the still photographers. It was not a total surprise when Akerson departed as the de facto White House press secretary to take a high-paid public relations job with a newsreel company.

Hoover's relationship with White House correspondents continued to deteriorate as the economy did. He blamed his poor relationship with the media for his political problems and eventually stopped holding news conferences, further injuring his public image. Hoover vowed, if reelected, he would "clean that bunch out whatever the consequences might be." He never got the chance, carrying only six of the 48 states in the 1932 election.

With Franklin Roosevelt, who would remain in office until his death in 1945, the White House introduced its first official press secretary. At last, there was someone designated theoretically as an always on-call stand-in for the chief executive, although as Carter Press Secretary Jody Powell would later note, there was no general agreement on precisely what the job entailed. Frequently the press secretary would become, as Reagan spokesman Larry Speakes said, "the second most visible person in the country, which can be not only an honor but a headache." Stepping into the role for FDR was Stephen Early, a hot-tempered southerner who had covered Washington for the United Press and its rival, Associated Press, and may have been the one who germinated the idea for the 30 carefully scripted "fireside chats" by Roosevelt on the radio. Early had departed the AP in 1927 to join the Paramount Newsreel Company.

When offered the press secretary post by President-Elect Roosevelt, Early, who would remain in the job for 13 years after originally intending to stay for only two, insisted on rules that remain to this day: He would have direct access to the president, there would be on-the-record comments attributable to the press secretary, and he would have an open-door policy to receive White House correspondents.

Roosevelt proved to be quite the contrast with Hoover, dispensing with written questions, although his answers for news conferences remained mostly for background use and some comments were still strictly off the record. The encounters were so lengthy that correspondents, most of whom had to stand for the entire session, broke into relieved applause when the marathons ended. Early in his first administration, a tradition began when a wire service reporter uttered "Thank you, Mr. President" to signal the end of the session.

Roosevelt also spoke to the traveling press corps on his train, his boat, and at his residences in Hyde Park in New York and Warm Springs in Georgia. He can even be credited with the creation of a prototype of the pool system, speaking to a group of wire service correspondents in his bedroom when he was not feeling well. That smaller group would then relay the comments to the other White House reporters. Overall, it was an ever-expanding corps, swelling to more than 100 accredited journalists, and Roosevelt, who had a reputation for being well prepared, met regularly with the larger group.

To summon the journalists, Roosevelt would push a buzzer, the signal for his secretary to alert the White House usher, who would clap his hands twice, prompting the reporters to rush past the Secret Service men and into the Oval Office.

In his first term, Roosevelt, the self-appointed "Dean of the White House School of Journalism," would hold 337 press conferences. The journalists were locked in the room until the president finished the session, preventing any individual reporter from darting out to scoop his competitors. (During the dozen years of his presidency, the total would swell to nearly 1,000 such gatherings.) Those who huddled closest to the presidential desk, with whom questions were planted, were known as the "giggle chorus" sycophants, their guffaws in response to Roosevelt's quips drowning out the comments for those farther back. "Most of the people in the back room are here for curiosity. Isn't that right?" the president once asked.

Some reporters considered the sessions as containing more quantity than quality. Roosevelt did not take follow-up questions—"No cross-examination," he would admonish.

Roosevelt, who once edited the *Harvard Crimson*, could be charming, playful, and dignified in his comments to the press. But he was a master at deflecting and diverting questions without giving direct answers most of the time. That is a complaint still heard among White House journalists dealing with twenty-first-century presidents. By the end of his second term, according to Merriman Smith of United Press, the Roosevelt news conferences had lost some of the panache they once had as the president "debated with reporters," frequently insulting and lecturing the press but still making the journalists in the room laugh. Smith's assessment would have aptly described the interactions we experienced with Trump in the White House seven decades later.

Roosevelt's administration contemplated creating a government-run Central Press Bureau to circumvent distribution of news about the administration by the Associated Press, Hearst News Services, and United Press. "I never expect an AP story to give my side in the lead," the president complained to the Society of Newspaper Editors in 1937.

Several US government offices from 1939 began supplying positive news intended for publication in rural newspapers. Once the country entered World War Two there was military censorship and an Office of Censorship, created by emergency executive order. Radio networks self-censored, eliminating any antiwar opinion from the airwaves and adding patriotic programs. In mid-1941, Roosevelt also established the Foreign Information Service, hiring playwright Robert Sherwood to run it. He recruited journalists to prepare broadcasts for Europe to air on private shortwave stations. That enterprise, with theatrical and radio producer John Houseman in New York overseeing broadcasts, commencing with "Stimmen aus Amerika" (Voices from America) in German on February 1, 1942, transmitted by radiotelephone to London for medium-wave retransmission by the BBC to continental Europe.

The project morphed into the Voice of America, under the Office of War Information. OWI was run by CBS newsman Elmer Davis. Roosevelt ordered Davis to "formulate and carry out, through the use of press, radio, motion picture, and other facilities, information programs designed to facilitate the development of an informed and intelligent understanding, at home and abroad, of the status and progress of the war effort and of the war policies, activities, and aims of the government." By 1943, in a nod to the technology and the desire for more effective communications of the president's words in wartime, Roosevelt's remarks before the assembled journalists had evolved to be termed "radio and press conferences." By then, about 85 percent of American households had at least one radio.

FDR broke new ground in press relations in other ways. He began a tradition of social interactions with the media. Roosevelt invited reporters to garden parties. Some attended state dinners, and a privileged few even joined the more casual Sunday night family suppers. Correspondents had access to the White House tennis courts and a new swimming pool. The president participated in games of water polo with the press.

Roosevelt, however, faced waves of criticism from certain influential newspapers, even in an era of national unity during the war. Media baron William Randolph Hearst, despite being an FDR supporter in earlier days, used his newspaper to continually disparage the New Deal. The *Chicago Tribune* and *Los Angeles Times* also routinely criticized Roosevelt's economic policies. There were more pernicious attacks on the president in more obscure journals—akin to those the Founding Fathers had faced—Roosevelt was a Communist, a secret Jew (or a puppet of a Jewish cabal), or demented. On the radio airwaves, which Roosevelt used to his advantage to frequently speak directly to the nation, the president had his critics, most infamously the anti-Semitic Canadian-American Charles Coughlin, a Catholic priest based near Detroit, with tens of millions of listeners, originally an FDR supporter. He was forced off the air in 1939, having by then been tagged as a Nazi sympathizer.

Roosevelt's attempt to tightly control coverage continued to target the mainstream media. In 1944, the president suggested to correspondents returning with him from Warm Springs to Washington that he be allowed in advance to review their stories. Days before he died a year later, Roosevelt still jokingly admonished journalists that they couldn't get their facts straight, closing what would be his final news conference with familiar words: "By the way, this is all off the record."

The Kansas City haberdasher who succeeded Roosevelt, his vice president, Harry Truman, spoke plainly, exhibiting little of the charisma that made the four-term president a star communicator. Truman, who had once worked in the mail room of the *Kansas City Star,* came off as rather dull on the radio and provided a dim presence on the emerging medium of television. As a critic of big business, he did not enjoy widespread support among newspaper publishers, who controlled the opinion pages, but he did gain respect after defying expectations he could not be elected at the top of the ticket in 1948. Truman seemed to connect directly with people. It may have been his whistle-stop campaign tours that allowed him to defeat the clear favorite, Republican nominee Thomas Dewey, who was the governor of New York and had lost the general election four years earlier in his quest to deny Roosevelt a fourth term.

Truman held 324 news conferences during his 93 months as president. While he had said in 1946 that press freedoms were among those "for which we were fighting [in World War Two] and essential to our democratic way of life," Truman had a dimmer assessment about journalists in private. In a 1955 letter to Dean Acheson, his former secretary of state, Truman noted that "presidents and the members of their Cabinets and their staff members have been slandered and misrepresented since George Washington." Journalists, he added, were "paid prostitutes of the mind."

Because briefings were not aired live on the radio, presidents retained a level of control of the flow of information unimaginable today. For example, Truman made a remark at a press conference on March 30, 1950, about Republican Senator Joseph McCarthy, who had begun claiming the State Department was infiltrated by communists. "I think the greatest asset that the Kremlin has is Senator McCarthy," the president quipped. Quickly realizing his comment would be counterproductive, Truman persuaded reporters to change the quote to: "The greatest asset that the Kremlin has is the partisan attempt in the Senate to sabotage the bipartisan foreign policy of the United States."

Dwight Eisenhower, the first Republican president since Hoover, initiated the first full on-the-record White House news conferences. He made further history on January 19, 1955, with a televised news conference, despite apprehension about what he called a "little experiment," expressing hope that "it doesn't prove to be a disturbing influence."

John F. Kennedy held the first live broadcast presidential news conference, considering television a means "to go around the newspapers." Aides recall he intensely rehearsed for these sessions, considering them the equivalent of preparing for a twice-monthly final exam. The initial event, on January 25, 1961, did not occur at the White House but rather at the State Department to accommodate more than 200 reporters and truckloads of television equipment. Kennedy opened with statements on several subjects, including an announcement that two long-imprisoned

US Air Force pilots, whose U-2 planes had been shot down, had been freed by the Soviet Union. The president then answered 37 questions.

Kennedy came to the presidency with the most familiarity with the media since newspaper publisher Warren Harding. Kennedy, after World War Two, thanks to connections of his rich and powerful father, businessman Joe Kennedy, landed a job as a reporter for the International News Service. He covered several major stories, including the opening session of the United Nations, the 1945 electoral defeat of British Prime Minister Winston Churchill, and the Potsdam Conference to plan the postwar peace. Kennedy would subsequently be elected to the US House of Representatives three times before winning a US Senate seat in Massachusetts in 1952. By the time he was elected president in 1960, Kennedy had received a Pulitzer Prize (in 1957) for his biography, *Profiles in Courage,* a book crafted by Ted Sorensen, who would serve as his special counsel and primary speechwriter during his presidency.

Kennedy, as did his successor Lyndon Johnson, voraciously scanned newspapers and magazines and had close ties with numerous publishers. Kennedy "really enjoyed being with newspaper people," according to his first press secretary, Pierre Salinger. One correspondent observed Kennedy's savvy in pitting reporters against each other with strategic leaks. Some knew of JFK's infidelities. But this was an era when reporting scandalous details about a president's intimate life remained off-limits. Salinger recalled in a *Washingtonian* magazine interview in 1993 that a reporter once asked him directly about Kennedy's sex life. "'Look, he's the president of the United States. He's got to work 14 to 16 hours a day. He's got to run foreign and domestic policy. If he's got time for mistresses after all that, what the hell difference does it make?' The reporter laughed and walked out. That was the end of the story. For sure, I couldn't get away with that in the '90s."

When reporters crossed him, Kennedy was not above retaliation. He ordered the FBI to place a tap on the phone of *New York Times* correspondent Hanson Baldwin, claiming the military reporter had committed a security breach. Kennedy also unsuccessfully pressured the newspaper's publisher to reassign Saigon correspondent David Halberstam for skeptical reporting about the pro-US regime in South Vietnam. Despite the Camelot mystique of the first family, Kennedy blocked the release of information in real time amid Cold War events, including the disastrous Bay of Pigs Invasion, the Soviet shootdown of a U-2 spy plane, and the Cuban Missile Crisis. White House correspondents and others complained about "managed news." During a meeting of the American Society of Newspaper Editors, Eugene Pulliam, a conservative Indiana publisher, told Salinger that "much information is being withheld, not for security reasons, but to protect individuals' mistakes."

Salinger, who said he saw Kennedy six to eight times daily, was not with the president on the tragic day in Dallas. The press secretary had boarded a plane with Secretary of State Dean Rusk, part of a high-level US mission to the Far East to pave the way for a 1964 presidential trip to Japan, when word came of the shots fired at the Kennedy motorcade in Texas. Even before the confirmation was received that the president was dead, Rusk had ordered the plane to turn around and return to Honolulu. The following day after arriving back at Andrews Air Force Base, Lyndon Johnson called Salinger. "I want you to stay on the job," said the new president, telling the press secretary he needed him more than Kennedy did. By the time LBJ left office in January 1969, there would be three subsequent press secretaries, an indication of the challenge of working for a politically savvy, press-obsessed, and volatile president.

A tall Texan, Lyndon Baines Johnson became the first US president since Theodore Roosevelt to assume office due to the assassination of his predecessor. Johnson, as had been Roosevelt, was an adept politician, having become the youngest Senate majority leader in history, and well acquainted with the media. Johnson was also in the media business. His wife, known as Lady Bird, was the owner of KTBC AM, FM, and TV—a lucrative media empire in Austin, the capital of Texas. Johnson obsessed about his media coverage. Early editions of the following day's newspaper were delivered to his bedside. There were multiple television sets in the rooms he frequented at the White House and at his Texas ranch. The president could be seen strolling the White House grounds with a transistor radio to his ear. There were noisy teletype machines in the White House spewing reams of copy from the wire services. As if he were an assignment editor in a newsroom, Johnson would read stories as they appeared on the clacking machines and frequently summoned underlings to give his reaction. It was not uncommon for press secretaries to be told to call one of the wire services and demand a correction. Aides would later describe Johnson variably as paranoid, erratic, impulsive, dominant, or depressed (more than a quarter of presidents through the first 36 scrutinized suffered from a mental disorder while in office that hindered their ability to do the job, according to a Duke University study in 2006). Johnson's appetites for sex, food, drink, and cigarettes ran to excess.

In his first six months in office, Johnson had 26 sessions with the press, frequently impromptu. Later in his administration, Johnson would try to get all questions submitted in advance for televised news conferences, but that did not happen. There were extended sessions on background with reporters, usually lasting two hours. One of the marathon sessions continued for seven hours. Johnson also socialized with reporters, inviting some to swim naked with him in the White House pool. During the 1964 presidential campaign, aboard *Air Force One,* Johnson held a briefing for accompanying reporters while disrobing until he was nude. It is unlikely any US president—past, present, or future—grants such full transparency in the manner of Johnson. He also invited journalists to accompany him in the White House family quarters, in the presidential limousine, and aboard helicopters. However, the president expected loyalty for his largesse, interpreting sober reporting about his administration as hostile and a betrayal.

Johnson ordered Salinger to reprimand offending journalists and then report back to him as to how they responded to the browbeating. Eventually Salinger, still grieving Kennedy's death and drinking heavily, had enough of the crass Johnson, who would frequently summon underlings, including Cabinet secretaries, while sitting on the toilet. Salinger decided to run for the US Senate in California, wrangled an appointment to the vacant seat when the incumbent died, but he lost to his Republican opponent in the general election.

Johnson appointed his longtime aide George Reedy, a former United Press congressional reporter, to replace Salinger. Reedy, reluctant to take the position, was summoned to the White House while hospitalized with gallbladder trouble. After getting his physician's consent to leave the hospital and arriving at the White House where he was informed of his new position, Reedy briefed reporters. Just as Donald Trump, decades later, instructed his press secretaries to improve their appearance, Johnson frequently demanded that the usually rumpled Reedy dress better and get a haircut.

Johnson briefly banished the traveling White House press pool from accompanying him on *Air Force One,* a routine that had begun in the Eisenhower administration. The pool reporters were "spies" in the mind of Johnson, who claimed they were on the plane only to try to embarrass the president. As the war in Vietnam escalated, so did the frustration of White House reporters with Johnson and Reedy. Newspapers began to publish stories about the "Credibility Gap" of the administration. In 1965 Reedy passed the baton to White House Chief of Staff Bill Moyers, whom Johnson also talked into taking the job. But the complaints from reporters about the administration—"outright prevarications, half-truths, concealments and misleading denials," as *Newsweek* columnist Charles Roberts phrased it—continued. Johnson gradually soured on Moyers, complaining that he was too close to rival and fellow Democrat Robert Kennedy and that he leaked too much information. Moyers, who made little secret he desired a more prominent job in government, perhaps as secretary of state, lasted until December 1966, when he became a New York newspaper publisher and subsequently one of the stars of fledgling public television.

The final press secretary of the Johnson administration, George Christian, had been an International News Service reporter in Austin and a public relations veteran of Texas politics. He stayed in the job for two years, longer than any of his three predecessors. Johnson gave Christian practically total access to any meeting he held and frequently summoned him to his bedroom early in the morning. Christian is credited with one important innovation in White House press operations—creating a space where correspondents could sit while questioning the press secretary—a forerunner of the briefing room, which debuted in the early 1970s during the administration of Richard Nixon.

As president-elect, Nixon, who first was elected to Congress in California in 1946 after leaving the navy, told reporters he did not need a traditional press secretary. By the time Nixon took office as president, Ronald Ziegler—a former Disneyland "Jungle Cruise" tour guide—had been named to the job. A veteran of Nixon's political campaigns, Ziegler, at 29 years of age, came to the White House with no journalism experience and quickly gained a reputation with the press corps for stonewalling. His evasive replies earned him the nickname Zigzag. Ziegler, in 1972, would utter his most historical quote, responding to an initial press query regarding a break-in at the Watergate building, as not worthy of reply from the White House as it was "a third-rate burglary attempt."

Nixon's people in the West Wing desired moving the journalists, who cloistered near the lobby where the presidents' visitors arrived, to the more spacious Old Executive Office Building next door. UPI's Merriman Smith strongly objected. A compromise plan to build a sunken press room under the White House North Lawn was vetoed by a member of the powerful Commission of Fine Arts, which reviews architectural development in Washington. After Nixon gave Smith and two other journalists a tour of a West Wing area, they came to an agreement. Where the swimming pool (built by FDR), sauna, massage rooms, dog kennels, and a florist had been, a modern briefing room with 40 desks, glassed-in booths, and cubicles for broadcasters was built. Not everyone was pleased as the reporters could no longer monitor the comings and goings of the president's visitors. *New York Times* correspondent James Naughton said the space was "decorated to resemble a high-class mortuary."

Top aides hoped to give Nixon a makeover, at least in the eyes of the press. The goal was to humanize the veteran politician. That would become the least of Nixon's problems.

Nixon kept a list of journalists "out to get us." The Nixon White House ordered the FBI to investigate some reporters. As president he had hoped, at best, for a relationship with the press that, as he put it in his memoirs, was "an uneasy truce." He never expected to get a fair shake because he saw most reporters, news executives, and others who craft the messaging in Washington and New York as liberals and the political opposition, part of an industry he believed was dominated by Jews who were "left-wing," "way out," "radical," and "for peace at any price, except where the support of Israel is concerned."

Nixon was known to personally approve which reporters were allowed to fly on *Air Force One* and temporarily banned some news organizations, including the Associated Press, *New York Times, Newsweek, Time,* and the *Washington Post* from social events.

While several of his predecessors had averaged two to three dozen news conferences annually, Nixon throttled back on such encounters. The president queried the White House Correspondents' Association in 1970 about how he could improve press conferences, and the organization replied he should have more of them. Nixon did not heed the advice and the following year held only nine, deciding instead to sit for televised conversations with high-profile network television journalists. Despite Nixon's accomplishments of ending the war in Vietnam and opening diplomatic relations to China, his presidency was doomed by the Watergate burglary and subsequent cover-up.

"The only time the press corps will ever be happy is when they write my obituary," Nixon remarked in mid-July 1973 (nearly 21 years before he died) amid an avalanche of Watergate revelations. Ziegler received hundreds of questions per month at White House briefings solely about Watergate. Nixon, however, blamed the media for the scandal and at a televised news conference on October 26, 1973, called the relentless Watergate coverage "frantic, hysterical reporting."

Nixon's supporters would blame the press for hounding the president from office. But the two reporters most responsible for exposing the criminal acts of the Nixon administration, Bob Woodward and Carl Bernstein of the *Washington Post,* were hailed as heroes. Their reporting and fame boosted enrollment at journalism schools for a generation. Watergate also cemented a more skeptical approach to reporting on the president and the White House. It also ended—with rare exception—the level of socializing that had gone on behind the scenes between presidents and favored journalists and an unwritten rule that certain things heard and seen would never get reported.

Gerald Ford, the first to reach the highest office never having been elected president or vice president, promised openness, candor, and honesty with the press. He recruited a fellow Michigander, Jerald terHorst, a veteran White House correspondent for the *Detroit News* who had been covering Ford since 1948, as his press secretary. But within weeks, the spokesman would resign in protest of Ford's surprise absolute pardon for Nixon, becoming the first press secretary to quit in protest over a presidential policy decision. The scoop of terHorst's resignation was achieved in advance of Ford's planned announcement of it by *Newsweek* correspondent Tom DeFrank (next to whom I would frequently sit for briefings in the press room during the Trump administration). Veteran UPI White House correspondent Helen Thomas would later say that terHorst's resignation set a standard of integrity for White House jobs, a notion that would be greatly tested during the later years of Trump's term.

During his very brief tenure terHorst did make a couple of changes involving the press pool that endure—the press vans in the motorcade are no longer forced to stop at the gate when the president returns to the White House, and reporters are allowed access to the South Lawn for *Marine One* arrivals and departures. terHorst likely didn't envision future presidents stopping for extended Q&A sessions with dozens of reporters amid the whir of helicopter blades.

Succeeding terHorst was the first press secretary with a background in television news, NBC correspondent Ron Nessen, who had covered Ford both as vice president and president. Among others who were under consideration for the post was Bonnie Angelo of *Time,* who would have been the first female press secretary, but she declined a preliminary offer. That glass ceiling wouldn't be shattered for another 19 years, when Dee Dee Myers was selected by Bill Clinton.

Nessen, on taking the job, promised his former colleagues: "I will never knowingly lie." Although it was now Ford's White House, Nixon continued to loom large over the building, and in Nessen's first month of answering questions in the briefings, half of the queries were about the former president. The stench of the Nixon scandal did not quickly abate. Seven months later, Nessen was said to have remarked, "It is going to take me six months to get the smell of Watergate out of the press room."

A half century later, Americans are likely to remember Ford foremost as a klutz for his physical stumbles, an image reinforced by comedian Chevy Chase portraying a frequently slipping commander-in-chief on *Saturday Night Live,* which debuted on NBC during the Ford administration. Both Nessen and Ford himself would appear on the program, a harbinger of decades to come when presidents and administration officials would also seek mass appeal outside the traditional highbrow news and talk programs. This ground arguably was broken when a stilted Nixon, as a presidential candidate in 1968, appeared—against the advice of his campaign managers—on NBC's *Rowan & Martin's Laugh-In* to deliver the trademark line of the socially conscious sketch comedy program: "Sock it to me."

Democrat Jimmy Carter socked it to Republican Gerald Ford in the 1976 presidential election, becoming the first challenger to defeat an incumbent president since Franklin Roosevelt ousted Herbert Hoover in 1932. Carter came to the White House with a promise to reporters "to be close to you." During his first year in office, Carter held 22 formal news conferences in the fourth-floor auditorium of the Old Executive Office Building, adjacent to the White House. Carter, in general, kept the media at more than an arm's distance, finding press conferences unhelpful and shunning the Washington media establishment. Despite the historic Camp David Middle East peace accord, he faced generally unfavorable news coverage due to an energy crisis and scandals, usually involving his hard-drinking brother, Billy. Iranian radical students seized American hostages in Tehran and held them for 444 days. A failed US military rescue attempt would help seal the fate of his presidency.

Carter's press secretary for the entirety of his presidency, Jody Powell, had started out as a driver for Carter during his successful campaign for governor of Georgia in 1970. Powell had become a confidante to Carter since then and in the White House was a key adviser, consulting with Carter frequently on top issues and crises, including how to respond to Iran. Powell created a powerful and centralized operation, consolidating staff previously not under the press secretary's control—the speechwriters, photographers, and researchers. Reporters grumbled that Powell was most often tardy—briefings didn't begin on time. By 1978, the mood in the room was acrimonious.

"There never was a honeymoon with the press but just a one-night stand," Powell told the president, as Carter recalled in his memoirs. The office of media liaison, under Powell's press office, sought ways to short-circuit the cynical and skeptical Washington-based news media. One innovation was a radio actuality service issuing short pieces to be inserted into broadcasts with distribution to hundreds of local stations. Critics blasted it as a government domestic propaganda service.

A landslide victory for Ronald Reagan made Carter the first elected president to be denied a second term since Franklin Roosevelt's defeat of Herbert Hoover in 1932. Later, Carter partly blamed the "irresponsibility of the press" for his loss.

Once again, the Republicans were back in power. The White House press corps braced for another change in party and personnel. Perhaps no president ever came to office as prepared to face microphones and cameras as Ronald Reagan. He had been a radio sports announcer, appeared in nearly 70 movies, and hosted two television programs before serving eight years as the governor of California.

The communications team Reagan assembled in the White House understood the persuasive power of the electronic media and it knew well-crafted optics and rhetoric could trump substance and context, an advantage for a photogenic and master communicator. The team initiated Saturday morning presidential addresses via radio, focused on photo opportunities, and courted small-market newspaper editors and correspondents for friendly White House chats with Reagan. There would be 46 televised news conferences, including six overseas, during Reagan's eight years as president. At his first one he used a lottery to decide who would get to question the president, but the innovation was unpopular and from the second news conference, Reagan merely pointed his finger at a desired reporter after glancing at a seating chart.

The aim of the presidential index finger was a matter of speculation. Several reporters would usually infer or pretend to believe Reagan had selected them. This was a technique still in use when I entered the White House, although Trump added a flourish of spinning his finger for a couple of seconds before zeroing in on a desired reporter.

Reagan had a less-than-flawless performance at the podium when it came to the facts. Both Reagan and Trump did not like preparing for press conferences and thus were frequently ill informed on numerous topics, resulting in plenty of gaffes and factual errors. Reagan, however, did not face accusations of lying and even managed a convincing performance when the Iran-Contra scandal threatened to sully his legacy. His storytelling routines about occurrences decades past were another matter, and it was generally accepted that Reagan exaggerated or invented some recollections, but he was not subject to the deep fact-checking of every utterance that would occur in later administrations. Reagan's press secretary, James Brady, with little initial access to important policy meetings, never overshadowed his boss. He was a well liked and jovial, if not a charismatic figure at the podium.

In an effort that also proved overly daunting for some of his successors in subsequent administrations, Brady sought to significantly reduce the number of journalists with White House press credentials. A legal precedent had been set in the Carter years that made it all but impossible to revoke credentials except on security grounds and, even then, compelled the Secret Service to state reasons and provide the right to appeal. Brady also sought to implement a dress code, noting TV crew members frequently wore T-shirts, sometimes with provocative slogans. They resisted requests to wear suits and ties, arguing successfully that such clothing interfered with the ability to operate their equipment.

After Brady was shot in the head and permanently disabled by the attempted assassin who nearly killed Reagan outside the Washington Hilton on March 30, 1981, White House officials moved to more tightly stage-manage the president's encounters with the media. Cautioned about peppering the president with questions on a myriad of subjects during photo ops, especially with foreign heads of state in the Oval Office, members of the press pool were asked and expected to keep questions on the topic of whatever the White House had deemed the "line of day." Attempts to query Reagan as he walked to and from his helicopter proved fruitless. White House journalists faced media criticism as a "palace court press." There were exceptions, notably Sam Donaldson of *ABC News*. As a local journalist in Ventura County, California, at the time, I saw Donaldson throw a tarmac temper tantrum, expressing his profanity-laced grievances after a smiling Reagan declined to answer his questions and boarded *Air Force One.*

Reagan, for his part, expressed frustration with news coverage but was not nearly as consumed by it as Johnson or Nixon, although at one point he did ask the FBI to investigate his staff in an unsuccessful attempt to find the source of leaks. Reagan jokingly suggested White House chandeliers might be bugged by the *Washington Post,* but he was not known for the level of paranoia or ill temper of other presidents, notably Johnson and Nixon.

Brady held on to the title of press secretary, but his acting successor, Larry Speakes, would admit in his memoirs he had twice attributed quotes to Reagan that the president did not say. It has been suspected that prior and subsequent press secretaries also committed that cardinal sin, but Speakes—who was well liked by the White House press corps— is the only one I'm aware of who has admitted it. Perhaps a clue to his duplicity was a sign on his desk: "You don't tell us how to stage the news and we don't tell you how to cover it." It wasn't until 1983 that the White House briefing room (now named for Brady) achieved the layout it has now. The deep leather couches and unassigned seats placed in the room in the Nixon era were replaced with rows of theater seats assigned for the first time to specific news organizations.

Marlin Fitzwater was a veteran government spokesman by the time he was summoned to the White House in September 1983 as a deputy press secretary. On his arrival in Washington some three decades earlier, he had been rejected by some of the biggest newsrooms in the capital, including the *Wall Street Journal,* UPI, and the *Washington Post.* The selection of Fitzwater to succeed Speakes was a compromise. Nancy Reagan, who wanted her former press secretary, Sheila Tate, was in a standoff with Chief of Staff Don Regan, who pushed Ann McLaughlin, a former spokeswoman at the Treasury Department, for the position. The first lady kept close tabs on Fitzwater, calling him frequently to discuss how he should approach certain topics. Reagan would be out of office before it became widely known how fiercely the first lady had defended her husband's image and sought to manage his workload. She was also powerful enough to force out Regan as chief of staff, dissatisfied with his handling of the Iran-Contra scandal.

George Herbert Walker Bush took office as the forty-first president in 1989 with a glittering résumé of public service capped with eight years as vice president. Bush, the son of a US senator, was a decorated World

War Two naval pilot, a Yale graduate, a House member (but twice defeated in quests for a Senate seat), ambassador to the United Nations, and director of the Central Intelligence Agency. He was the first sitting vice president since Martin Van Buren in 1836 to be elected to the higher office. Lacking Reagan's star power, Bush was seen as a safe pair of hands by political moderates, although he was regarded with some suspicion by those both on the right and the left.

Bush surpassed Reagan in conducting about 200 news conferences during his four-year term. He, too, claimed unfair treatment by the media. Bush was labeled as soft on China after the Tiananmen Square massacre. In one of the most embarrassing presidential moments in US history, during a banquet in Japan in 1992, Bush, said to be suffering from intestinal influenza, vomited on Prime Minister Kiichi Miyazawa and fainted onto the floor. The videotape was repeatedly broadcast. Another incident, closer to the 1992 election—his on-camera amazement with a barcode scanner for groceries, gave the impression he was out of touch with the lives of ordinary Americans. Bush was also bedeviled by the perception he had broken his famous pledge of "Read my lips, no new taxes."

When Bush took office, Marlin Fitzwater stayed as press secretary, achieving a remarkable record of seeing seven White House chiefs of staff come and go over two presidencies. Fitzwater would later recall that Bush had a sophisticated understanding of how journalists operated and the needs of the press secretary. Fitzwater was the bridge between the two administrations who traveled from the Reagan side, where the press office was determined to stick to the line of the day in its daily interactions with White House reporters, to Bush territory, where it was the journalists who decided the most important topic. Bush, since his days as vice president, had been accused of not having "vision"—meaning he could not place issues into a larger context or rhetorical frame, so critical for packaging a candidate's (or president's) messaging. That lack of clarity and principles to shape public opinion and influence Congress meant "the public does not know why it should care if he gets his way," wrote conservative columnist George Will. Giving control of the narrative in the daily press briefings to the reporters asking the questions reinforced the criticism that Bush lacked vision and was a factor in the president's loss to Bill Clinton in 1992.

When a teenaged William Jefferson Clinton shook hands with President Kennedy in the White House Rose Garden in 1963, UPI correspondent Helen Thomas was there.

"Little did I know at the time that there was a future president in the wide-eyed group in public service," she wrote in her book, *Front Row at the White House: My Life and Times.* Thomas still sat in the front row of the briefing room when Clinton returned to the White House in 1993. Four years later, on her seventy-seventh birthday, Clinton presented the doyenne of the White House press corps with a birthday cake.

Thomas, who clearly expressed left-of-center views when she moved from UPI to Hearst as a columnist, was among those who scrutinized Clinton's foibles, including the West Wing affair with intern Monica Lewinsky, which led to the president's impeachment for lying under oath and obstruction of justice. Thomas believed she and her colleagues adequately did their job and were not overly aggressive because they were "lied to for nine months." In a 1999 interview with National Public Radio, Thomas said, "We did not ask enough questions."

Clinton and his press team certainly believed the press asked too many questions, going back to the 1992 campaign when women began to come forward, alleging Clinton had engaged in extramarital relationships. In addition to having a magnetic personality, he played the saxophone on late-night TV, chatted with friendly TV hosts, and appeared on youth-oriented MTV. Clinton, tagged "Slick Willie" by his detractors, survived the storms of the election season to defeat Bush with a campaign war room helmed by George Stephanopoulos and James Carville, who ensured speedy responses for the around-the-clock cable news networks. After Clinton's inauguration, the White House press team abruptly ended the open access reporters traditionally enjoyed to part of the Executive Wing by sealing the passageway from the press room to the communications suites, an area known as "Upper Press."

"It was our judgement that we ought not to have reporters here where people are working and doing business," White House Press Secretary Dee Dee Myers explained six months after Clinton took office, but assured journalists would make up for the loss of spatial access by having more frequent briefings. Facing a backlash and ensuring negative publicity from national reporters, Clinton went around them to reach the public as some of his predecessors had done. In eight years, Clinton made 455 weekly radio addresses, held televised town hall meetings, granted interviews to local radio stations, and to a degree no previous president had, interacted with Black-owned media. Clinton did not shun the protective pool of reporters who would accompany him every time he left the White House, including on his frequent early morning jogs.

"In his early years, Clinton was inclined to respond to shouted questions from the press pool covering his jog. He seemed to pride himself on being willing to respond to reporters, especially if it was on a subject he liked. Occasionally, his responses would prove troublesome for him, and his second chief of staff, Leon Panetta, admitted he told Clinton that he was under no obligation to answer press questions on his runs," Mark Knoller, the longtime CBS Radio White House correspondent, told me.

Clinton had a temper and lectured or berated those around him. Unlike most other occupants of the Oval Office, Clinton could erupt during on-the-record interviews. In one encounter, an interview for *Rolling Stone*, Clinton complained he was sick and tired of the way he was treated by the "knee-jerk liberal press," an outburst one might expect from a Republican but not a Democratic president.

Clinton got socked from both the left and the right. Conservatives sought to force him out of office through relentlessly questioning his character. But Clinton's team successfully fought back, going on the offense with assertive media management. While Clinton's presidency survived, his legacy was permanently tarnished.

Decades later, most Americans who can remember the Clinton presidency are unlikely to cite any of his policy accomplishments but will recall the stories about the Whitewater investigation, conspiracy theories (with no evidence) about the death of Deputy White House Counsel Vince Foster (whose shredded suicide note complained that *Wall Street Journal* editors "lie without consequences"), and, of course, the Monica Lewinsky scandal, which dominated the evening newscasts of ABC, CBS, and NBC in 1998.

Clinton exhibited natural talent in interviews and usually came across as a charismatic and gifted communicator. Despite everything else that confronted his administration in the first term, he easily won reelection over a statesman, war hero, and well-qualified Republican senator, Bob Dole.

Myers made history as the first woman to serve as presidential press secretary starting when Clinton took office in 1993, and contemporaries say she never received proper respect from the male-dominated staff and many reporters, who found her ill informed. She also never sat in the traditional big office occupied by the press secretary. Myers, at the age of 31, lacked experience in journalism or in government public relations.

She had been a spokesperson for the unsuccessful president campaign of Michael Dukakis in 1988 before joining the Clinton campaign.

"I was young. I was 31. I was the first woman and I was from California. So that's sort of the trifecta of how not to show up," she recalled on the *Political Breakdown* podcast the day after Biden was inaugurated. "I was a bit of an exotic creature and establishing authority was challenging."

As would be the case decades later when Karine Jean-Pierre found herself breaking barriers as press secretary, Myers was quickly overshadowed by a white male. In Myers's case, it was George Stephanopoulos, a veteran of the Dukakis and Clinton campaigns, and in the Biden White House it was the polished John Kirby who handled the meatier matters of global geopolitics.

The Clinton White House also experimented with daily briefings on C-SPAN, the pioneering public service cable and satellite television channel, but it quickly stopped. Myers said it was "not found to be productive" and when Stephanopoulos (who would have a subsequent successful on-camera career at *ABC News*) took over the podium for the main daily briefing (although Myers retained the press secretary title) only the first five minutes of the briefings were seen live. Myers's successor at the lectern also did not earn good reviews from the audience in the room, further burnishing the image of a White House in disarray.

In his memoir, Stephanopoulos spoke of the toll the job took on him— his face broke out in hives and he suffered from depression. When David Gergen, who had been Reagan's media adviser, returned to the White House, he again allowed media access to Upper Press. Myers took over the main daily briefing. She would be replaced as press secretary in December 1994 by the State Department spokesman, Mike McCurry, who had been approached about the job by Chief of Staff Leon Panetta without Myers's knowledge. She found out from a Reuters dispatch that McCurry would be taking her job.

McCurry was credited by the press corps with improving relations between the journalists and the White House. His daily briefings at the lectern were televised live, and the press secretary gave interviews to TV reporters on the North Lawn.

"I think cable television got hooked on putting the briefings on television, and then everyone reverted to theatrical roles" during the Lewinsky scandal when serious reporting stopped, McCurry told the *Columbia Journalism Review* in 2015. McCurry's deputy, Joe Lockhart, a veteran of high-profile Democratic campaigns who temporarily left politics to work for ABC, CNN, and NBC, including as an on-air reporter, succeeded him. Lockhart had the unenviable task of defending Clinton during his impeachment trial. He earned another footnote in presidential history when in 2017 he sold, for $8.1 million, his Kalorama neighborhood home to former President Barack Obama, who had been renting it since leaving office.

Clinton's successor, Republican George W. Bush (son of the former president, George H. W. Bush), hired veteran Capitol Hill press aide Ari Fleischer to turn his frequent malapropisms into attractive policy statements, although in the early years of his presidency, he would make unannounced appearances at the daily televised briefings to respond to a few questions.

As a candidate in 2000, Bush learned an early lesson that politicians should assume any microphone is always a live microphone. Turning to running mate Dick Cheney, the Texas governor pointed out *New York Times* reporter Adam Clymer, calling him "a major league asshole." Bush never apologized. After becoming president, he joked Clymer was actually a "major league asset." The trivial piece of presidential press history resurfaced when, in January 2022, President Joe Biden lost his temper with Fox News's Peter Doocy, calling him a "stupid son-of-a-bitch."

Fleischer devoted most of his attention during his 37 months in the job to the major players of the mainstream media sitting in the first two rows of the briefing room. Due to the 9/11 attacks on his watch, Bush was thrust into the role of a wartime president as America sought revenge in Afghanistan and broadened the conflict to include an invasion of Iraq on the mistaken belief that Saddam Hussein had nuclear weapons. In 2008, Bush acknowledged to *ABC News* the biggest letdown of his presidency was "the intelligence failure in Iraq," but he would "leave the presidency with my head held high." Fleischer, after clashing with some of Bush's aides, had exited in 2003, with a quip that he wanted "to unwind, do something more relaxing, like dismantle live nuclear weapons."

Fleischer's deputy succeeded him at the briefing room podium. Scott McClellan, a Texan with deep Republican roots in that state, helped craft the message for the president's successful reelection effort against future Secretary of State John Kerry. McClellan came to be regarded as a turncoat after he resigned in 2006 and wrote a memoir two years later, while Bush was still in office. He accused the president of "self-deception" to justify political goals and wrote that the West Wing suffered from "a permanent campaign mentality." The book was titled, in a not-so-subtle manner, *What Happened: Inside the Bush White House and Washington's Culture of Deception.*

"I fell far short of living up to the kind of public servant I wanted to be," McClellan wrote, but he also had criticism for the news media, calling it "complicit enablers" in the White House's "carefully orchestrated campaign to shape and manipulate sources of public approval" in the lead-up to the Iraq war back in 2002 and 2003. The year his book was published, McClellan endorsed Barack Obama for president.

Before Bush left office, there would be two more White House press secretaries: Fox News anchor/commentator Tony Snow, who served less than a year before taking medical leave for a losing battle with colon cancer, and Dana Perino. She was accidently hit in the left eye with a boom microphone during the scuffle after an Iraqi journalist thew a pair of shoes at Bush during a news conference in Baghdad in December 2008.

Bush projected a sunny personality. He sought to overcome the perception he was not intelligent and a lightweight compared to other presidents. The 9/11 attacks, the US-led campaign ousting the Taliban and the battle against al-Qaeda in Afghanistan, and the US invasion of Iraq temporary quelled much of the negative media coverage of Bush. But once the president declared, "Iraq is free" under a "Mission Accomplished" banner aboard an aircraft carrier, critical news coverage of Bush resumed. By his final months in office, only 11 percent of those surveyed by Pew considered Bush a president who was above-average or outstanding, compared to 42 percent for the scandal-tainted Clinton.

Barack Obama had scant experience dealing with the Washington press corps at the time of his inauguration in January 2009. Certainly, he had garnered attention as a barrier-breaking major party presidential candidate during the campaign, but by no means had he been a well-known figure during his nearly four years as the junior US senator from Illinois. He had first come to national attention in 2004 when, as a state senator, he delivered a keynote speech at the Democratic Party's national convention. Much of the mainstream media venerated Obama during the 2008 campaign, but the honeymoon doesn't last long after settling in at 1600 Pennsylvania Avenue. Obama certainly did not help his cause by eschewing the schmoozing with key journalists, editors, and publishers, as well as senior senators and House lawmakers who had skillfully aided the public image and legislative acumen of some of his predecessors. Obama was no backslapper and known for keeping his composure during the few hostile interviewers he encountered in his eight years in office. Well into his second term, Obama was still considered an enigma even among those who covered him closely.

"The people who cover the president know him the least," Peter Baker, a White House correspondent for the *New York Times,* told the *Columbia Journalism Review* in 2014. "People ask me all the time, 'What's he like?' As if I knew."

More than any previous administration, the Obama White House attempted end runs around the traditional press corps to get out its messaging, including increased use of social media. (Obama showed up there six years into his presidency.) Social media proved vital to the administration's push of the Affordable Care Act (also known as Obamacare), which sought to provide comprehensive healthcare coverage to more Americans.

The administration's focus on alternative media methods was a White House effort "to conceal its workings from the press, and by extension, the public," according to the article in the *Columbia Journalism Review.* And under Obama, "evidence suggests that the relationship between the president and the press is more distant than it has been in a half century."

Historian Harold Holzer put Obama alongside John Adams, Abe Lincoln, and Woodrow Wilson "as the most aggressive presidents in blocking press scrutiny and making professional life difficult for his critics." The Obama White House engaged in spats and essentially froze out from interactions with the president the most nonpartisan broadcaster to cover politics, the C-SPAN public access channel. During his formal encounters with the White House press corps, Obama religiously adhered to a prepared list of reporters whom he would call on, and he excelled at responding at length with nonnewsy answers to run out the clock. Obama was also highly disciplined during the pool sprays in the Oval Office and elsewhere, avoiding responses that generated news. He did speak with poolers off the record on *Air Force One,* but these sessions were not considered insightful and a far cry from Lyndon Johnson's soul-baring marathon inflight sessions. The Department of Justice, during Obama's presidency, also brought more charges against journalists in cases involving leaked information than all previous administrations combined. In one case, it fought, ultimately unsuccessfully, for seven years to try to compel *New York Times* reporter James Risen to identify his confidential sources about a bungled operation in Iran to disrupt that country's nuclear operations. A former Central Intelligence Agency officer, Jeffrey Sterling, was convicted in 2015 of disclosing highly classified information to the journalist.

Also targeted during the Obama administration: Fox News correspondent James Rosen, whom the Justice Department named an unindicted "criminal co-conspirator" for allegedly exposing secrets about North Korea. The Obama administration responded to the inimical Fox News like an enemy combatant. The president and his top officials eschewed appearing on the channel, which since his candidacy had allowed its paid commentators to portray Obama as a socialist and pushed conspiracies the president was perhaps born in Kenya and not Hawaii; that he was secretly a Muslim, a Black separatist, or even a terrorist.

"We're going to treat them the way we would treat an opponent," White House Communications Director Anita Dunn told the *New York Times* in October 2009. "As they are undertaking a war against Barack Obama and the White House, we don't need to pretend that this is the way that legitimate news organizations behave."

Four months earlier, Obama had told NBC that Fox News was "entirely devoted to attacking my administration." Out of office in 2017, Obama, on a trip to India, said if he had watched Fox News, he wouldn't have voted for himself. "I would watch it and say who is that guy? This character Barack was portrayed in weird ways."

Tasked with messaging for the relatively reticent president were three successive press secretaries, all white males—Robert Gibbs, Jay Carney, and Josh Earnest. Gibbs grew up in Alabama, had worked on Capitol Hill, and had been the press secretary for a time during John Kerry's unsuccessful presidential campaign in 2004 before becoming an adviser to Obama's senate race that year. He famously quipped that left-wing critics of Obama were "crazy" and should be drug tested. Gibbs frequently used sports metaphor at the lectern and engaged in fierce exchanges with reporters, some of whom found him abrasive. After his time at the White House, Gibbs became a spokesman for the McDonald's fast-food chain.

Carney, who had been Vice President Biden's spokesman, had spent 20 years at *Time* magazine, including three years as Washington bureau chief. Clocking three years as press secretary, he enjoyed a relatively long tenure, but by the end of it he criticized his interlocutors in the briefing room who frequently mocked him. Like Gibbs, Carney left for a lucrative position as a corporate flack, in his case with Amazon and Airbnb.

Earnest had been part of the Obama team since the presidential campaign, during which he served as Iowa communications director. When Obama appointed him, he issued a statement saying his name described his demeanor. "Josh is an earnest guy, and you can't find just a nicer individual, even outside of Washington." During his final daily briefing, Obama surprised Earnest on the podium, noting he had topped a *Politico* annual survey as the best press secretary, but Earnest had avoided being "too solicitous towards the press." As was the case with his two predecessors, Earnest found himself in corporate public relations after government service as the top spokesman for United Airlines.

21

Each presidency produces its own style of press relations. Early in a new administration White House correspondents bristle when proposals are made to change the rules of the game. Even before Trump took office there was an uproar when incoming officials suggested evicting the correspondents from their West Wing space and relocating them to either the Old Executive Office Building next door or the White House Conference Center on Lafayette Square.

"The interest of the team is to make sure that we accommodate the broadest number of people who are interested and media from around the country and around the world," then Vice President–Elect Mike Pence said on CBS's *Face the Nation.* The White House Correspondents' Association, established in 1914 during the Wilson presidency, objected to "any move that would shield the president and his advisers from the scrutiny of an on-site White House press corps." The reporters were not relocated, but there remained the challenges of frequently closed doors and having to snare one of the spokespeople as they walked back from the Pebble Beach media tents on the North Lawn driveway following live interviews on the Fox News Channel.

Trump, in contrast, made himself available for interviews with a frequency perhaps unprecedented in US history. Most of those opportunities went to Fox or the other media outlets owned by Rupert Murdoch, as well as several upstart conservative publications and broadcasters. Trump did sit for interviews with wire services and media outlets, such as CBS and the *New York Times,* which were clearly not in his partisan orbit.

Despite the frequent and casual interactions with White House journalists, Trump only held one formal news conference during his first year in office. By contrast, in their initial year, Obama held seven and George H. W. Bush conducted 27 such encounters.

To his credit, Trump did not revert to prescreening questions as did many of his early twentieth-century predecessors. The majority of reporters to whom he gave extended access were those he knew could be relied on not to ask hostile or embarrassing questions.

Despite the sheer number of questions during his presidency to which he responded, Trump is likely to go down in history as the president who had the most acrimonious relationship with journalists.

"I have a running war with the media," Trump acknowledged during a visit to the headquarters of the Central Intelligence Agency on his first full day as president on January 21, 2017. Irked about news stories and photographs showing his inaugural crowd smaller than Obama's, Trump claimed the media was lying,

"I think they are going to pay a big price," he told the CIA employees as the accompanying press pool recorded the threatening prediction.

Trump's press secretary, Sean Spicer, also vowed the new administration would "hold the press accountable."

By August, Trump's assault on the mainstream media had become so frequent and severe that hundreds of US newspapers jointly responded with editorials. After the *Boston Globe* warned that Trump was signaling to despots abroad "that journalists can be treated as a domestic enemy," the president called the newspapers' campaign "collusion" and continued his attacks, declaring the press to have an agenda driven by hate. The situation would not get better.

22

When does "off the record" become "on the record?" Officials reply, "never." Journalists have developed a fuzzier response, based on being the recipients of such conditional statements since George Washington.

Harold Brayman, the late president of two Washington media institutions, the National Press Club and the Gridiron Club, dated the presidential practice back to Grover Cleveland in his book *The President Speaks Off-the-Record.*

Towson University's White House Transition Project Director Martha Joynt Kumar has noted that when presidential press conferences went from off the record to on the record, their frequency dropped drastically. Compare Calvin Coolidge's average of 93 sessions annually to the couple of dozen per year during the Eisenhower and Kennedy administrations.

The term "off the record" has appeared in print since the early twentieth century.

Theodore M. Knappen, in a front-page article in the *New York Tribune* on November 15, 1918, a few days after the end of World War One had been declared, details War Industries Board Chairman Bernard Baruch having "an informal discussion with the newspaper men in which nothing was 'off the record.'"

The Associated Press defines the term bluntly: "The information cannot be used for publication."

A former US defense secretary, Donald Rumsfeld, cynically cautioned, "with the press there is no 'off the record.'"

Despite the rules and promises, particularly newsworthy quotes spoken off the record by the president or other senior administration officials frequently will quickly, albeit clandestinely, circulate. Reporters whisper. Summary confidential emails are sent by reporters to their editors. Officials leak to one another. Call me old-fashioned, but if a fellow journalist relays something they heard off the record, I do not report it nor do I launder it into a background quote. In the Trump era, however, the rules became less rigid.

John Kelly, as his stress-filled tenure as White House chief of staff pushed the retired Marine general to the breaking point, did not appear to be incensed when some of his not-for-publication comments saw the light of day. It was unclear whether he didn't recall the ground rules for what he said or he didn't care.

A new precedent was set when the *Toronto Star* published off-the-record comments Trump had made about NAFTA negotiations with Canada during an interview with Bloomberg. The wire service denied leaking the quotes to correspondent Daniel Dale, although the president himself unleashed a tweet accusing Bloomberg of blatantly violating "this powerful understanding." Two sentences later, Trump appeared to be less angry, stating, "At least Canada knows where I stand."

It didn't stop Trump from speaking to journalists off the record. And leaks again occurred. Sometimes it was Trump himself tweeting out comments he or others had made off the record. Trump never blamed himself but frequently accused others of violating confidences. That happened in July 2018, when the president held what was supposed to be a private meeting with A. G. Sulzberger, the publisher of the *New York Times*. Trump took to social media to talk about the encounter. The newspaper publicly challenged Trump's version of the events.

After the Trump-Sulzberger kerfuffle, a *Times*'s national politics reporter, Matt Flegenheimer, in 2018 wrote a piece explaining how he has heard many after-the-fact pleadings from politicians who regretted their words:

> As a national political reporter for The Times, I have heard all manner of after-the-fact pleading from politicians who regretted their words.
>
> Politicians who insisted an on-the-record comment was actually off the record. (It was not.)
>
> Politicians who acknowledged that, yes, they'd said the thing they said, but what if we pretended they hadn't? (Not how this works.)
>
> Politicians who promised unspecified future scoops, if only I'd convert their ill-advised comments from on the record to off the record. (No deal.)
>
> As a general principle, a reporter's best course of action is to establish jargon-free parameters in plain English at the start: Can a source be

quoted by name? Can we use the information if we leave out the name? Can we at least describe the source's job?

Twice, in early 2019 after off-the-record lunches with television news anchors (who are gossips by nature of profession), Trump's off-the-record comments went quickly into the wild. And, again, Trump was angry—on Twitter—accusing the mainstream media of having gone "totally bonkers." There were no repercussions—something that almost certainly would not have been the case in the Roosevelt White House. But it was not for lack of trying on Trump's part. During 2019 and 2020, when Stephanie Grisham was press secretary, the president repeatedly pressed her to expel the press corps from the White House.

"At his behest I extensively researched what it would take to remove them from the complex, and once it was made clear that we'd likely be sued and lose, I researched different places we could put them other than the press briefing room," Grisham wrote in her memoir.

The former press secretary said she deliberately stalled and eventually the clock ran out on the Trump presidency.

Occasionally in the White House methods of reporting reverted to the FDR era. Nothing has the potential for confusion among denizens of the digital era as the "pen-and-pad" session. While audio recorders and TV cameras have become ubiquitous, there was a time when such technology was barred from the reporting process.

As a young reporter in Las Vegas in the late 1970s, I found nothing proved as challenging as courtroom reporting. Imagine being a kid with scant experience as a journalist and knowledge of jurisprudence limited to civics textbooks dispatched to the courthouse to report on an arraignment of a mobster. The first rule of legal reporting—unless or until convicted, Tony "the Ant" Spilotro is an *alleged* mobster. The qualification by adjective seen as protection against libel claims.

Courtroom action unfolds quickly. Much of it, at least to the non-lawyers, is in arcane legal lingo. Reporters cannot ask the attorneys or the judge to repeat themselves, slow down, or clarify what they're saying. The journalists are usually not allowed to record the proceedings, although some judges in recent decades have allowed cameras in their courtrooms. The court itself depends on its own "reporters," who are skilled at typing on a dictation machine to prepare the official transcript. When considering an appeal, this is the trial record the appellate court consults. Even if there are audio and video recordings, a transcript is pre-pared by a team of specialists.

At the White House, some briefings are still strictly pen and pad, which frequently further confuse the rules regarding attribution. Most of these sessions take place in the office of the national security adviser or a similar high-ranking official. Unlike the Oval Office, Roosevelt Room, or many other places where administration officials meet the press, the national security adviser's office is considered a secure space in which to hold classified discussions, known as a SCIF (for Sensitive Compart-mented Information Facility) and pronounced "skiff." This means report-ers cannot bring any electronic devices—audio recorders, laptop com-puters, or cell phones. Even Fitbit-type watches are surrendered and deposited in West Wing equipment lockers before entering the SCIF. Some officials, speaking in these pen-and-pad sessions, are more forth-right than when they know their words are recorded—even if the audio will not be permitted to be broadcast. They do not reduce their speed of talking. So, for journalists from the postdictation era, there's no way to literally record every word.

The most confusing outcomes of these pen-and-pad sessions have come from the official alternating between speaking on background (at-tributable to a "senior White House official") and off the record (where none of the information is supposed to be used in any news reports). Keeping track of what was on background and what was off the record has led some to publish or air information that was not supposed to be re-leased. There's been more than one time when I've had to ask for clarifica-tion whether a particular comment was on background or off the record.

It is prudent for government officials to make clear to reporters when they are not speaking for attribution and even then, they should be care-ful what they utter. If it is racist, offensive, off-color, or whatever, most politicians in the twenty-first century have learned they are actually never totally off the record.

All journalists and public servants should become familiar with what happened in August 1976, when the secretary of agriculture was on a commercial flight to California for the Republican National Convention. Singer Pat Boone asked the agriculture secretary, Earl Butz, why the Re-publican Party was not attracting Black voters. Butz explained in graphic and unprintable language "what the coloreds want" in terms of sexual intercourse, footwear, and bathroom habits. (I've decided not to include the precise wording here. Suffice to say those inclined can find the quote with an online search or peruse this book's bibliography.)

The Associated Press did not censor Butz's words on its wire, although apparently only a couple of newspapers, one in Ohio and another in Wisconsin, dared to print them. Other newspapers said readers could visit the office to read the remark, and some editors offered to mail them the unexpurgated quotation. Even I, as a novice teenaged reporter in Nevada, in that preinternet era, managed to quickly learn what Butz had said. I still recall thinking I had never heard anything as disgusting in my life.

Enough people also figured out what Butz had said so that by early October, President Ford forced him to resign after the Cabinet member halfheartedly apologized, saying his jokes were sometimes too colorful and his "bad racial commentary" did not reflect "my real attitude."

It was a watershed moment in American history. Crude, racist, or misogynistic remarks, even uttered in private, were no longer tolerable by public figures—at least until Trump managed to stay atop the Republican ticket despite the airing of the *Access Hollywood* audio.

The frequency of on-the-record White House press briefings waxes and wanes. The rarer they are, the more intense they become and the more likely they are to be televised. This places intense pressure on competitive correspondents to be called upon, whether to fire off a zinger that will go into heavy rotation on newscasts and late-night talk shows or merely to ask a question that will hopefully result in newsworthy insight into administration policy. Although my assertion here may be met with skepticism, I assure you that I am always seeking the latter. Sean Spicer and Sarah Sanders, in the Trump administration, as proxies for the president, became heroes to the Republican president's base for unleashing their own auditory arrows at front-row inquisitors, thus playing their part to try to make American great again.

For Trump's detractors, who quickly regarded his spokespersons as purveyors of officially sanctioned lies, those occupying the podium were video villains. Regardless of what the public thought, those with raised hands wanted to ask a question, or two or three.

It was an adjustment for those holdovers from the relatively halcyon lame-duck end of the Obama administration when Josh Earnest, who was at the lectern at least 350 times, would hold court for as long as an hour, satisfying all potential questioners, including Raghubir Goyal of the possibly defunct *India Globe* (supposedly a self-published in Washington,

DC, newspaper he claimed to have distributed to family and friends). Goyal is best known for puzzling inquiries regarding mango imports or India-Pakistan relations. One afternoon when the final question went to Goyal and I was left with a raised hand and an unanswered question, I immediately confronted Sanders in her office and vented my supercilious frustration over the credentialing of those with apparently the most dubious of connections to journalism.

"Oh, Goyal," she said in her Arkansas drawl with a smile. "We'll never get rid of Goyal. He brings us fruit."

This was a helpful revelation. The staffers in the White House press office were overworked like the rest of us and are human beings who appreciate a tasty treat (and if adhering to US government ethical guidelines, are permitted to accept gifts worth less than $10).

A more overt method of raising the odds of being called upon during the routine briefings and presidential press conferences involves sartorial self-selection. During the Reagan years, red was the color of advantage. As noted by the Associated Press after a March 1985 news conference, at least 10 of the 18 reporters recognized by the president wore red—four women in red dresses and six men with red neckties.

"I know that Nancy upstairs would die if I didn't call on you in that pretty red dress," Reagan said to the first reporter he called on, Helen Thomas of UPI. "That why I wore it," Thomas replied. The second question went to Michael Putzel of the AP. "Where's your red tie?" Reagan asked. "Doesn't aways work," Putzel replied, wearing a green tie. In the news conference, Reagan, wearing a maroon tie with gray stripes, credited Jane Meyer of the *Wall Street Journal* with having unleashed the scarlet fad in the briefing room. As Putzel noted, wearing red did not guarantee getting a question nor would strapping on a row of blinking LED lights compel a contemporary president or press secretary to select the colorful questioner. They have their favorites whom they regularly call upon, as well as those they shun.

My own trick—and I have no scientific analysis to ascertain whether it increases my odds—is to wear a nontraditional multicolored tie, eschew a dark-colored suit (worn by most of the men) for something gray or beige while brightening the overall appearance with a yellow or blue shirt. The combination will never win fashion kudos, but it is certainly eye-catching.

23

I don't know who said half the fun is getting there, but when it involves a very long flight, that's not true. To quote baseball legend Yogi Berra, it was déjà vu all over again when I found myself as the radio pool reporter for a second time accompanying the president to a summit with North Korea's leader, Kim Jong Un. The initial summit had been in Singapore. The subsequent meeting was in Hanoi. From Joint Base Andrews it was a 20-hour and 20-minute journey, including two fuel stops.

We were not informed before we departed the Maryland base where we would be landing for the pit stops and we were not able to report those locations until we were on the ground at RAF Mildenhall in Suffolk, England, and subsequently Al Udeid Air Base, headquarters of US Central Command, in Qatar. When we landed at Mildenhall, it was midnight local time and we were allowed to get off the plane. Trump did not disembark. If the president gets off the plane, he goes down the front steps. We leave down the back stairs.

As I stretched my legs in the middle of the night near the tail of *Air Force One,* I noticed none of the other dozen pool members joined me. But a group of White House staffers did, including Press Secretary Sanders and her principal deputy, Hogan Gidley. The group meandered to the terminal. I followed. No one else engaged with me, but I was not told to stay back so I trailed the White House staff. There was a lounge in the terminal, but base staff had difficulty finding the keys to the door. We stood in the lobby of the VIP lounge for a few minutes before everyone went back outside. Personnel from the 100th Air Refueling Wing who were Americans at this British base gathered to pose for a group photo with Sanders and acting White House Chief of Staff Mick Mulvaney in the center. I stood next to Gidley to observe this Kodak moment. I snapped a picture on my iPhone to put on Twitter and turned to one of the airmen to get the proper name of his unit. Gidley told the

Preparing for a live TV report from atop a hotel in Singapore in June 2018 where President Trump had a historic meeting with North Korean leader Kim Jong Un.

airman I was a reporter, essentially acknowledging I was there doing my job, and he expressed no objection. This exchange became important a couple of hours later.

My first indication of trouble occurred when I returned to the port side of the aircraft where a Secret Service agent crisply informed me that I must be "wanded" because I ventured out of his visual range and thus popped the press pool bubble. White House staff can come and go as they please and don't become "dirty" when they are out of visual range of the security detail. It is a reminder that the journalists, despite our White House hard passes, are civilians. So, before reboarding, I assumed the pose with arms outstretched to be scanned for any metal objects. I thought nothing more about this minor infraction until we were in flight about an hour later.

White House staff on *Air Force One* have internet access, but the press pool does not, except in extraordinary circumstances. Apparently, my dispatch to the radio pool emailed prior to takeoff for Qatar and my subsequent tweet of the very innocuous photo of Mulvaney and Sanders posing with the airmen had caused a stir in the forward cabin. I became aware of this from the sole White House staffer who sat in our section of the plane—a comfortable rear seat with a little desk for internet access—directly across from the toilet. This seat is occupied by our in-flight wrangler, usually a young junior aide from the press shop. This particular wrangler had always been quite nice to me, but at that particular moment, there was no sunshine from her in the middle of the night. "You weren't authorized to tweet that photo," she said.

For a moment my brain tried to figure out which picture she was referring to as I had tweeted several during our fuel stop. I tried to clarify, but she cut me off.

"You know what photo I'm talking about."

And then it occurred to me. "You mean the thing with the airmen?

"Yes."

Someone with authority in the plane had obviously complained to our wrangler. Several administration officials, I knew from my list of verified followers, followed my account and one of them likely scrolling through their feed had spotted it.

"Well look," I said, "the deputy press secretary was standing right next to me. He knew that I was a reporter and what I was doing." That took a bit of wind out of her admonishment. "I'll talk to Hogan about it," I quickly added. But I never did. And no one raised the minor issue again, as by the time we had landed at Hanoi, the White House press office had likely been overwhelmed with a dozen more important issues.

24

At the White House on a Wednesday morning, a member of the medical office swabbed inside my nostrils to collect a sample for the routine COVID-19 rapid test all members of the protective pool of reporters covering the president's activities underwent daily. It was a brief and painless procedure. I had undergone it more than a dozen times in recent months—always with the same "negative" result. That has also been the case as well for my colleague on the White House beat, Patsy Widakuswara, with whom I alternated campaign coverage when it was VOA's turn in the rotation among radio networks.

As the day's designated radio pooler for the round-trip to Minnesota on *Air Force One* on September 30, 2020, I was responsible for ensuring all the networks would have broadcast-quality audio as quickly as possible whenever the president spoke—from the time we left Joint Base Andrews in Maryland to our postmidnight return on the same tarmac.

The president's first stop in Minnesota, known as the Land of 10,000 Lakes, was a massive multimillion-dollar estate on the shores of Lake Minnetonka. At a fundraiser at the Shorewood home of wealthy Republican Party donor Martin Davis, during which the accompanying media waited outside in our vans, Trump mingled with several dozen guests, who were reportedly required to show a negative COVID test within 24 hours prior to the event. We could not observe if the participants wore masks or engaged in social distancing. Such recommended precautions were certainly not evident at the president's next stop in Duluth, where an airport rally was held. Thousands of enthusiastic supporters attended—crammed in bleachers on the tarmac and in the hangar. Only about a fifth of the crowd wore any type of face covering, ignoring the state's health orders. Trump spoke for only 45 minutes. His normal rally remarks usually stretched beyond an hour. This, I noted at the time, was unusual. But it was chilly and windy on the north shore of Lake Superior on that last day of September.

When we made the sprint back to the warm airplane, the group of reporters and photographers surmised the president did not want to spend additional time exposed to such inclement weather. Later we would learn Trump already felt unwell, that he fell asleep for part of the two-hour flight back to Maryland, and an ill Hope Hicks, counselor to the president, had decided to isolate herself on the plane. She tested positive for the coronavirus the following morning, something the public did not know until Bloomberg's Jennifer Jacobs broke the story later that Thursday.

Trump, during his travels the previous day, had not made remarks before boarding or stepping off the plane, and he did not come back to the press cabin at any time to speak to us. That was unusual but not unprecedented. We also had no contact with Hicks that day. White House Chief of Staff Mark Meadows chatted for about 10 minutes with the poolers on the plane during the flight home from Minnesota. He said he had tested negative for COVID-19. What he did not reveal at the time was that Trump had tested positive for COVID-19 four days previous during the Saturday White House Rose Garden announcement of his nomination of Amy Coney Barrett to the Supreme Court, which had already become known as a coronavirus "super-spreader" event for the number of people infected. I had also covered that event, standing in the rear, attempting to keep my distance from the other journalists. I did not end up testing positive, but among those who did who were seated closely together at that outdoor event were White House Press Secretary Kayleigh McEnany, former Counselor to the President Kellyanne Conway, two US senators, and at least two members of the White House press corps.

Trump, according to Meadows in his memoir, had taken a second rapid test and it was negative. The president continued with his normal schedule, considering the second test "full permission to press on as if nothing had happened."

In a decision that would later be criticized, Trump flew to his private club in Bedminster, New Jersey, for a roundtable meeting and fundraiser with supporters on Thursday after news of Hicks's diagnosis had been made public. Several White House aides who had been in proximity to Hicks did not join the trip.

Asked why the president went ahead with the journey, White House Press Secretary Kayleigh McEnany subsequently told reporters that "it was deemed safe" by White House operations. At the outdoor fundraiser, the president was kept more than six feet from a group of about 18 donors, who did not wear masks, according to campaign sources. While the president was in New Jersey, I was on an Amtrak train to Delaware, where I would resume coverage of the Joe Biden campaign.

Although we would not depart with the Democratic Party candidate to Michigan from Delaware until Friday, the campaign required all pool reporters traveling with Biden to take a COVID-19 test the prior day. This was done at a Wilmington hotel by a pair of technicians from a chain pharmacy, and the antigen test was similar to the one conducted at the White House. Unlike the procedure in the White House, where we are not informed of the results unless it is "positive," the reporters in Wilmington waited on the spot while their mucus was analyzed by the humming Abbott ID NOW machine, which, after about 15 minutes, would spit out a piece of paper with the results.

"COVID-19: Negative. Procedural control valid," read my test result.

At that point, I assumed I was good to go and returned to my downtown hotel to rest for a Friday morning gathering, where we would join the Biden motorcade near his residence for the ride to the New Castle airport. When word came of Hicks's positive test and her presence on the *Air Force One* flights the previous day, I notified the Biden campaign, which consulted with medical advisers, and it was decided that out of an abundance of caution, I stay back on Friday. It would be a few hours later, with a @realDonaldTrump tweet, we learned one more passenger on *Air Force One* had tested positive for the coronavirus: the president himself.

Trump, an admitted germaphobe who rarely exercised at the age of 74, survived his exposure to COVID-19, thanks to first-rate medical care, experimental treatments, and a three-day hospital stay.

The president, although visibly out of breath and appearing to wince in pain, made a triumphant return to the South Lawn of the White House, climbing the South Portico stairs to the balcony, removing his mask, and giving a thumbs-up.

"Don't let it dominate you," Trump said of the virus in a video that was taped on his arrival at the White House. "Don't let it take over your lives." The disease, we learned months later, had almost taken Trump's life. The White House chief of staff, Mark Meadows, feared the president, who at one point was gravely ill, would die.

White House correspondents, in any administration, assume loyal staff members will go to great lengths to hide presidential illnesses.

Such concealment is a tradition going back to George Washington, who was incapacitated for weeks by a near-fatal bout of influenza in his first term. Abe Lincoln's battle with smallpox was downgraded by aides to a milder "varioloid" of the disease. Chester Arthur, in 1882, flatly denied he suffered from Bright's disease (nephritis), as revealed by the Associated Press. He died of complications from the kidney disease less than two years after leaving office.

Grover Cleveland, in his nonconsecutive second term, was diagnosed with a cancerous tumor in his upper-left jaw, an epithelioma that had killed President Ulysses Grant after he left office. Cleveland hid the illness from his Cabinet and Vice President Adlai Ewing Stevenson, who would have become president totally unprepared had Cleveland died during surgery. The high-risk radical operation (Cleveland was severely overweight) to remove the president's cancer was performed on a yacht. While the president recuperated at his summer home in Massachusetts, reporters were told Cleveland was fine except for a "slight attack of rheumatism." When word leaked that the president had undergone surgery for a malignant growth, his de facto press secretary Daniel Lamont lied to skeptical reporters, insisting Cleveland underwent a trivial dental procedure.

When William McKinley was bedridden with influenza both in 1900 and 1901, his de facto press secretary, George Cortelyou (who would become postmaster general, secretary of commerce, and then secretary of the treasury under Theodore Roosevelt), denied the president was ill.

Woodrow Wilson caught the Spanish flu in April 1919 while in France to attend the Paris Peace Conference. Reporters were told it was merely a cold. Later in the year, a stroke debilitated Wilson, who had a history of cerebrovascular disorders. The president's wife, Edith, and his physician, Cary Grayson, conspired to keep the true extent of his condition hidden from the Cabinet, the public, and Wilson himself. Wilson may have been near death, but the White House issued a press release falsely stating the president was recovering. The lack of information led to wild rumors spreading across the country about the president's health, including that he had gone insane or had contracted syphilis in Paris.

Warren Harding, arguably, had some of the worst medical care of any US president. His homeopath dispensed pills based on their color, rather than their ingredients. Harding's father had been a homeopath. Charles Sawyer—to whom Harding gave the rank of brigadier general in the Army Medical Corps—famously misdiagnosed the president's heart attack as ptomaine poisoning, possibly from eating tainted crab following a trip to Alaska. Harding died.

Today it would be impossible to conceal the use of crutches and wheelchairs by a sitting president. That was not the case in the 1940s with Franklin Roosevelt, who had contracted polio in 1921. The American public was never told by the media that FDR was confined to a wheelchair, and constituents did not see any film or photographs of him being lifted into and out of automobiles. In June 1937, *Life* magazine ran a photograph of the president at a distance being rolled in his wheelchair to visit an ailing adviser at Bethesda Naval Hospital. Subsequently all photographers were banished from naval property when Roosevelt was on the premises. Whenever rogue photographers dared to break the unwritten rule concealing the president's infirmity, Secret Service agents would intervene to block their view or rip the film from their cameras.

During Roosevelt's run for a fourth term in 1944, Dr. Frank Lahey concluded Roosevelt would likely die of congestive heart failure before the end of his next term. Reporters were never told Roosevelt was terminally ill, and when he became sick, they were told the president had a bout of influenza. But Roosevelt's deteriorating condition was obvious to reporters 13 months before he died while he was running for reelection. Reporters did not share their observations with their readers and listeners, although photographs revealed the president had lost weight and looked pallid. Eighty-two days into his fourth term, Roosevelt succumbed to a cerebral hemorrhage at the age of 63.

War hero Dwight Eisenhower had been a four-pack-a-day smoker before going cold turkey in 1949. Elected president in 1952, he came into the job with a history of serious health issues. During his four years in office Eisenhower suffered a heart attack, a bowel obstruction, and a stroke—the latter caused aides to worry that the president was left mentally impaired.

Eisenhower's successor, John F. Kennedy, lived in near-constant lower-back pain due to osteoporosis. His poor health, including Addison's disease, which is a life-threatening adrenal condition, and persistent digestive issues were kept a closely guarded secret. Kennedy, according to medical records, as president was taking codeine, Demerol, and methadone for pain; the stimulant Ritalin; meprobamate and librium for anxiety; barbiturates for sleep; thyroid hormone; injections of gamma globulin to boost his immunity; and occasionally additional drugs. Reporters were constantly told the president was in excellent physical condition.

Besides several cancer scares during his two terms, Ronald Reagan was dogged by rumors of dementia long before there were signs of Alzheimer's disease in his second term. On the day Reagan was shot outside the Washington Hilton early in his first term (March 30, 1981), reporters were told the president had walked into the hospital under his own power. What was not revealed is that as soon as Reagan, who had lost a lot of blood, was inside the facility, he collapsed. The medical team was certain his condition was grave.

Reporters who covered George H. W. Bush thought that by the end of his second term there was something wrong with the president, who was said to have an irregular heartbeat. Press Secretary Marlin Fitzwater revealed in his memoirs they were right. Bush suffered from a thyroid problem and the medication had zapped his vigor, reducing the president to a low-energy version of his former hyperactive self.

When Trump's personal doctor, Harold Bornstein, in 2015 declared the Republican candidate would be the healthiest president ever elected, the assertion was met with considerable skepticism. Several years later the gastroenterologist admitted to CNN that Trump had dictated the superlative bill of health. "I didn't write the letter. I just made it up as I went along," said Bornstein. Slightly more credence, perhaps, was given in early 2018 to the assessment of Dr. Ronny Jackson (who survived scandal and became a Texas Republican congressman). Jackson praised Trump's "excellent genes," declared the president in pristine cardiac health, and said his patient scored 30 out of 30 on the Montreal Cognitive Assessment test. "Person, woman, man, camera, TV," Trump uttered two years later, attempting to demonstrate he had scored "extra points" in the Jackson-administered cognitive test.

Another medical mystery in the Trump administration occurred on a Saturday afternoon in November 2019 when the president made an unexpected two-hour visit, traveling by armored SUV, to the Walter Reed National Military Medical Center in Bethesda, Maryland. The White House claimed it was an interim part of the president's annual physical exam, but no details were released. The visit had not been listed on Trump's advance schedule released to the media nor on a private, internal White House agenda.

When I pressed White House Press Secretary Stephanie Grisham the next day with follow-up questions about the hastily arranged visit amid rumors Trump had suffered a heart attack or a stroke, she replied, "We're not going to get into security and movement protocols when it comes to the President, but as my statements said, he's in good health and it was a routine checkup as part of his annual physical. I've given plenty of on-the-record statements that were truthful and accurate—the press who are actively trying to find and report conspiracy theories really need to stop."

Some 10 months later, a book by *New York Times* reporter Michael Schmidt revealed he had learned in the hours leading up to the hospital trip that Vice President Pence had been informed to stand by in case he needed to take over presidential power if Trump were anesthetized. Pence said he did not recall any such alert, although subsequent reporting indicated the president had a colonoscopy and Trump declined to have anesthesia administered so that his second-in-command would not be able to take over, even briefly. Other reports said Walter Reed medical staff had been required to sign nondisclosure statements in connection with the president's visit, which rankled them. The fresh revelations prompted Trump to tweet a denial he had suffered any type of health issue the previous September. In typical style, he blasted the media, saying it was "perhaps another candidate" (Biden) who had suffered a series of ministrokes.

During his failed reelection bid, Trump would challenge Biden to take a mental test, claiming the Democratic challenger was "old and out of it." Questions about Biden's cognitive acuity were raised on a seemingly daily basis by his detractors during the 2020 campaign, after his election, and well into his presidency.

As a White House correspondent, I was frequently asked if Trump is crazy or Biden senile. I would preface my responses with the obvious caveat that I hold zero medical qualifications but, as best as I could observe, no and no. Based on my interactions with both presidents on a frequent basis, I observed Trump in self-control and Biden displaying no overt signs of dementia in their interactions with the press corps.

Journalists, commentators, and scholars wade into hazardous territory when armchair psychiatry mixes with partisan politics. It may be an evaluation best left to the medical professionals—or maybe not. When Barry Goldwater became the Republican Party's presidential nominee in 1964, some 1,000 mental health experts deemed him "psychologically unfit to be president." Goldwater's tenure in the US Senate totaled more than a quarter of a century. His rhetoric and high-minded conservatism, which once had him labeled as an "extremist" and "lunatic," puts him closer to the current political mainstream, considering the senator endorsed legalization of abortion and marijuana, and after he was out of office expressed support for gays serving in the military.

What the public and pundits from afar are quick to diagnose as pathological is much more likely to be manifestations of personalities. Both Trump and Biden could be prickly, cranky, and impatient and desiring to dominate the conversation—not unusual traits for the wealthy and famous. Of the two, Trump was far less diplomatic and displayed an infamous streak for holding grudges and seeking revenge for perceived grievances. Some credentialed critics during his presidency labeled him a sociopath or a narcissist. Some members of his Cabinet reportedly did consider him crazy and there were discussions about invoking the Twenty-Fifth Amendment of the Constitution, which empowers the vice president and Cabinet officials to declare the president "incapacitated." Some close to Trump contend he became more erratic and paranoid before his 2020 election defeat, tying the change in behavior to his hospitalization for COVID-19.

Biden has a short fuse he attributes to his "Irish temper." Like many of his age, Biden also did not hesitate to repeat well-trodden biographical stories varnished with hazy recollections over decades. Biden, who overcame childhood stuttering, also acknowledged when stressed that the words do not always emerge smoothly off his tongue. Sometimes what he said, after announcing he was not too old to run again, made for puzzling interpretation—"God save the Queen, man" at the end of a gun control speech in Connecticut, and telling reporters Russian President Putin was losing the war in Iraq (he meant Ukraine).

What is no secret is that Biden has had episodic atrial fibrillation, suffered two brain aneurysms, and had his gallbladder and several nonmelanoma skin cancers removed. Based on recent and more distant presidential history, it should be no surprise, despite the irritation of staff and supporters, that reporters repeatedly pepper press secretaries with questions about the health of their bosses.

Despite what reporters might relay, many in the audience are likely to draw their own conclusions, based on partisan prejudices, whether a president is insane or senile, fit or feeble.

25

The modern news media have the privilege and responsibility to question the president directly, as well as his officials, not only about the leader's health but other matters of public interest. There is a popular perception that decorum deteriorated in presidential press relations in the new millennium. During the Trump presidency, as the Republican greeted visiting dignitaries as they alighted from their vehicles under the West Wing entrance, Brian Karem, then covering the White House for *Playboy,* shouted at the president: "What do you know about Epstein's girls?" This was a reference to Trump's friendship, decades previously, with financier Jeffrey Epstein, found dead in his New York City jail cell in August 2019 while awaiting trial on sex-trafficking charges. Karem, notorious for heckling Trump's press secretaries during briefings, briefly had his White House credentials suspended after a Rose Garden altercation with former Trump aide Sebastian Gorka. (Full disclosure: I also had a contentious exchange that same evening with Gorka, who relished bullying reporters, but I did not face any punishment from the White House.)

In August 2019, Karem, through a leading law firm, Gibson Dunn, sued White House Press Secretary Stephanie Grisham, seeking immediate restoration of his hard pass, citing protections of the First and Fifth Amendments. (The legal complaint filed by Karem's lawyers also referenced my clash: "On his way out of the Rose Garden, Gorka insulted another member of the White House press, calling Voice of America's White House Bureau Chief an 'ass hat.'") Karem gave little heed to objectivity in his coverage of the Trump administration and appeared to revel in being a polarizing figure. Even Karem found the behavior of another gadfly in the room during Biden-era briefings beyond the pale. Simon Ateba, from Cameroon, who runs a website focused on Africa news, faced criticism for yelling questions out of turn at press secretaries and was generally accused of being insensitive to whoever was speaking.

"Mind your manners when you're in here," Karem ironically admonished Ateba after the latter interrupted an appearance on the briefing room podium by the cast of the TV show *Ted Lasso*.

While both Karem and Ateba were objects of scorn among some of their peers, accused of attention-seeking behavior, few likely realized their caustic approach followed an early American approach to journalism that was partisan, biased, and even scurrilous, depending on the motivations of publishers, editors, and reporters.

The dichotomy between the powerful and the press goes back to the first US president, George Washington, who despite being a Revolutionary War hero general, was notoriously thin-skinned in the face of partisan press coverage of his presidency. Washington, until near the end of his first term, enjoyed a honeymoon period with the nascent American press, which quickly became divided along Federalist and Democrat-Republican party lines. The Federalist newspapers backed Washington and were influenced behind the scenes by Treasury Secretary Alexander Hamilton. They advocated for a robust central government and favored reestablishing ties with Britain. The other party, known as the Jefferson Republicans, favored France over Britain and was wary of federal power over the rights of the states. Washington feared the intensity of the acrimony expressed by the partisan presses could be the catalyst for the young Union to split.

Thomas Jefferson, as secretary of state, helped orchestrate the anti-Federalist press coverage, which included printed attacks on President Washington. Republican editors claimed that Washington was imperious and desired to become king, and that he was a thief and age had robbed him of his mental faculties. (Does that sound familiar?)

When the general-turned-president rode off to western Pennsylvania to lead forces suppressing the Whiskey Rebellion, some papers accused him of abandoning the duties he had been elected to conduct. Washington was most incensed by a newspaper caricature of his head placed on a guillotine (a reference to his leaning toward London rather than France). In a subsequent Cabinet meeting, Jefferson and other secretaries looked on as Washington threw a tantrum and declared all his acts in government had been done with the purist motivation. It was feared that Washington, then and there, might choose to return to the farm rather than continue to endure the attacks by printer's ink.

Jefferson, meanwhile, complained the Federalist papers would not cover the 1792 financial panic, absolving the president of any blame.

Jefferson would finally quit the Washington Cabinet at the end of the following year, severing the bipartisan governance under America's first president. Washington wrote to Jefferson complaining about his four years of unfair press coverage and that he had been subjected to "the grossest, and most insidious misrepresentations." Some of Washington's contemporaries believed the media attacks contributed to the first president's decision to call it quits after completing two terms. Washington's announcement that he would retire and not seek a third term led to the unprecedented summoning of a journalist to the Executive Mansion in Philadelphia in September 1796. David Claypoole, editor of the *American Daily Advertiser,* a rare nonpartisan gazette, was told by Washington he would be given the scoop in the form of exclusive publication of the president's farewell address. Immediately after the issue hit the streets of Philadelphia, other newspapers in the city reprinted the valedictory message of the president and over a period of months it was disseminated in newspapers across the young country. The opposition papers hounded Washington all the way back to Mount Vernon. The *Aurora* declared the retiring president as "the source of all the misfortunes of our country."

The *Aurora* and other Republican papers published the attacks as part of their campaign to see Jefferson as the second president over Washington's preferred choice and narrow victor, John Adams.

Washington's successor was perhaps even more thin-skinned and had none of the iconic status and charisma of the retired general. For several months the opposition press continued their attacks on Washington, ignoring the new president. When relations worsened between the United States and France, the *Aurora* assailed Adams as "a man divested of his reason" and called for his resignation.

Unlike Washington, Adams decided to act against his detractors. The Congress, controlled by the Federalists, passed emergency legislation, known as the Alien and Sedition Acts, which Adams signed in 1798. The statutes included language declaring it illegal to "write, print, utter or publish" any false, scandalous, or malicious criticism intended to put the US government or its leaders "into contempt or disrepute." The law, however, blatantly excluded the vice president from such protection, meaning it would still be fair game on Adams's rival second-in-command, Thomas Jefferson, the leader of the political opposition. The vice president, as the most prominent Democrat-Republican, launched a covert counterattack against the action of the Federalists and the president, ghostwriting challenges, along with James Madison (known to history as the Virginia and

Kentucky Resolutions), arguing the new law was unconstitutional as it violated the First Amendment's guarantees of freedom of speech, or the press.

Under the Sedition Act, Adams consented to the arrest of Thomas Cooper, a former English radical who had advocated freedom of the press, denounced the Act, and called the president a "power-mad despot" in Pennsylvania's *Sunbury and Northumberland Gazette*. Cooper was convicted and sentenced to six months imprisonment and fined $500, plus court costs. Adams next targeted a more prominent foe for censorship: Benjamin Franklin's grandson, *Aurora* publisher Benjamin Bache. But before the 29-year-old could be brought to trial, he died of yellow fever. That did not deter the Adams administration, setting its prosecutorial sites on Bache's successor, William Duane, who had married the late editor's widow and alleged to have accused the president of taking bribes from the British. Duane was arrested and charged but never convicted on various charges—including sedition—the first and hopefully only reporter ever ordered arrested by the US Senate (after he obtained a copy of controversial pending legislation regarding the upcoming 1800 election and printed it). Duane was beaten and whipped by a Federalist mob but escaped further legal harm when ally Thomas Jefferson was elected president. (Duane, decades later, would briefly serve as treasury secretary but was fired by President Andrew Jackson when he blocked Jackson's controversial attempt to remove federal deposits from the Second Bank of the United States.)

It was Thomas Jefferson who would become the first president to suffer unwanted media scrutiny of his personal life after a former supporter of his switched newspapers and allegiances. Thomas Callender was among America's first prominent pamphleteers and had ended up in prison in Richmond, Virginia, for nine months following a conviction for seditious communications. Callender had accused Adams of being "mentally deranged," alleging the president planned to crown himself king and was grooming his son, John Quincy, as heir to this planned throne. He labeled the Federalist president a "hideous hermaphroditical character, which has neither the force of a man, nor the gentleness and sensibility of a woman."

Jefferson pardoned Callender, but the coeditor of the reliably Republican *Richmond Examiner* thought the new president owed him much more (the payment of his $200 fine and a cushy government job). Jefferson did cough up $50, not an unsubstantial sum in those days, and after that cut off Callender. The scorned journalist vowed revenge, moving over to a rival pro-Federalist newspaper, the *Richmond Recorder*. There Callender published a scoop unlike any in the young republic's history and one that would continue to reverberate centuries later.

On September 1, 1802, on page 2, the *Recorder* story headlined, "The President Again" contained this lead:

> IT is well known that the man, whom it delighteth the people to honor, keeps, and for many years past has kept, as his concubine, one of his own slaves. Her name is SALLY. The name of her eldest son is TOM. His features are said to bear a striking although sable resemblance to those of the president himself.

DNA testing and scholarship concluded, 200 years later, Callender's explosive story was true. According to the Thomas Jefferson Foundation, the slave-owning president likely fathered at least six of Sally Hemming's children.

Ten months later, Callender met his demise. Drunk and destitute, he drowned in three feet of water by the shore of the James River.

Other Federalist editors continued to be charged under the Sedition Act once vehemently opposed by Jefferson. Harry Crosswell (pen name Robert Rusticoat), editor of *The Wasp* in Hudson, New York, was convicted after accusing Jefferson of having been previously married and attempting to seduce the wife of a friend. A lawyer named Alexander Hamilton, who would go on to greater fame, represented Crosswell on appeal and the prosecution's case fizzled.

While Jefferson never specifically denied the printed accusations about his personal life, he did complain that Federalist editors "never utter a truth" and that every syllable written about him in opposition papers "is distorted."

Jefferson also faced press reports, which peaked in 1802, that he was in such poor health as to be about to die or set to resign. Jefferson outlived that fake news by two dozen years.

26

The president-elect was warned—there was a conspiracy to prevent the counting of the electoral ballots and disrupt his inauguration. There was even talk of seizing Washington by military force in a deeply divided nation. It was not Joe Biden receiving the alarming reports after his 2020 election but Abraham Lincoln following the vote of 1860.

"There was also an assassination plot against the president-elect to prevent him from arriving in Washington at all," according to Lincoln historian Harold Holzer. Members of a white supremacist secret society and a Baltimore militia, both committed to preserving slavery, had discussed seizing Washington by force before looking to sabotage the train carrying Lincoln to his inauguration.

Lincoln was inaugurated as the sixteenth president of the United States on March 4, 1861. By then Southern states had begun seceding to form the Confederate States of America. To get to the ceremony in Washington, Lincoln avoided going through the slaveholding city of Baltimore, as had been announced, instead detouring to Harrisburg, Pennsylvania, disguised as an ordinary passenger in a sleeping car on a night train. The plot to kill the president-elect (who was assassinated in 1865 after winning a second term) "turned out to be little more than rumor and drunken boasting and Lincoln was afterward so embarrassed that he had listened to any of it that he almost went to the other extreme in disregard of his personal safety," according to Princeton University professor Allen Guelzo.

Some Americans in 1860 were incensed by unfounded charges about the legitimacy of the popular and electoral votes, as were some in 2020. "It was even more ridiculous than the recent charges by Donald Trump," Holzer said of the claims that Lincoln was not legitimately elected because he prevailed in the North but had no electoral votes in the South.

Lincoln won the election "on the strength of the electoral college vote, but with only 39 percent of the popular vote. However, the states where he won the popular vote—and thus the electoral vote—gave him whopping margins of victory, so there was never any question about challenges to electors in those states," according to Guelzo, director of Princeton's Initiative on Politics and Statesmanship of the James Madison Program in American Ideals and Institutions.

In another parallel to recent events, a mob tried to force its way inside the US Capitol to disrupt the electoral vote count on February 13, 1861. Unlike the insurrection at the Capitol 160 years later, authorities were prepared. General Winfield Scott, a Southerner and hero of the Mexican War in charge of defending Washington, had even sent a cannon to Capitol Hill. The general made it known that any intruder would be "be lashed to the muzzle of a twelve-pounder and fired out the window of the Capitol." For emphasis, he added, "I would manure the hills of Arlington with the fragments of his body." That intimidated the group, according to historians.

A major difference between 1861 and 2021 was that all the senators and many of the House members from the breakaway states had already permanently departed Washington. "So, there was no one there really to take votes and object to the state counts. And that's one of the other reasons why it actually went much more smoothly than it did in 2020," said Holzer, director of the Roosevelt House Public Policy Institute at Hunter College.

The vice president of the United States, who is the president of the Senate, in both 1861 and 2021 did not tamper with the ceremonial but crucial electoral vote count. On the fateful day in 1861, Vice President John Breckinridge of Kentucky (the runner-up presidential candidate from the Southern side of a split Democratic Party) presided over the event. Two months later, civil war began when Confederate forces attacked a US Army fort in the harbor of Charleston, South Carolina.

"We are in a battle for the soul of America," Biden declared on the first anniversary of the January 6, 2021, deadly attack on the Capitol, accusing Trump of trying to unravel the country's democratic system by continuing to repeat lies about the 2020 election. Trump insisted, without evidence, there was "massive vote fraud" in several states he lost.

A special House committee investigated in 2022 the siege of the Capitol and the violent attempt to disrupt the electoral vote counting in 2020. The US election system had improved since Lincoln's days, but lawmakers and others thought more reform was still needed to keep pace with technology.

"In those days, state electors were elected in many states by the legislature, not even by voters. There was a lot of possibilities for fraud, or at least overpoliticization that ignored the will of the people," noted Holzer. "We don't have that now. We have electronic and computer counts. We have poll-watchers, we have the popular vote."

Numerous technical issues with the certification and counting of the electoral votes remained concerningly vague, however, according to Michael Morley, a law professor at Florida State University and a member of the National Task Force on Election Crises. "It's an issue that four years ago wouldn't have been on anyone's political radar," Morley told me in 2022.

The danger for the next presidential election in 2024 in a deeply divided nation was "both the possibility, as well as a public perception of the possibility, that the outcome of the election could be determined by politically motivated decision-making rather than the dictates of the law and what the actual outcome of the vote is," said Morley. In late 2022, such concerns prompted a bipartisan group of US senators to examine ways to modernize the law concerning the electoral ballots.

The 1887 Electoral Count Act, finally revised in 2022, was woefully out of date, according to Republican senator Susan Collins of Maine. Collins explained that lawmakers, after the January 2021 siege of the US Capitol, explored how to raise the requirements for members of Congress to challenge state-certified election results and ensuring the vice president's role is purely ceremonial when the electoral votes are certified.

It was critical, according to Collins, to prevent a repeat of the situation in which Trump pressured his vice president, Mike Pence, to overturn electoral results. A fix, called the Electoral Count Reform Act, was attached to a year-end government funding bill in December 2022. It was approved by Congress and signed by President Biden. It clarifies that the vice president's role in the counting of Electoral College ballots is ceremonial and states' electors cannot be refused.

Some prominent lawmakers on Capitol Hill contend the 2022 reform does not go far enough, and the only way to ensure there is no future attempted subversion would be to abolish the Electoral College, allowing Americans to directly elect their president.

Many Trump appointees in the West Wing were among those surprised that the president, after he lost his reelection bid, continued to insist, at least publicly, that he had won. Trump's election denialism was a recycled page from his playbook of his successful 2016 campaign. Following his second-place finish behind Senator Ted Cruz in the Iowa caucuses, Trump, during the subsequent New Hampshire primary campaign, insisted to voters that "Ted Cruz didn't win Iowa, he stole it."

27

Not only is the modern-day president accompanied by a pool of reporters during travel, but frequently the vice president is as well.

Mike Pence's visit to the Mayo Clinic on April 28, 2020, was not expected to generate much news, but I was along for the ride from Joint Base Andrews to Minnesota as the radio pool reporter on *Air Force Two*. The trips with Pence were much more relaxed for the media pool than those of *Air Force One*. News editors, producers, and the public widely view any vice president as a mere placeholder in case something happens to the chief of the executive branch of government. Pence, in a flight jacket, with wife Karen at his side, frequently appeared in the press cabin for an off-the-record brief, trivial chat to exchange pleasantries.

The vice president's visit to one of America's premier medical facilities in Rochester, Minnesota, was intended to highlight an experimental treatment for COVID-19 using antibodies found in plasma from other patients who had recovered from the coronavirus. Inside the Mayo Clinic we followed Pence as he met with staff and patients.

"When I hear about the innovation that's been developed here and the opportunity to scale some of the new tests that you've developed here at the Mayo Clinic, I know that we've only just begun to expand new platforms of testing around the country. And it will be owing to the ingenuity, the creativity, and the expertise of the extraordinary men and women here at Mayo Clinic," said the vice president.

I recorded his utterances throughout the tour on my digital recorder attached to a directional microphone that was at the end of a long boom pole I was holding. It was hardly a newsy quote, keeping in line with Pence's reputation as second fiddle to Trump. Pence tended to leave the headline-making to his boss (who had chosen Pence as a running mate after repeatedly being advised it would not be prudent to select his preferred number two, his daughter Ivanka). On this visit, everyone on the tour, including Food and Drug Administration Commissioner Dr. Stephen Hahn, Minnesota Governor Tim Walz, and US Representative Jim Hagedorn, wore masks. Everyone, that was, except Pence. I took a photo on my iPhone to send with one of my radio pool reports and also to post on Twitter. The images of a maskless Pence soon would be more widely distributed by the pool photographers and videographers in the room. Around the same time the Mayo Clinic posted on social media that it had informed Pence of the mandatory mask policy prior to his arrival. Pence's chief of staff, Marc Short, quickly found out about the tweet and chewed out a Mayo Clinic public affairs staffer, prompting the medical center to delete the post. That drew more attention to it.

Amid the national political polarization on mask-wearing and the lack of any real news from Pence's tour, the resulting headlines were inevitable. "Pence Meets with Mayo Clinic Patients, Staff while Not Wearing Face Mask" was the online headline that evening on the *Washington Post* website. "Since I don't have the coronavirus, I thought it'd be a good opportunity for me to be here, to be able to speak to these researchers, these incredible health-care personnel and look them in the eye and say thank you," Pence said in his defense for not wearing a mask. That quickly prompted a stronger backlash on social media with critics noting mask-wearing does not obscure anyone from looking people in the eye.

The late-night TV comedians, who usually devote their material to Trump, suddenly were roasting Pence. "You know, the only reason he didn't wear a mask is because Trump won't wear one," ABC's Jimmy Kimmel remarked—more of an honest observation than a joke.

The vice president's office began to have a serious public relations problem that needed to be addressed to preserve the reputation of a politician who clearly aspired to run for president (subsequently becoming a Republican candidate in 2023, pitting him against Trump). *Fox News* host Laura Ingraham defended Pence, bringing on her program the White House press secretary, Kayleigh McEnany. "The media obsession with Mike Pence wearing a mask is really just ridiculous," said McEnany in response to Ingraham asking about "mask-shaming." The press secretary said the media, "instead of focusing on mask palace intrigue, perhaps they can focus on delivering news to the American people."

Karen Pence then went on *Fox News* and stated her husband was not aware of the Mayo Clinic's mask mandate until after the visit. The chief White House correspondent of *Fox News,* John Roberts, on the morning of April 30, tweeted about the second lady's comment, noting it contra-

dicted a "Mayo tweet that he was made aware of the policy before beginning the visit." That was correct. I retweeted John's tweet, adding: "All
of us who traveled with him were notified by the office of @VP the day
before the trip that wearing of masks was required by the @MayoClinic
and to prepare accordingly."

That's that, I thought and did not imagine what I viewed as essentially
a minor amplification of the *Fox News* journalist's tweet would set off
alarm bells in the office of the vice president. Within minutes I received
a phone call from an irate Katie Miller, who was Pence's press secretary
and the wife of Trump's West Wing éminence grise, Stephen Miller.

Mrs. Miller accused me of violating the off-the-record terms of a planning memo that had been sent to me and the other reporters in advance
of the vice president's trip. I laughed and attempted to explain to Miller
her argument was ridiculous as the trip was over. The contents of the
planning memo were no longer a sensitive matter. Yes, indeed, we do
keep confidential off-the-record logistical notices about the movements
of the president and vice president, but after the trips have ended, the
past-tense whereabouts of officials are no longer a security concern. My
tweet had come nearly 48 hours after the trip to Minnesota had ended.
Miller was not having it. She insisted I had violated the agreement and
must be punished. I gently cautioned the 27-year-old press secretary this
was not going to be the best look for her or the vice president.

I had no previous disagreements with her and having interacted with
government officials for more years than she had been alive, I felt certain this was not a good move on her part. Apparently, Miller viewed my
advice as a threat. So, I gave up and did not try to further dissuade her
from the path of dispensing punishment. Shortly thereafter, I was notified by the White House Correspondents' Association that Pence's office
had banned me from further travel on *Air Force Two*.

When reporters sought confirmation of my travel ban from the vice
president's office, Miller (who would test positive for COVID-19 within
days) backtracked slightly. I figured she probably had not cleared this action with Short, whom I had always considered rather level-headed and
mature compared to many of the West Wing officials. She said lifting the
ban from the vice president's plane was contingent on whether I apologized for my sin.

"My tweet speaks for itself," I said, issuing a rare public personal
statement and no apology. "We always have and will strictly adhere to
keeping off the record any White House communications to reporters

for planning purposes involving logistics that have security implications prior to events. . . . All White House pool reporters, including myself and my VOA colleagues, take this very seriously."

Some prominent people came to my defense on social media about the post facto release of logistical details.

"Let's be clear. He did not leak sensitive information. He tweeted publicly available information. No apology necessary," tweeted Brett Bruen, who had been the White House director of global engagement in the Obama administration.

During Pence's next public appearance, at a General Motors automotive plant in his home state of Indiana, the vice president wore a mask.

The vice president's office blaming me for the mask mess gave rise to speculation that the Trump administration had an ongoing campaign against the Voice of America. VOA, as a US government–funded independent news agency, had been the subject of recent White House criticism. My *Air Force Two* ban came less than three weeks after the administration launched a bizarre and unprecedented attack on VOA, with the White House accusing it of promoting Chinese propaganda in reporting about the coronavirus outbreak. Their "evidence" was a video clip from Associated Press Television posted on April 7 by the English-language Twitter account of VOA News showing residents of Wuhan in China watching a light show following the lifting of that city's pandemic lockdown.

Dan Scavino fired the first executive branch salvo toward VOA. The White House social media director called it a "disgrace" that VOA was in the Chinese propaganda business. A former manager of one of Trump's golf clubs, Scavino's tweets had been deemed by the US Office of Special Counsel to be violations of the Hatch Act, which bars executive branch employees from engaging in electoral activities.

I was both angry and concerned. Others perceived that Trump and Pence had put a target on me and VOA and that the QAnon conspiracy theorists and other fringe characters took notice. I sent a message directly to Scavino, telling him if anyone in the administration had issues with VOA's coverage, they should contact our bosses to directly address it with them, "but when you use that type of language in a tweet it does result in personalized threats of harm to our journalists (including me)." I attached an example of one of the numerous such threats my colleagues and I had begun receiving. (I would later file official reports with the Federal Protective Service after more explicit death threats.)

Scavino, to his credit, quickly responded. "Got it." He said he would "share with my boss, too," presumably Trump. The West Wing attacks on VOA, however, escalated.

The White House subsequently issued an official statement in its "1600 Daily" newsletter, which had 2.5 million subscribers, headlined: "Amid a Pandemic, Voice of America Spends Your Money to Promote Propaganda."

"VOA too often speaks for America's adversaries—not its citizens," declared the White House comment, also posted online.

VOA's director, Amanda Bennett, felt compelled to respond.

"One of the big differences between publicly-funded independent media, like the Voice of America, and state-controlled media is that we are free to show all sides of an issue and are actually mandated to do so by law as stated in the VOA Charter," Bennett wrote in a long statement that included links to numerous VOA stories that had highlighted China's response to COVID-19. "We have never promoted propaganda for anyone," Bennett told the *Washington Post.* "We cover stories from all different sides. That's part of the reason we are so trusted by people around the world."

The Congressional Research Service, which works for members of Congress, their committees, and staff on a nonpartisan basis, issued a brief insight memo on April 28 titled "President Trump Criticizes VOA Coverage of China's COVID-19 Response." It concluded: "Some policy observers argue that VOA suffers from a lack of direction and funding, and a sufficiently aggressive approach toward countering Chinese propaganda. Others suggest that the Trump Administration's recent accusations that VOA supports Chinese propaganda are overblown, and that VOA's independence from U.S. government pressure should be protected."

Two days after the CRS report, an official at the Centers for Disease Control and Prevention (CDC), a federal agency based in Atlanta under the Department of Health & Human Services, sent an email to its staff instructing that all media requests from VOA should be ignored.

To many of us inside VOA, and others in the media world, something was going on that really had nothing to do with a video posted to a Twitter feed. There had been clear indications since the previous year that Trump was unhappy with VOA and Radio Free Europe/Radio Liberty and those running the parent agency for those entities, the US Agency for Global Media. (USAGM also oversees Radio Free Asia, the Middle East Broadcasting Networks—composing Alhurra TV and Radio Sawa—and the Office of Cuba Broadcasting, which runs Radio and TV Marti.)

During an October 3, 2019, speech in the Villages, a master-planned senior citizen community in central Florida, Trump veered off the topic of the hour-long event, which was the signing of an executive order on Medicare. The president, ignoring the prepared remarks on the Teleprompter, suggested starting "our own network" to counter the global reach of CNN and its "fake news." The president also spoke of VOA and RFE/RL in the past tense: "We used to have . . . Radio Free Europe and Voice of America, and we did that to build-up our country, and that's not working out too well."

Thirteen days before I rode on *Air Force Two* to Minnesota, Trump had launched a verbal fusillade on VOA. During an April 15, 2020, coronavirus news conference in the White House Rose Garden, Trump threatened to adjourn Congress to push through his stalled judicial and other nominees.

"An example is Michael Pack. He's my nominee for the CEO of the Broadcasting Board of Governors, and he's been stuck in committee for two years, preventing us from managing the Voice of America." BBG no longer existed, having been replaced by USAGM.

"And if you heard what's coming out of the Voice of America, it's disgusting. What things they say are disgusting toward our country," Trump continued.

There it was—the real reason those from Trump on down were attacking VOA was to bring attention to the president's stalled nominee to run USAGM, whom some on the Republican side of the aisle in the Senate had privately expressed qualms about confirming as he was being investigated for possible tax violations. (Pack in 2022 would settle a lawsuit filed by the DC attorney general's office over use of donations to a nonprofit organization he had created to fund filmmakers.)

Although no one asked about VOA during the question-and-answer portion of Trump's Rose Garden event (which was, again, supposed to be focused on fighting the coronavirus), some prominent media figures and celebrities quickly came to VOA's defense on social media.

Andrea Mitchell, the highly respected doyenne of *NBC News,* noted on Twitter that since its creation in 1942, "Voice of America has never been attacked so fiercely by a President as just now. Its journalists have done [an] exemplary job reporting China's false claims about COVID 19. No evidence to White House claims VOA repeats Chinese propaganda." Actress and activist Mia Farrow also noted that VOA went back to 1942, and "the accuracy, quality and credibility of the Voice of America are its most credible assets, and they rest on the audiences' perception of VOA as an objective and reliable source of U.S., regional and world news." Paul Farhi of the *Washington Post* remarked in a tweet: "Kind of amazing that Trump would seek to adjourn Congress amid a national health emergency because he can't get his nominee approved to oversee VOA."

The following month, at a private lunch with Senate Republicans on Capitol Hill, Trump complained about Pack's stalled nomination and referred to VOA "as the voice of the Soviet Union" (defunct since 1991). Trump taking to the bully pulpit proved effective. The Senate confirmed Pack a little less than two months later by a 55–38 vote with Democrat Joe Manchin of West Virginia voting with the Republicans. Democratic senator Robert Menendez of New Jersey led the party's objections, contending Pack should not be confirmed while a small nonprofit organization he ran was under investigation by the office of the Attorney General of the District of Columbia.

Democrats were also opposed to Pack, who headed a relatively obscure conservative think tank in California, because he had previously collaborated on documentary projects with Steve Bannon, Trump's former chief strategist. Bannon had urged the president to take control of VOA and overhaul it, saying publicly it was "a rotten fish from top to bottom." For Bannon—who took inspiration from the Bolsheviks for his government reform plans—VOA was just another instrument of the Deep State he desired to dismantle.

Pack, under President George W. Bush, had run Worldnet, created in the Reagan administration to use satellite television as an instrument of public diplomacy. Worldnet was eventually absorbed by VOA. Pack had also worked as a senior executive in the television production division at the Corporation for Public Broadcasting. That background gave VOA journalists hope Pack would arrive with an understanding and respect for their mission.

When Pack was finally confirmed, Trump celebrated on Twitter. "Nobody has any idea what a big victory this is for America. Why? Because he is going to be running the VOICE OF AMERICA and everything associated with it." Pack had vowed to keep VOA's parent, USAGM, independent from the whims of the White House during his confirmation hearing. "The whole agency rests on the belief the reporters are independent, that no political influence is telling them how to report the news and what to say," said Pack. "Without that trust, I think, the agency is completely undermined."

We were about to find out whether Pack would keep his pledge. The chairman of the House Foreign Affairs Committee was clearly skeptical. "It's taken nearly three-and-a-half years for the White House to fill the top job at our international broadcasting agency, and I'm troubled that the Senate has confirmed not an experienced manager of a news organization, but someone with long ties to right-wing individuals, organizations, and media," Representative Eliot Engel of New York said in a statement. "The Administration has recently launched a volley of attacks on the Voice of America for not being sufficiently pro-Trump, even though the law requires that our broadcasters remain unbiased and free from interference by any administration. I hope that Mr. Pack understands this law and will not permit USAGM to be turned into Trump TV."

Engel promised that the Committee on Foreign Affairs would keep a close eye on Pack, the writer and director of a two-hour film, funded by conservative donors, about US Supreme Court Justice Clarence Thomas that was composed of interviews with the jurist and his conservative activist wife, Ginni Thomas.

28

It was not long—June 16, to be precise—before Engel felt compelled to issue another statement. "I have learned that Michael Pack, the new CEO of the US Agency for Global Media, intends to force out a number of the agency's career senior leadership tomorrow morning," said Engel. "My fear is that USAGM's role as an unbiased news organization is in jeopardy under his leadership. USAGM's mission is 'to inform, engage, and connect people around the world in support of freedom and democracy'—not to be a mouthpiece for the President in the run up to an election." Engel remarked that President Trump had an "obsession with the myth of the so-called 'Deep State'" and that had jeopardized national security by depriving the State Department of "untold years of experience, sometimes breaking the law in the process."

Before Pack departed USAGM—he was sent packing on the day President Biden was inaugurated—some of his actions at the agency would be deemed illegal by a federal judge.

Engel's statement came a day after the two journalists in charge of VOA resigned.

"Pack, as the Senate-confirmed chief executive officer of USAGM, has the right to replace us with his own VOA leadership," Director Amanda Bennett and Deputy Director Sandy Sugawara wrote in an email to staff in which they announced their resignations. "Nothing about you, your passion, your mission or your integrity changes," they added. "Michael Pack swore before Congress to respect and honor the firewall that guarantees VOA's independence, which in turn plays the single most important role in the stunning trust our audiences around the world have in us," they added. "We know that each one of you will offer him all of your skills, your professionalism, your dedication to mission, your journalistic integrity and your personal hard work to guarantee that promise is fulfilled."

Within 48 hours, in a move dubbed the "Wednesday Night Massacre," Pack announced the removals of the heads of Radio Free Asia, Bay Fang; Radio Liberty/Radio Free Europe, Jamie Fly; and the Middle East Broadcasting Network, Alberto Fernandez. In the same announcement, Pack said he expected USAGM's new board of directors, chaired by himself, to approve his actions. Pack also removed all the respective boards of the USAGM entities, putting into place his own team. They included bringing in people from other federal agencies, including the Department of Housing and Urban Development and the Office of Management and Budget.

The head of the Senate's foreign relations committee, New Jersey Democrat Bob Menendez, was quick to react, calling the firings an "egregious breach" of the mission of the broadcasters' parent agency and accusing Pack of a political mission to destroy the USAGM's independence and undermine its historic role.

Pack, at this stage, was still pledging to honor "the independence of our historic journalists around the world." But the new USAGM CEO said he would now "examine some of the problems that surfaced in the media in recent years" and make the agency more effective. He did not specify what were those problems. By mid-August, the purge had deepened in the upper ranks of USAGM. Pack ousted the agency's chief financial officer, Grant Turner, who had been interim chief executive prior to Pack's arrival. Pack also removed USAGM's general counsel, David Kligerman. Among the rank and file, Turner and Kligerman were considered apolitical and had good reputations. Turner had held government positions in both the George W. Bush and Obama administrations. Turner issued a statement saying that his ouster was without merit and that he had been trying to do his job by calling Pack and his team to account for gross mismanagement of the agency. Kligerman, noting his bipartisan tenure as a civil servant, said there was no other conclusion to draw for his removal, "except that it is in retaliation for attempting to do my job in an apolitical manner and to speak truth to power."

A subsequent review by the State Department's Office of Inspector General, released in August 2022, concluded Pack's hiring of a prestigious law firm, which billed USAGM $1.6 million to investigate the agency's senior executives, constituted "a waste or gross waste of government resources" and there were "serious violations of federal law and regulation" for the unauthorized payments.

After Pack's arrival, the agency had taken the highly unusual action of suspending the security clearances of Turner, Kligerman, and four others, allegedly in relation to USAGM's hiring of foreign nationals. The State Department's OIG, during the Biden administration, exonerated all six of the USAGM suspended executives.

"These reports are an important step in holding those responsible for egregious waste, fraud and abuse accountable," USAGM Chief Strategy Officer Shawn Powers, one of the executives whose security clearance had been suspended and later restored, said at the time of the release of the inspector general's findings. "They send an important signal that political persecution of civil servants will not be tolerated."

While most of the journalists in the headquarters at VOA are US citizens, for some of the language services there was a critical shortage of qualified and experienced media professionals so those with legal permanent residency in the United States would be hired, and, in some cases, nonresidents would be hired and given J-1 visas.

Pack contended that VOA and other USAGM entities were misusing the J-1 visa program and this constituted a national security issue. Others, including former USAGM head John Lansing (who went on to be the president and CEO of National Public Radio), viewed Pack's focus on the foreign staffers as a smoke screen. Pack's team specifically targeted for removal from their positions some high-profile journalists with "foreign" names, according to several VOA managers.

When some of the J-1 visa holders expressed fear they would be targeted for retaliation if forced to return to their home countries, USAGM responded by suggesting if that was really the case, they should apply for political asylum.

In September 2020, nine Democrat members of Congress sent Pack a letter saying his failure to authorize renewal of the visas was "more than callous treatment of a class of employees and contractors who have put their unique skills and insights to use in service of the USAGM's mission."

One US senator, Jeff Merkley, a Democrat from Oregon, even proposed a bill to grant a temporary extension to the VOA journalists affected by the J-1 issue. Late the previous month, the USAGM human resources department had issued termination letters to several J-1 visa holders, whose work authorizations had or were due to expire in coming months. USAGM told the employees it was terminating the contracts because their J-1 visas had expired, meaning they were "no longer authorized to work in the United States."

By this point, more than a dozen of VOA staff members (including me) had expressed our concern about Pack's public remarks in a letter to acting VOA Director Elez Biberaj. (Dozens of additional current and former VOA journalists would sign onto the letter in subsequent weeks.)

"Pack's actions risk crippling programs and projects for some countries that are considered national security priorities," stated the VOA journalists' letter.

Of particular concern to us was that Pack, on a politically conservative podcast, claimed some staff had been improperly vetted and foreign intelligence services had been interested in penetrating US government-funded media agencies since they were created. "It's a great place to put a foreign spy," Pack said. Not one VOA journalist had been accused of being a spy.

"This is a very dangerous thing to say to suggest that journalists are spies. It makes every journalist suspect and to some degree puts every journalist in danger," John Daniszewski, vice president of the Associated Press and editor at large for standards, told my VOA colleague Jessica Jerreat. Throughout this period, VOA continued to report—relatively unhindered—on what was happening at VOA.

The visa issue stemmed from a long-running bureaucratic dispute between USAGM and the Office of Personnel Management over responsibility for the background checks conducted prior to hirings. That responsibility, prior to Pack taking over, had been given to the Pentagon's Defense Counterintelligence and Security Agency in February 2019, even though no VOA journalists have any privileged access to classified information. On the Federalist podcast, Pack had also joked in response to a question about how best to drain the swamp that he would look into banning masks and turn off the air-conditioning in the VOA headquarters.

We did not laugh.

VOA, RFE/RL, and RFA journalists, over the years, have faced accusations from unfriendly governments that they were intelligence agents. On a visit to North Korea in 2013 for a reporting assignment, the officials of that totalitarian government with whom I interacted assumed I was a fluent Korean-speaking intelligence officer operating as a US-government journalist. They also told me they knew CNN's broadcasts were directed by the CIA, so make of that what you will.

It was one thing for officials of a hostile authoritarian regime to believe VOA journalists were spies. It was another matter for the head of our parent agency to suggest VOA reporters might be spying on behalf of foreign governments.

"We fear that the current USAGM leadership is failing not only the news organizations . . . and our audiences, but also our stakeholders, including the American public," said the VOA journalists' letter to Biberaj.

The timing of Pack's action came as a pair of former Radio Free Asia journalists faced espionage charges in Cambodia for allegedly installing equipment covertly to broadcast reports back to the service after RFA closed its Phnom Penh bureau.

Some media outlets characterized the letter to Biberaj as an open revolt against our leadership. I do not think any of those signing the letter would have characterized it so dramatically. We would later discover, however, how upset the USAGM political appointees were with the letter. What it set into motion behind the scenes would eventually threaten my career and those of some of my colleagues.

29

By October 2020, it was revealed, first by NPR, that two political appointees of Pack's USAGM had been investigating me to prove bias against President Trump. I was still reporting from the White House—no one at VOA manipulated the copy I filed. The federally mandated firewall remained intact, as far as I knew, and I certainly did not self-censor. I was aware of the upheaval layers above me inside USAGM. It was increasingly a distraction, but little beyond that.

A lengthy dossier (which I did not see in its entirety until the Biden administration) claimed my reporting and tweets had been unfair to Trump and had broken VOA standards and social media policies. This, according to the confidential report, denoted a "conflict of interest." The NPR story, which described me as "perhaps the most public face of VOA," revealed the findings of the dossier had been quietly presented in September to VOA's acting director.

The evidence appeared flimsy, according to others who read the dossier. It included dueling political comments made by two of my siblings on my personal Facebook page in response to a posting of one of my VOA reports from the White House. In reporting about the dossier, the left-wing Intercept news organization characterized me as "scrupulously neutral." Pack made no bones about finding a head on a pike for public display. In another podcast interview with a conservative journalist, he said people needed to suffer the consequences. "And I think I'm getting the Voice of America to do that now."

According to several academic researchers who published a book in 2023, *Capturing News, Capturing Democracy: Trump and the Voice of America,* that head on a pike was to be mine.

"The investigation into Herman had little to do with VOA's news output. Instead, participants consistently told us that Pack's main concern seemed to be the influence that Herman might be exerting via his personal use of social media, and his relationships with prominent journalists at other US media outlets," according to the book's authors.

The two Pack aides spearheading the investigation, Frank Wuco and Samuel Dewey, had long-standing Republican and conservative ties. Wuco, a right-wing talk show host, had propagated baseless conspiracies, including that former President Obama had been born in Kenya, then House Speaker Nancy Pelosi was a Nazi, and former CIA Director John Brennan had converted to Islam. Dewey, an attorney, was under a restraining order to stay away from his own father against whom he had made death threats.

I had never met either Wuco or Dewey and I was not approached by anyone at USAGM in the preparation of the dossier.

Pack directly pressured Biberaj to fire me or at least remove me from the White House beat because I had "liked" a political cartoon posted on Facebook and had internally compared Pack's tactics to the McCarthyism "Red Scare" campaign of the 1950s.

Biberaj, under intense pressure, held firm, essentially becoming the firewall protecting VOA's independent journalists from political retaliation.

A lawsuit on behalf of the ousted USAGM executives filed by the Gibson Dunn firm alleged Pack's aides created the dossier to have me reassigned. That resulted in judicial pushback with Chief Judge Beryl Howell of the US District Court for the District of Columbia issuing a preliminary injunction prohibiting USAGM officials, including Pack, from interfering with the editorial independence and First Amendment rights of the journalists at VOA and the other networks it oversees.

Howell cited the internal investigation, saying it "imposes an unconstitutional prior restraint not just on Herman's speech" but also on the speech of VOA acting program director, Kelu Chao, and other editors and journalists at VOA and the networks.

Chao, who in the Biden administration would be appointed acting USAGM CEO after Pack was fired along with five USAGM officials placed on administrative leave in August 2020, had gone to federal court to argue that Pack's actions were unlawful, violating the First Amendment and the statutory firewall established to prevent outside interference.

The judge, in her 76-page memorandum opinion in the case of *Turner v. US Agency for Global Media,* instructed Pack and other USAGM officials not to make or interfere with personnel decisions related to individual editorial staff at VOA and its sister networks; not to directly communicate with editors and journalists, with the exception of the heads of those networks, or unless they have a director's consent; and not to conduct investigations into content, journalists, and alleged breaches of ethics at the networks.

The injunction was issued a week after Trump's Justice Department argued, it turned out unsuccessfully, in a legal filing that the free speech protections of the First Amendment did not apply to VOA journalists because we were federal government employees.

VOA and other USAGM outlets "are not intended to promote uncritically the political views and aspirations of a single U.S. official, even if that official is the U.S. president," wrote Howell in her opinion.

The Reporters Committee for the Freedom of the Press filed a brief in support of ousted interim USAGM CEO Grant Turner and his fellow plaintiffs, emphasizing that journalists at VOA can assert First Amendment rights against USAGM notwithstanding our status as federal employees.

While Chief Judge Howell, in her preliminary opinion, declined to hold VOA journalists' rights are equal to those of any other journalist, as the Reporters Committee and the plaintiffs had urged, she did agree that USAGM and the Department of Justice were wrong to suggest VOA reporters have no First Amendment rights just because the government pays our salaries. This was something my colleagues and I had taken for granted for decades. Now a federal judge solidified it in a legal decision.

Reporters covering the USAGM vs. VOA story considered the internal conflict unprecedented.

"I have covered media for more than 20 years, and I have covered controversies in Voice of America before," NPR media correspondent David Folkenflik told the Nieman Foundation at Harvard. "I don't think we've seen anything like this. This is the kind of war being waged upon broadcasters and the agency by the leadership of the agency itself."

The situation had become so alarming for USAGM and VOA staffers that by the end of 2020, at least 11 whistle-blower complaints had been filed with the US Office of Special Counsel, a federal watchdog. One of the most distressing actions had been the removal of Steve Springer, the standards and practices editor of Voice of America. Springer, a journalist with more than 40 years of experience in journalistic ethics and best practices, was clearly sidelined because among anyone in the organization, he had the most institutional knowledge of how the firewall worked.

The US Office of Special Counsel eventually concluded that US-

AGM leadership—singling out Pack—"repeatedly violated the Voice of America firewall" and "engaged in gross mismanagement and abuse of authority." The six USAGM executives who had blown the whistle on Pack's actions were fully vindicated in June 2021 when the State Department's OIG informed them the suspension of their security clearances was unjustified and retaliatory. By that time, all had returned to their jobs following Pack's removal by President Biden, but the inspector general suggested that that USAGM consider additional corrective action—including awarding the executives attorney's fees and other reasonable compensatory damages. The OIG stated that the dossiers compiled on each executive included rumors, gossip, and uncorroborated statements.

The OIG report also found the Pack-era USAGM disregarded the danger to VOA journalists with refusals to renew J-1 visas. The report determined that USAGM, under Pack, disregarded national security risks and COVID-19 safety guidelines and that some of Pack's political hires at US-AGM willfully failed to cooperate with investigators as required under agency and State Department guidelines.

Attorney David Seide of the Government Accountability Project (GAP), a nonprofit organization protecting whistle-blowers, who represented Turner, said the inspector general's findings that Turner and his colleagues "were wrongly retaliated against is not surprising. What is shocking are OIG's discovery of the many more ways Pack and his political appointees—while running USAGM for a mere six months—managed to break the law, abuse authority, endanger public health and safety and grossly mismanage the agency."

It was later revealed that under Pack, USAGM had hired, on no-bid contracts, two law firms to investigate the sidelined executives. That cost US taxpayers at least $4 million, a violation of federal contracting rules.

Pack's improper retention of one of the law firms, McGuire Woods, according to Seide, "violated additional laws, rules and regulations." He requested that OSC refer the matter to the Department of Justice. OSC has kept mum on that, responding to inquiries from Seide and journalists that it is unable to comment on or confirm possible referrals to DOJ.

Pack was also found to have illegally fired the board of the Open Technology Fund, another USAGM entity, which promotes international internet freedom, and replaced them with Republican Party activists.

The events between June 2020 and January 2021 would be scrutinized during an independent review by the Office of Special Counsel, which issued a 144-page report in November 2022, after it conducted interviews with a number of those involved, including me. Pack and most of the other Trump political appointees declined to answer questions. The OSC team of three outside experts reviewed thousands of documents and records. It concluded Pack abused his authority when he:

- **improperly suspended the security clearances of six senior executives and another management employee and placed them on administrative leave** without a legitimate basis after they made protected disclosures, thus violating Presidential Policy Directive 19 (PPD-19);
- **attempted to debar the Open Technology Fund** to prevent them from receiving any federal funding, in violation of federal rules;
- **violated the International Broadcasting Act of 1994 by attempting to enshrine a provision into grantee bylaws and employment contracts imposing limitations on removal of CEO-appointed board members and presidents,** specifically by restricting the grounds for their removal to conviction(s) for a felony or misdemeanor requiring imprisonment; and
- **directed employee-related materials covered by the Privacy Act be sent to individuals outside of the government** against the advice of an external law firm that stated this could violate the law.

The Office of Special Counsel also said Pack's actions put at risk numerous internet freedom projects, "including in countries that are State Department priorities," by trying to block federal money going to OTF.

The OSC added that Pack engaged in gross mismanagement when he sidelined VOA's standards and practices editor, Steve Springer. The office also determined Pack's hiring of an outside law firm to conduct investigations was an act of gross mismanagement and gross waste. Further, it concluded, Pack's punching through the firewall, including his determination to take punitive action against me, were inconsistent with statutory mandates.

"Given the timing of the investigation, the publicly stated hostility toward the letter, and the effort by political appointees to identify the White House Correspondent as a central party involved in the letter, the investigation appears retaliatory in nature in response to protected disclosures, whatever the merits were of concerns regarding his social media activity," stated the OSC report.

Weighing in on the debacle, the editorial board of the *Washington Post* called the OSC review's conclusions "damning," and that lawmakers should take action to clearly define the limits of the authority of the chief executive of USAGM.

The OSC report was "a timely reminder of the damage a single appointee can cause during just eight months in a job—and a harbinger of what a second Trump administration might look like," said the June 2023 newspaper editorial.

The work USAGM is doing "is as important as ever," opined the newspaper in conclusion. "The agency says its programming in Russian and Ukrainian has been viewed more than 8 billion times since Russia's invasion and that 1 in 4 Iranians uses circumvention tools it supports to access information blocked by the regime in Tehran. Those are healthy signs its credibility, which depends on being perceived as factual and independent, has survived."

30

After Joseph R. Biden Jr. was elected as the forty-sixth president of the United States in November 2020, it was clear the clock was ticking for Trump's political appointees at USAGM. The drama, however, continued following the election during a period in which Trump propagated the "Big Lie," claiming without evidence that his Democratic Party opponent had somehow stolen the election, denying him a second term. Then came the violence at the US Capitol on January 6, 2021—the first time it had been stormed by a hostile force since the War of 1812—with pro-Trump rioters attempting to thwart the ceremonial counting of the electoral votes and threatening to kill Vice President Pence and House Speaker Pelosi, among others, whom they saw as obstructionists standing in the way of a second Trump term.

For the journalists of the Voice of America, it was clear our parent agency would soon be under new management, but the focus in the interim was reporting on a country verging on constitutional crisis while we tried to avoid the distraction of the interference from the political appointees of the outgoing administration.

With little more than a week before Biden's inauguration, my VOA colleague on the White House beat, Patsy Widakuswara, was removed from her position as the senior correspondent. (I was White House bureau chief at this point, assuming the title after Peter Heinlein had retired and Patsy came onto the beat and inherited my previous position.)

Patsy, who had come from VOA's highly regarded Indonesia service, is a stickler for facts, but perhaps more tenacious than most. She works hard, she works long, and she does not quit until the assignment is complete— even if it is an around-the-world journey on *Air Force One* (the type of adventure that by the end of the Trump administration I found exhausting).

In the view of VOA Director Robert Reilly, who had been appointed by Pack, Patsy inappropriately peppered Secretary of State Mike Pompeo with questions following a January 11, 2021, speech he delivered at VOA's headquarters. In his remarks, Pompeo had lambasted VOA because it was not uncritically promoting the Trump administration's positions to the rest of the world. Pompeo said VOA's broadcasts had often "demeaned" the United States and it should adopt a more patriotic tone.

"It's not fake news for you to broadcast that this is the greatest nation in the history of the world," the secretary of state added. VOA staffers took umbrage, especially with the remarks coming less than a week after what many Americans and those abroad regarded as an insurrection attempt at the US Capitol.

After the address, Reilly engaged in a back-and-forth session with Pompeo, lobbing softball questions. None of the VOA journalists in the audience was allowed to ask Pompeo any questions. That did not sit well with Widakuswara and many of our colleagues. Patsy quickly decided to try to do something about it.

As Pompeo prepared to leave the premises, Patsy flung several questions at America's top diplomat. Among them: What did he intend to do to improve the international reputation of the United States? Did he regret saying the presidential transition for Trump would proceed smoothly into a second term?

Pompeo, known for an explosive temper, ignored her. Widakuswara then went back inside and confronted Reilly about why he did not ask Pompeo any of the questions VOA journalists had submitted. Reilly had no idea he was being confronted by one of his White House correspondents.

"You don't know how to behave," the VOA director told Widakuswara, adding she was "not authorized" to ask questions and she was "out of order." Reilly's deputy, Elizabeth Robbins, within hours, sent word to our bosses in the VOA newsroom to inform Widakuswara she was being demoted to a general assignment reporter, effectively immediately, and she should promptly turn in her White House press badge.

Patsy had been scheduled the following day to be the radio pool reporter on *Air Force One* for President Trump's visit to the Alamo in San Antonio, Texas.

The White House Correspondents' Association was forced to scramble for a last-minute replacement. The WHCA president, Zeke Miller of the Associated Press, was incensed about the action taken by the VOA bosses.

Miller, in a statement, said Widakuswara's removal from her post was "an assault on the First Amendment" and the retaliation against her "for doing her job, asking questions, is an affront to the very ideals Secretary of State Pompeo discussed in his speech Monday."

The action against the VOA correspondent "gives comfort to efforts to restrict press freedom around the world," Miller concluded.

A total of 26 VOA journalists quickly demanded that Reilly and Robbins resign after a series of alleged retaliatory measures and firewall violations culminated in the reassignment of Widakuswara. Our statement accused Reilly and Robbins of violating VOA's journalistic code in giving a senior government official "a free platform to speak live on our channels" by arranging the live broadcast of Pompeo and then removing Widakuswara after she tried to question the outgoing secretary.

"VOA does not speak for the US government. VOA staff do not accept treatment or assistance from US government officials that is more favorable or less favorable than that of staff of private sector news organizations," said the statement.

The Government Accountability Project informed USAGM and VOA leadership, along with the Office of Special Counsel, the Office of the Inspector General, the House Foreign Affairs Committee, and other lawmakers, that those signing the petition calling for the resignations were deemed protected whistle-blowers.

Pompeo was still sore about his reception at VOA two years after he left the State Department. In his book, published in early 2023, the former secretary of state said those at VOA who had opposed his appearance in the building "exposed an internal contradiction" that "the people who collect a check from Uncle Sam didn't want the voice of American diplomacy to be broadcast on VOA."

Pompeo wrote that under the Biden administration, "I assume VOA has gone back to sliding into irrelevance and leftism at a time when the global battle against Chinese and Russian disinformation is at a fever pitch."

The action taken against Widakuswara immediately following Pompeo's speech generated further public criticism of Reilly, who had arrived at VOA with baggage, despite having previously held the director's post for about a year in the administration of President George W. Bush. Reilly replaced Elez Biberaj, who had been acting director and made a gallant effort to resist Pack's interference in the VOA newsroom. In public comments between his VOA stints, Reilly had written a controversial book, *The Closing of the Muslim Mind: How Intellectual Suicide Created the Modern Islamist Crisis.* Another publication by Reilly, in line with his long campaign against gay marriage and homosexuality, was titled *Making Gay Okay: How Rationalizing Homosexual Behavior Is Changing Everything.* To say that Reilly's arrival unsettled VOA's employees who were Muslim or gay (or both) would be an understatement.

When Reilly was appointed by Pack the previous month, House Foreign Affairs Committee Chairman Eliot Engel was livid. "Michael Pack should be packing up his office, not packing the leadership of U.S. broadcasting entities with right-wing ideologues and bigots," Engel said in a December 9, 2020, statement. "Robert Reilly, Mr. Pack's new pick to run VOA, is best known for spewing anti-LGBT hatred in print and on the airways. The idea that he's been given the reins of an institution with the history and legacy of VOA is a disgrace and an embarrassment. VOA journalists shouldn't have to endure the reputational harm of having to work for someone with views so backward and out of step with American values."

A group of VOA whistle-blowers, on December 14, had sent Pack a letter calling for the immediate recision of Reilly's appointment. The letter noted his brief tenure in the Bush-era VOA had been filled with controversy, including his move to try to close five overseas news bureaus, and that the Broadcasting Board of Governors had deemed him incompetent. The letter to Pack also said that while Reilly as a private citizen was free to express opinions on Islam and homosexuality, as obnoxious as they may be, his appointment to run VOA would further stain its reputation for balance and objectivity. Pack ignored the plea.

Reilly's predecessor, Amanda Bennett, three days before the journalists wrote to Pack, published an opinion piece in the *Washington Post*, saying while normally she would never speak out publicly against her successor, Reilly's controversial views compelled her to characterize him as a dangerous choice to run VOA. Bennett also pointed to previous comments Reilly had made that VOA should "advance the justice of the American cause while simultaneously undermining our opponents."

Even as Pack's resignation was requested immediately by the White House after Biden was inaugurated, a last-minute attempt was made to fire at least four USAGM employees by those who worked for the Trump appointee. After Kelu Chao on inauguration day was appointed by the new president as Pack's interim replacement, Reilly was able to hang on for only a couple of days. He was removed by Chao, who named Yolanda Lopez as VOA's interim director. Lopez herself had been removed by Reilly from a senior position only days earlier.

The most tumultuous period for the Voice of America had ended, but not the wider debate, which is likely to continue for years, about the level of autonomy for a government-operated broadcaster or whether VOA should be privatized, as is the case with Radio Free Europe/Radio Liberty and Radio Free Asia, whose funds are provided by Congress and administered under USAGM but are not federal entities. These differences may seem subtle and technical, but they have significant operational and journalistic ramifications.

When lecturing about US international broadcasting and public diplomacy, I remind audiences the struggle for the soul of VOA has been going on since the 1940s. It is an institution that has served the country and its international audiences remarkably for such a long time, and it will be the role of our stakeholders, especially members of Congress and the American people, to determine in what form it should endure.

In their concluding chapter of *Capturing News, Capturing Democracy: Trump and the Voice of America,* British academic researchers Kate Wright, Martin Scott, and Mel Bunce state: "We believe that US citizens will only realize how urgent the need to protect VOA is, when they grasp how easy it would be for the network to be captured by a future government with authoritarian leanings, and how easy it would then be for government appointees to turn VOA into a major US news organization."

I have been asked what was it like to cover a president and an administration who were accusing my media organization of spewing propaganda and personally targeting me and some of my closest colleagues. It was distracting and annoying. It appeared to accelerate the graying of my hair, some family and friends noted. Mostly I internalized the onslaught and did not deeply reflect on the period until it came time to write this book, which I did belatedly. Eighteen months passed after Trump left office before I was ready to relive the four years of his administration.

I had known about three years into the Trump administration that I soon would need to dial back my pace a bit. I was, on average, working every day, about 18 hours a day, even if I was not in the White House or on reporting trips during that time. If my work had been able to be measured by an RPM dial on a dashboard, I was consistently in the red zone.

Trump was an all-consuming president for the reporters who covered him. In August 2019 I informed several key editors in the VOA newsroom I wanted to make clear, regardless of who won the presidential election the following year, I did not want to cover the full term of another administration. Perhaps I could do the first year, ideally even less. I was getting burned out.

I stuck around for the first eight months of the Biden administration and took refuge for several months in our standards-and-practices unit for a breather from day-to-day political journalism and to try my hand at a different and challenging task. Following that, I jumped back into reporting but without the burden of tracking a president's every public move.

In retrospect, the attacks on VOA and me only had added to the pressure, but I had no way to quantify it. I had tried, when it was occurring, to brush it off and place it into a historical perspective. Others before me had been in far more peril.

During the Nixon years, numerous journalists had been on the president's enemies list (yes, he compiled a list—two lists actually). From the media: Dan Rather, Marvin Kalb, and Daniel Schorr at *CBS News;* Lem Tucker and Sander Vanocur at *NBC News;* the totality of the *New York Times, Washington Post,* and *St. Louis Post-Dispatch;* numerous columnists; and nearly three dozen correspondents, reporters, and editors.

Nixon had the FBI spy on some of the journalists, told the IRS to audit their tax returns, and attempted to censor others. It was alleged that the Nixon White House even plotted to assassinate one particularly problematic columnist, Jack Anderson. Conspirators discussed poisoning Anderson, tampering with his car so it would crash, or staging a mugging in which the journalist would be stabbed. The plot was called off, according to former Anderson intern Mark Feldstein, only when the hit squad was given a more urgent assignment: placing a bug in the Democratic Party's headquarters in the Watergate office building.

31

As is the case with many journalists who don't appear on the nightly news or have a big-city newspaper byline, my name would be even more obscure than it is inside the United States if not for Twitter.

The Voice of America is an external media entity. We do not direct our coverage at Americans, and the United States is not a target for distribution of our content. The web and social media know no geographical boundaries (except countries where online access is actively blocked by repressive governments). What I posted on Twitter, however, was actively consumed inside the United States just as much as outside the country, although I have always viewed my social media output as primarily explanatory for a non-American audience, in line with VOA's mission. Whether from inside the Oval Office or on a tarmac after disembarking *Air Force One,* Twitter allowed me to instantly communicate snippets of vital information to—I didn't know who—anyone in the world, including my next-door neighbor. The power of retweets amplified my eyewitness reports to an even larger audience. Sometimes our editors in the VOA newsroom in Washington would cobble together brief news reports for our 47 language services and web page based on a series of tweets as I raced to keep pace, as a pool reporter, with the president on overseas trips.

I never intended tweets to give a complete or nuanced picture of events. As journalism is the first draft of history, tweets are the first draft of journalism, I told people. I had honed my technique over the years as I became acquainted with the platform and my following grew, while realizing the speed and power of social media.

Ever since the beginning of my career in broadcast journalism, starting in local radio in Las Vegas, mentors such as Bill Buckmaster at KORK Radio instilled in me the critical need not only for accuracy but the value of immediacy. It didn't get any faster than Twitter as electrons raced

India's Taj Mahal is normally crowded with tourists. But the 42-acre site was cleared of outsiders when President Trump and the first lady, along with accompanying US and Indian escorts, visited in February 2020. The traveling White House press pool was there to record the event.

around the world from server to server, computer to cell phone at the speed of light. It took Twitter until late 2022 to introduce an edit button. Until it was introduced you could delete a tweet or correct information in a subsequent message, but you couldn't edit what was already dispatched.

Despite my embrace of emerging communication technology, including being an early adopter of bulletin board systems, UseNet and Compuserve, I was initially wary of commercialized social media platforms. Facebook in the mid-2000s appeared to be a dubious time-suck, with a near-cultlike devotion to such games as *Farmville.* I did not feel compelled to join the fun. It wasn't until one evening late in November 2008, when it became clear something terrible was happening at several locations in Mumbai (previously known as Bombay) in India, that I became a lurker on Twitter. I was based in New Delhi as VOA's South Asia bureau chief. Initial reports on Indian cable television news channels were sensational and unreliable, including speculation about warring rival gangs of Nigerians (however implausible that was in India). The most accurate and fastest information came from terrified witnesses inside several five-star hotels who used their Blackberries (the smartphone of its day) to relay to the world there had been explosions and gunfire. The terror attack would continue for four days and shortly after it was over—with 175 people dead—I was on Twitter.

Initially I had no intention of being an active tweeter, viewing Twitter as a digital successor to the radio police scanner—a device to monitor emergency responses in real time but information that would need to be independently verified before broadcasting. It would be awhile before I realized that Twitter was a valuable and reliable two-way information system.

Two and a half years later when I was one of the first international journalists in Fukushima as reactors melted down at a commercial nuclear power plant after the facility was crippled by a tsunami triggered by the largest earthquake to strike Japan in recorded history, Twitter helped make me a prominent international reporter. I was unaware that the information I posted to Twitter on radiation readings recorded daily by local governments was some of the quickest and most accurate real-time data to the rest of the world. I was more focused on recording TV reports and web stories from the affected communities, and the tweets were information I posted when I had spare moments, except when powerful aftershocks and fresh tsunami warnings were issued.

Twitter would come to play a larger role in my professional life after I got to the White House. The credit or the blame, depending on one's political perspective, goes to Donald Trump. The wealthy host of the *Celebrity Apprentice* program issued his first @realDonaldTrump tweet on May 4, 2009, and it was innocuous enough: "Be sure to tune in and watch Donald Trump on Late Night with David Letterman as he presents the Top Ten List tonight!" Less than eight years later he would take over the @POTUS account and the Oval Office from Barack Obama, but arguably his most powerful instrument of power would be his personal Twitter account.

Until Twitter threw him off the platform on January 8, 2021, two days after the riot at the US Capitol, Trump issued 26,237 tweets and retweets as president on his personal account—an average of 18 per day—with upwards of 80 million followers and retweets of his tweets reaching the rate of 1,000 per minute. A statistic most enlightening about Trump's personal Twitter account is that, as president, he never followed more than 48 accounts, but if he wanted ample feedback, all he needed to do was glance at his mentions column. All that time on Twitter did not boost Trump's public support. He entered the presidency with a favorability rating of 45 percent, according to Gallup, and left office (after losing his bid for a second term) twice impeached with a job approval rating of 34 percent, the lowest of his four-year presidency.

After billionaire Elon Musk purchased Twitter, Trump's permanent suspension was rescinded in 2022, shortly after the former president formally declared he would try to win back his old job during the 2024 election. Twitter's new owner, however, while welcoming back Trump and others on the political right who had been banished, began removing some journalists from the platform.

Trump's suspension stemmed from rhetoric fomenting an insurrection and took place under the previous Twitter ownership. My "permanent suspension" resulted from tweeting about other journalists suspended from Twitter for tweeting about a banned account that tweeted publicly available flight information about new Twitter owner's Elon Musk's private jet.

US Senator Ben Cardin was among the prominent people tweeting their concern about the takedown of my account and those of the other journalists.

"This is not only wrong for the American press, it is bad for truth-telling around the world," said the Maryland Democrat, a member of the

Senate's finance and foreign relations committees. "The mission of @ VOANews is to send real news to people in countries where free speech & independent journalism are not allowed. This work is part of America's long-standing policy to inform audiences in countries that are not free. Restore the accounts!"

Musk subsequently tweeted the journalists' accounts were "restored." That was misleading. In my case I would not be able to tweet to my 115,000 followers, view my own time line, or see the accounts I follow unless I removed three tweets mentioning @ElonJet. I appealed and found myself sentenced indefinitely to this deeper level of Twitter purgatory. The only recourse I had, according to Twitter, was to withdraw my appeal and remove the offending tweets, which Musk inaccurately characterized as public dissemination of "assassination coordinates."

None of the suspended journalists revealed Musk's real-time location. They did mention the banned account that tracks his private jet.

For four years as a White House correspondent, traveling with Trump many times, I tweeted in real time the location of *Air Force One* and the president's whereabouts. This was considered public information, released by the White House to all its accredited journalists. No one at Twitter or anywhere else ever accused us of tweeting assassination coordinates.

After Musk purchased Twitter, I set up accounts on other emerging social media platforms. I saw these new accounts as insurance policies—alternatives but not replacements for Twitter should my favored site's servers begin to melt down due to the layoffs of techs and other personnel. I did not plan to abandon Twitter, where up to 100 times daily I reposted—without offering opinion—my news stories, on-the-site observations of breaking news, and retweets of stories from other mainstream journalists and news organizations.

I expected to lose my Twitter appeal, although I sensed a victory in the court of public opinion.

My insurance policies—Mastodon, post.news, and Spoutible—were already providing benefits. At the moment I was banished from Twitter, I had about 3,000 followers on Mastodon. That increased more than tenfold within a week. On post.news, a simpler and more user-friendly site, I also quickly gained thousands of followers. While the totals paled in comparison to my Twitter followers, I noticed something unexpected and remarkable—the engagement (comments, likes, and reposts) far exceeded what I had recently experienced on Twitter. I was not certain why, but it may have been that many Twitter accounts had been abandoned, were bots, or the users are merely very passive observers.

Some who fled what they considered a toxic environment on Twitter were exploring other platforms and preferred no longer to be exposed to politics, disaster, and other mayhem (they told me so). But the majority—95 percent, according to an unscientific online poll I conducted on Mastodon—encouraged me to post even more news than I did on Twitter.

The news items that initially generated the highest level of engagement on these other sites: the turmoil at Twitter and Musk's expulsion of reporters.

32

In the fleeting minutes before the inauguration of his successor, I witnessed Donald Trump enjoy the perquisites of the presidency for a final time—an escorted motorcade moving slowly through the streets of Palm Beach, Florida, as he waved from behind the windows of an armored vehicle to hundreds of supporters holding banners, cheering his name, and some urging him to run again in 2024. Trump was accompanied home by the now former First Lady Melania Trump, a small number of still-loyal aides, and a dozen members of the White House press corps. The motorcade pulled through the gates of the Mar-a-Lago estate less than 30 minutes before Trump lost the powers of the presidency. The final White House traveling press pool accompanying Trump was not permitted to go through the gates. Journalists there to document the moment of history sat in the press vans watching on our cell phones and laptops Joseph Biden take the oath of office. It was the most anticlimactic moment of my journalism career. In that parking lot in Palm Beach County, Florida, on January 20, 2021, I whispered to no one in particular, "It's over." What *it* was, from a historical perspective, I realized would take some time to answer. There was a subtle sense of relief. I had stood near the president countless times. I frequently asked Trump questions and usually got answers that—depending on his mood and actual knowledge about the subject—could be puzzling, obscure, emotional, or humorous but rarely satisfactory. (I would soon make a similar assessment of some of my exchanges with President Biden.)

When I wasn't listening to Trump's voice on a near-daily basis, I read his tweets, from early morning until late into the evening. He had consumed my life for four years.

Hours before landing in Florida, Trump had departed the White House for a final time, taking the *Marine One* helicopter to Joint Base Andrews in Maryland, where I and the other pool reporters boarded *Air*

Force One. It was chilly and—despite my layers of clothing, including an *Air Force One* Presidential Guest flight jacket I thought suitable to wear to mark the historic occasion—I was shivering. I took a couple of selfies with some of the other press pool members, including Reuters's Steve Holland, whom I had nicknamed the Trump Whisperer for his effective questioning technique, and CNN's Jim Acosta, who had regularly riled the president.

Trump was greeted by a military band performing "Hail to the Chief" (although some instruments froze up due to the icy wind) and a 21-gun salute from a battery of four black Army cannons. There, for under 10 minutes, he addressed several hundred supporters, although thousands more had been invited by a mass email. Trump delivered a more subdued, casual, and condensed version of the stump speech from his frequent "Make America Great Again" rallies that he had hoped would win him reelection the previous year.

"We love you," some in the crowd shouted as Trump began his final speech as president.

"I wish the new administration great luck and great success. I think they'll have great success. They have the foundation to do something really spectacular," said Trump without referring to his successor by name.

Trump, who had been criticized for downplaying the coronavirus pandemic, made a rare mention of the "incredible people and families who suffered so gravely" from COVID-19, referring to it as "the China virus." The forty-fifth US president cryptically promised to "be back in some form" and then concluded his remarks by telling the cheering crowd, "Have a good life. We will see you soon."

Trump also thanked Vice President Pence, who was not present as he was attending Biden's inauguration. Trump, less than two weeks previous, had expressed support for the insurrectionists who sought to drag the vice president from inside the Capitol for assassination by a hangman's noose.

The Trumps climbed the steps to *Air Force One* and turned around to wave several times, before departing for Florida. Trump, as was the norm for four years, had broken with tradition until the very end, avoiding Biden's inauguration. Before touching down in Florida, *Air Force One* did a low-altitude flyover of the Florida coast to give the Trump family on board an aerial view of Mar-a-Lago.

Trump's presidency had ended in shambles. In its waning days, he was impeached a second time, the latter after the House of Representatives, including 10 Republicans, charged him with incitement of insurrection. Trump faced trial in the Senate, where he was acquitted.

In the January 6 speech on the Ellipse, with the White House in the background, he had exhorted supporters at the "Stop the Steal" rally to march on the Capitol, where lawmakers, led by Vice President Mike Pence, were counting the electoral votes to finalize Biden's victory.

The mayhem caused death, injury, and damage resulting in federal charges against nearly 900 people—an event many Democrats and others quickly characterized as an attempted coup—and became the largest criminal investigation in FBI history. That event temporarily weakened Trump's grip on the Republican Party as many of its key politicians asked themselves whether the former president would help or hurt them in congressional elections less than two years away. Their concerns were well founded. In 2022 Republicans did manage to regain control of the House but not the Senate, and many of the Trump-backed candidates failed to win election.

In a Gallup poll released the week he left office, Trump departed with a 34 percent approval rating, the low point of a presidency that already had the weakest average favorability rating of any since the survey began in the 1940s. Yet he remained popular among Republican voters, with an 82 percent approval rating.

Despite condemnation from some of his party's lawmakers and even members of his Cabinet who resigned in protest over his postelection rhetoric, Trump retired from office the 2024 GOP front-runner and announced on November 15, 2022, he would seek a second nonconsecutive term as president, hoping to emulate Grover Cleveland.

Trump's business partners, from golf tournament partners to banks, began shunning him after the violence at the Capitol, and financial pundits predicted that out of office, he would struggle to remain a billionaire before the next presidential election. Trump had been silenced on major social media and began to confront legal charges in New York and in other states before the next presidential campaign. In his wake, Trump left behind a pandemic whose global spread he had blamed on China. In the final year of his presidency, the president had been hospitalized after becoming infected by the coronavirus. Opinion polls indicated the majority of Americans believed his administration's response had made the pandemic worse.

On the day he headed home to Florida (having previously switched his residency from New York to the southern state), Trump supporters pointed to his administration's achievements, including destruction of the Islamic State caliphate, the Abraham Accords, criminal justice reform, and speeding approval of generic drugs. Many historians, in the immediate years after his presidency, predicted Trump's legacy will not be those accomplishments but rather what he said and did between Election Night 2020 and January 6, 2021.

After launching his 2024 campaign, Trump continued to court controversy, including hosting a white supremacist for dinner at his Mar-a-Lago estate and calling for "termination" of the US Constitution so he could be immediately reinstated as president. Nineteen months before the 2024 election, Trump would find himself in a New York City courtroom to enter not-guilty pleas to nearly three dozen felony counts stemming from hush-money payments to a former adult-film performer, Stormy Daniels. There would be subsequent indictments.

While Trump goes down in history as the first former US president to face federal criminal charges, there was one president who was arrested while in office—although it was more of an embarrassment than a scandal. The full story was not told until decades later and the press accounts may have been embellished. The basic facts, however, are not in dispute: Ulysses Grant, on two consecutive days, was stopped by a policeman for speeding in his carriage. Police had set up patrols in Washington after public complaints of speeding carriages, including one accident in which a mother and child were hit and seriously injured. The president, an avid fan of horse racing, got off lightly the first time he was stopped. The policeman issued a warning after Grant apologized and promised to never again speed. But the next day—at 13th and M Streets NW in Washington, a few blocks from the White House, the same officer, William West, a Black man who had fought for the Union Army in the Civil War, informed Grant he was being placed under arrest. The president and several of his buddies, who were also racing their carriages, went to a police station. Grant was ordered to put up $20—a substantial sum in those days—as collateral. A trial was held the next day. Grant did not appear, but others who did were ordered to pay heavy fines and rebuked by the judge for speeding.

Grant is quoted as saying after the incident: "Let no guilty man escape, if it can be avoided. No personal considerations should stand in the way of performing a public duty." The president was apparently a serial offender. DC Police Chief Cathy Lanier, in 2012, confirmed that department records showed Grant, during his presidency, was cited three times for speeding.

Trump's legal troubles—not only the hush-money case but also the dozens of felony counts of mishandling classified documents after leaving office, his pressure on Georgia state officials to find him more votes, and his words and actions on January 6, 2021—led to speculation he might have to campaign for president behind bars. He would then become the second party presidential nominee and prisoner in American history.

Trade unionist Eugene Debs, during his fifth and final time as the Socialist Party's nominee, was incarcerated in a federal penitentiary in Atlanta after being convicted of sedition under the Espionage Act for speaking out in Canton, Ohio, against America's involvement in World War One. Debs's campaign buttons in the 1920 election pictured him in his prison jumpsuit and declared: "For President—Convict No. 9653." On Election Day, Debs received nearly 1 million votes—3.4 percent, a third-place finish behind two Ohioans, Republican victor Warren Harding, who was a US senator, and Democrat James Cox, the state's governor. Harding commuted Debs's ten-year sentence on Christmas Day 1921.

Debs still had his loyalists a half century later, another Socialist who would subsequently run for president (as a Democrat), Bernie Sanders. He produced a 30-minute filmstrip about Debs, which was marketed to schools and aired on two TV channels in Vermont.

Debs is a mere historical footnote a century after his involvement in presidential politics. It is more likely journalists and historians will still be referencing Trump in 100 years. What we cannot discern yet is whether Trumpism was an anomaly or a force that permanently alters the American political landscape.

EPILOGUE

VOA is a microcosm in the global media ecosystem. As is the situation in many newsrooms around the world, it has faced challenges transitioning from an analog to digital environment. Many individual journalists have adapted much better to digital than their employers. Newspapers for too long held on to newsprint before belatedly realizing they must rely on electrons instead of felled spruce trees for future profits. Local newspapers shriveled and died, unable to profitably transition to digital, creating news deserts. National Public Radio in the previous decade refused to promote podcasts on air, lest that anger affiliated stations on which the network relies for licensing of its programs. Television news programs were reluctant to stream on Facebook Live or YouTube for much the same reason: undermining the network-affiliate relationship, which has proved so profitable since the days of black-and-white transmissions.

For the individual journalist, a sizable audience potentially can be reached without relying on an increasingly archaic infrastructure. Independent journalists, not constrained by editors, can also thrive. But many of them traffic in disinformation and many readers cannot discern between well-researched and edited fact and unvetted fiction.

With a smartphone, I can stream instantly on Facebook Live or YouTube. I can, within seconds, compose texts with attached photos or videos and dispatch them to several social media platforms, potentially reaching millions of people around the world. Journalists—and news organizations—globally are also crafting and distributing stories on WhatsApp, Telegram, TikTok, and a cornucopia of other popular and emerging social platforms. And the reaction from the audience is interactive and instantaneous. No need to put a "Letter to the Editor" in the mailbox.

Most twenty-first-century journalists cannot carry out their work without social media. The majority in surveys confirm these tools are "indispensable" to their work, relying on them to find stories, reply to comments about their work, or monitor their beats. While my cumulative number of followers on social media—more than a quarter of million—might seem notable, the tally still does not match the potential reach I have through my employer, VOA, which has about four dozen language services, a total weekly audience above 300 million, and several Facebook accounts, each with millions of followers. But from my social media accounts I do notice much more engagement than from traditional media and occasionally my posts go viral when boosted by prominent followers who themselves have millions of followers, including Cabinet ministers of various countries, members of Congress, prominent journalists, and even the mysterious Zero Hedge, which has an outsized influence on equity markets. And that's one thing I've realized: the quality of your followers on social media is more important than the quantity.

Some journalists—because of their individual number of followers on their social media accounts—desire to become distribution platforms onto themselves, eliminating the need for a traditional employer. A few of them, creating accounts on Substack and other publishing platforms, may earn decent salaries this way, effectively working for themselves, emulating less serious influencers on the video platforms. In the early days of broadcasting, newscasters hawked products into their microphones—including cigarettes.

I saw some inkling of this future when the pioneer of backpack journalism, Kevin Sites, was hired in 2005 by Yahoo (then best known as an internet search provider) to cover every war zone in the world.

Sadly, the trend was not hiring more journalists like Kevin Sites. Rather, the industry evolved toward so-called reporters teleworking and repurposing the content of other journalists and publishers to create listicles or slap such content together with sensationalistic headlines. Offshore word factories have been established where a reporter who could be in Bangalore, India, monitoring online media, is paid to write stories about what is happening in Bangor, Maine.

Some online platforms have no compunction about inventing stories (and I'm not talking about *The Onion*, which is wonderful satire), propagating conspiracy theories, and sowing civil discord. Some have been linked to Russian disinformation campaigns. Consumers of content unsurprisingly became confused, and a lack of media literacy has meant many cannot easily discern between an objective investigative report compiled by a team of Pulitzer Prize–caliber news professionals and fraudulent material posted to their Facebook feed.

Social media propagates the wildest of conspiracy theories. I have experienced this firsthand.

Emerging from the Oval Office on March 17, 2021, President Biden briefly stopped to answer questions on the South Lawn before boarding *Marine One*. The president, wearing a black mask, gestured with his hands close to a group of microphones, which can be seen in the TV pool video. Biden leans forward and as he is replying to a question, saying, "not at the minute," he emphasizes the point with his right hand, which appears to go through a microphone with a large, gray furry cover that is attached to a boom pole.

As soon as the video was aired, some prominent personalities on social media, including former Major League Baseball player Aubrey Huff and wrestler Tito Ortiz, claimed the video had been digitally altered and the president really had not been speaking outside the White House. Rumors quickly spread: Biden was incapacitated. Biden was dead. The White House press pool was obviously a part of the conspiracy.

I was the journalist holding that big microphone that Biden's hand supposedly passed through.

When I became aware of the claims that the scene had been shot with an actor and digitized with a green screen (used for TV weather forecasts and in Hollywood to generate backgrounds), I felt compelled to tweet: "It's all real. Who actually believes this nonsense and more importantly who is spreading it?"

Some major media outlets, including AP, BBC, and Reuters, felt compelled to issue fact-checking explainers about how it was an optical illusion.

"There is no sign of manipulation or green-screening," Hany Farid, a professor who focuses on digital forensics at the University of California–Berkeley told the Associated Press. "In this higher resolution version, I see where the strange movement of the one mic comes from, but I think all that is happening is the mic is coming from below and President Biden reaches over it."

Farid noted that false claims like this one are not new. "There were similarly unfounded claims that Trump was releasing green-screened videos—this silly claim seems to be bipartisan."

Certainly, some remained unconvinced by the mass media explanations because they believe we are all part of the cover-up.

Sigh.

Another problem is confirmation bias where people tend to solely seek information to confirm their existing beliefs, shutting out information sources that could challenge their views. A healthy news diet should include sources that might taste bitter, providing our brains with nutritious content so that we can exercise common sense and discern between what is credible and nonsense, as well as understanding the views of those with whom we disagree.

More people have decided to take the news into their own hands, blurring the line between the traditional gatekeepers of information and a generation of independent online-only activists. In recent decades, videographers needed cameras costing tens of thousands of dollars, an expensive and high-maintenance analog videotape-editing suite, and a costly microwave or satellite transmission path to get the signal across the country or around the world. Now all this technology is contained in our smartphones. There's no barrier to entry—either concerning cost or experience. I have used my iPhone to stream ad-libbed video reports on VOA's main Facebook page and was amazed to see these broadcasts generate tens of thousands of views within minutes.

I am guardedly optimistic about what is ahead for the industry even though not everyone is an effective storyteller. And not everyone who can click on a photo app has the eye to create a compelling picture. The professional journalist is likely not headed for quick extinction in the digital era, and some of our best traditional journalistic institutions are managing to successfully transition.

The top tier—with great reputations and loyalty, especially those targeting the educated and wealthy—survive. And some of those pursuing the lowest common denominator—the bottom feeders—skewing toward sensationalism or even ignoring facts altogether, also flourish. However, as conspiracy theorists such as Alex Jones discovered in 2022, peddling hoaxes can result in financially deleterious verdicts rendered by judges and juries.

During the Industrial Revolution, readers in large US cities could choose from among a half dozen or more dailies. Both yellow and crusading journalism predate the twentieth century back to when our first presidents in the United States, angered by partisan gazettes printing falsehoods and uncomfortable truths, had to decide whether to ignore, rebut, or censor such publications.

Many of my contemporary colleagues are dispirited. Some retire early. Some go into public relations or marketing where they can earn substantially higher salaries and enjoy better job security. Some try to figure out how to become their own brand—using their significant social media followings to acquire patronage (or crudely, sponsorship). There is a private group on Facebook for such journalists named "What's Your Plan B?"—with nearly 18,000 members. Glancing at the requirements for job openings, it is routine now to see that employers expect their new hires to be more familiar with CSS than semicolons. Digital sites, in common with their dot-com brethren, prefer young blood willing to toil long hours without complaint for a byline and modest wages. No one, of course, should contemplate a career in journalism as a path to riches. It is better to view the profession as a noble calling, akin to a priesthood, but without requisite vows of poverty or celibacy.

College journalism departments have evolved after years of recalcitrance amid the evolution in the workplace. They now teach students web coding, data journalism, and infographics. Budding journalists may be savvy in data visualization skills, but they still need to learn the fundamentals of writing. A larger concern is news literacy, both among those who desire to be journalists and their audiences.

The lack of critical thinking skills, even in advanced Western countries, astonishes. It may get worse for future generations. A Stanford survey of middle schoolers found 80 percent took sponsored content (essentially, advertising) as real news stories, a statistic the researchers termed "dismaying," "bleak," and a "threat to democracy." Rumors, hoaxes, staged videos, and the most ridiculous conspiracy theories all spread instantly, much to the chagrin of news professionals. The worst thing the internet has done is to turn the digital natives into the digital naive.

Artificial intelligence (AI) is also expected to have a significant impact on journalism this century. Some of the ways this could happen:

1. Newsgathering and reporting: AI technologies such as natural language processing and machine learning can be used to quickly gather, analyze, and disseminate large amounts of data and information. This can allow news organizations to report on stories faster and more efficiently.
2. Personalization and customization: AI can be used to personalize and customize news content for individual readers, based on their interests and preferences. This could lead to a more engaging and satisfying news experience for readers.
3. Data-driven analysis: AI can help journalists to analyze and interpret large amounts of data, allowing for more accurate and objective reporting.

4. Job loss: On the other hand, the increasing use of AI in journalism could lead to job loss for human journalists, as certain tasks become automated.
5. Ethical concerns: There are also ethical concerns surrounding AI-generated content, such as the potential for misinformation and bias.

Overall, AI is expected to have both positive and negative impacts on journalism in the twenty-first century. It will likely lead to significant changes in the way that news is produced and consumed.

The previous paragraphs in sans serif type were not written by me. They are the work of ChatGPT, described as a "language model trained to produce text," in response to my online query in January 2023: "How will artificial intelligence impact journalism in the 21st century?" Like a good journalist, I went to the source. The remaining question is: Did this source—which is not human and does not think—give us a biased response?

Most journalists go to great lengths to properly source and fact-check their stories. Editors ensure balance, and publishers—those not pushing a blatantly partisan agenda—seek to give audiences a credible account. The news media, however, appears to have failed at explaining its quality-control process. Too many believe reporters invent falsehoods. One tech news online site, CNET, in late 2022 began writing articles using ChatGPT without initially informing readers. When the tech news website Gizmodo used AI to write under the byline Gizmodo Bot, a chronology of *Star Wars* movies and television shows, there was an immediate outcry among editorial staffers, who pointed out numerous errors and that posting the article online actively hurt their reputations and credibility and showed zero respect for the site's journalists. The *Columbus Dispatch,* a Gannett chain newspaper, in August 2023, paused use of AI after a hilariously robotic text attempting to describe a high school soccer match and a football game ("a close encounter of the athletic kind") went viral on social media.

AI can generate newscasts, using voice prints of real announcers or making up a new audio avatar—stations can even customize regional accents. And video manipulation can create "deep fakes," a convincing representation of someone famous saying something they didn't.

All of this will pose more challenges for reporters, especially those covering US presidents and government, who hope to rebuild or retain credibility with their skeptical and confused audiences.

After Trump regularly began spouting his "fake news" accusations, the Media Insight Project—an initiative of the American Press Institute and the Associated Press-NORC Center for Public Affairs Research—surveyed Americans in 2018 about what they thought that term meant. A majority, given the opportunity to select more than one definition, agreed it meant "made-up news stories from news outlets that don't exist" (71 percent); "journalists from real news organizations making stuff up" (62 percent); and "media outlets that pass on conspiracy theories and unsubstantiated rumors" (63 percent).

The survey also found that both the public and reporters support journalists explaining themselves more. Specifically, we need to proactively resolve doubts and address questions audiences may have.

Everyone should be able to evaluate the credibility of information they encounter. This is essential for democracies. The news media need to remain relevant to audiences and reach them where they are at. For the younger demographics, that destination is no longer a newspaper or a 30-minute evening newscast on a terrestrial TV channel as it was for their grandparents. According to a survey by the Pew Charitable Trust—across all age groups—the top categories for news interest are the same and in this order: crime, local community, and health. Sports and local government round out the top five. International news ranks ninth, ahead of entertainment.

The role of the media "as the interface for culture is gone," according to Brian Morrissey, the former president and editor-in-chief of Digiday, which focuses on the digital media and marketing industries. "It won't come back, and adjusting to the end of empire is always a messy affair. It will require a certain humility."

There appears no lack of enthusiasm among some of the well-heeled and risk-tolerant to launch what they tout as the next big thing in our industry.

"Time and again, billionaires who made fortunes in disparate fields swagger into the media business, only to get punched in the face, if not lower on the body," noted Morrissey in his newsletter, *The Rebooting*.

Most of us will only be capable of helping effectuate the next iteration of journalism and media as contributors and consumers.

"Many newspapers are shrinking and flailing, local news faces an existential crisis, investigative reporting has been cut back, opinion journalism has too often been reduced to name calling—and objective, fair, credible coverage of events is under attack from the right and left," wrote

Nicholas Goldberg in his final opinion column in the *Los Angeles Times* in 2023. "These are dangerous developments because it is journalists who provide much of the information and context that enable citizens to participate knowledgeably and effectively in a democracy. Let's stand up and support great reporting where it is still being done."

One notable but cynical assessment of journalists was made by musician Frank Zappa, who said the reporters writing about music were people who couldn't write, interviewing people who couldn't talk for people who couldn't read. Some would say the same thing about political reporting in this generation.

Surveys show that consumers, regardless of their level of apparent literacy, do not appreciate the fire-hose approach of the online media and its randomness. They want filtering. And the ability to search is important. The gatekeeper role is still desired. Both traditional and new media can still be portals in the digital era. And how can those of us in journalism remain relevant?

Edgar Allan Poe said in the nineteenth century: "We now demand the light artillery of the intellect; we need the curt, the condensed, the pointed, the readily diffused—in place of the verbose, the detailed, the voluminous, the inaccessible."

From Wuhan to the White House, may the foot soldiers persevere in conveying the artillery of the intellect.

ACKNOWLEDGMENTS

The detour from daily journalism to book writing is akin to shifting from slalom skiing to attempting mastery of cross-country skiing. The former is a quick and sometimes perilous ride to the finish line while avoiding obstacles. The latter is a numbing slog, requiring exquisite discipline to avoid total physical and mental exhaustion. There was no professional sabbatical for this endeavor, so I was frequently going downhill by day and cross-country evening and weekends.

During my 54 months in the White House, nearly everyone outside I encountered, including family members and friends, when I mentioned seemingly innocuous tidbits about my job, encouraged me to write a book. I usually replied, "There are dozens of journalists sitting in the briefing room in the West Wing doing just that. What can I add that they won't say?"

It turned out I did have a unique perspective that wouldn't have seen ink and paper without the encouragement and support of so many others.

Foremost was family: Rosyla Kalden, who tolerated my seven-day work weeks, including the extended and frequent travels with the presidents and candidates. She then kindly permitted me the luxury of time to write a book while helping to place my personal and professional lives into balance. My father Kenneth, brother Jay, and sister Lisa provided personal perspectives on the substantial changes in the American body politic that had occurred while I spent a generation living overseas.

Relatives long a source of encouragement since I first expressed an interest in journalism: Jerry and Carolyn Shapiro; Myron Herman; Bernice Jaeger and her late husband, Ivan, and their late daughter (and one of my cousins), Ginger. A thank you to all my other supportive cousins.

Close friends of many decades in California, including Kate Neiswender, Adam Gower, and Patricia Judice, gave valuable guidance. Closer to home came deep conversations about our craft with: Paul Beckett, Curtis Chin, Nirmal Ghosh, Jean Lee, Heather Timmons, and Martyn Williams.

Thanks to USAGM and VOA colleagues past and present, especially: Kurt Achin, Miguel Amaya, Carla Babb, Matthew Baise, William Baum, Amanda Bennett, Birgit Berg, Jim Bertel, Maggie Besheer, Elez Biberaj, Michael Bowman, Sean Burke, Mia Bush, Gary Butterworth, Kelu Chau, Nike Ching, Pete Cobus, Kate Pound Dawson, Penny Dixon, David Ensor, John Featherly, Holly Franko, Jim Fry, David Futrowsky, Bill Gallo, David Gollust, Adam Greenbaum, Carol Guensburg, Katherine Gypson, Alan Heil, Bill Ide, Sue Jepsen, Jessica Jerreat, David Jones, Steve Karesh, Amy Katz, David Kligerman, Yolanda Lopez, Colin Lovett, James McLaren, Steve Miller, Anna Morris, Purnell Murdock, Barry Newhouse, Aru Pande, Anjana Pasricha, Al Pessin, Anita Powell, Sean Powers, Carolyn Presutti, Michael O'Sullivan, Aru Pande, Eric Phillips, Michelle Quinn, Jim Randle, Steve Redisch, Amy Reifenrath, Cindy Saine, Mary Alice Salinas, Daniel Schearf, Douglas Schuette, Jeff Seldin, Bridget Serchak, Sharon Shahid, Brian Q. Silver, Salem Solomon, Steven Springer, Scott Stearns, Sandy Sugawara, Tom Turco, Grant Turner, Barry Unger, Hung Van, Sam Verma, Candace Williams, Sarah Williams, Khin Soe Win, and Paula Wolfson.

Special appreciation to a pair of incomparable and hygienic VOA colleagues with whom I shared the intimate VOA booth in the White House West Wing basement: Peter Heinlein and Patsy Widakuswara. Also on the White House beat, aboard *Air Force One* or during grueling overseas pool duty during those years (especially fellow radio poolers): Takaaki Abe, Jim Acosta, Francesca Chambers, Doug Christian, Greg Clugston, George Condon, Sara Cook, Bob Costantini, Jon Decker, Tara Gimbel, Fin Gomez, Steve Holland, Scott Horsley, Jennifer Jacobs, Tamara Keith, Kent Klein, Sagar Meghani, Doug Mills, Toluse Olorunnipa, Franco Ordonez, Steven Portnoy, Vivian Salama, Debra Saunders, Darlene Superville, Mineko Tokito, Karen Travers, and many others.

Kudos to the White House press secretaries, their deputies, the wranglers, numerous assistants to the president, campaign staffers, the White House travel office, the stenographers, the Secret Service protective detail agents, *Air Force One* and helicopter crews, motorcade drivers, and West Wing custodians. They all helped us do our job and, in some cases, kept us out of harm's way.

Mentors at different stages of my career: Rachel Ambrose and Myron Belkind, who spent their careers with AP, Myram Borders of UPI,

Bill Buckmaster and the late Ned Day. Alan Heil and Jennifer Janin, who were VOA colleagues, and the late John Lewis of CNN, as well as Hank Tester, Jeffrey Trimble, and Liz Vlaming.

Also in the media, those supportive during challenging times: Oliver Darcy, Paul Farhi, David Folkenflik, Brad Friedman, Mark Knoller, and Brian Stelter. Others who through their generous time and hard work supported VOA's mission and our editorial independence: Lee Crain, Sharon Papp, Raeka Safai, David Seide, and Mark Zaid.

Trusted friends in academia who have worked in or deeply understand media: Bernard Hibbitts, Balbina Hwang, Terril Yue Jones, Shahan Mufti, Desiree Simons, Kevin Z. Smith, and Doualy Xaykaothao.

Crucial help and advice with research, remembering names, or navigating the publishing world: The Authors Guild, the Library of Congress, the staff of my local branches of the Central Rappahannock Regional Library in Virginia, the University of Texas–Arlington Library Special Collections, the Sixth Floor Museum in Dallas, the JFK Presidential Library in Boston, the LBJ Presidential Library in Austin, Christy Burton and John Glionna in Las Vegas, Brian Gruber on Koh Phangan in Thailand, and Takeshi "Go" Kawasaki in Tokyo. Jill Swenson, who read early drafts of the manuscript and guided me toward finding the right publisher.

At the final stage at Kent State University Press: Clara Totten, Susan Wadsworth-Booth, Julia Wiesenberg, and Mary Young skillfully helmed the transformation of the manuscript into this book. I am also indebted to Valerie Ahwee for her professional copyediting and Darryl Crosby for the excellent bookplates.

SELECTED BIBLIOGRAPHY

Achenbach, Joel, and Lillian Cunningham. "The Hidden History of Presidential Disease, Sickness and Secrecy." *Washington Post,* Sept. 12, 2016. https://www.washingtonpost.com/news/to-your-health/wp/2016/09/12/the-secret-history-of-presidential-disease-sickness-and-deception/.

Acosta, Jim. *The Enemy of the People: A Dangerous Time to Tell the Truth in America.* New York: Harper, 2019.

Alberta, Tim. *American Carnage: On the Front Lines of the Republican Civil War and the Rise of President Trump.* New York: Harper, 2019.

Algeo, Matthew. *The President Is a Sick Man: Wherein the Supposedly Virtuous Grover Cleveland Survives a Secret Surgery at Sea and Vilifies the Courageous Newspaperman Who Dared Expose the Truth.* Reprint, Chicago: Chicago Review Press, 2012.

Allsop, Jon. "Trump, Michael Pack and the Complicated Role of Voice of America." *Columbia Journalism Review,* June 17, 2020. https://www.cjr.org/the_media_today/trump_michael_pack_voice_of_america.php.

American Oversight. "In the Records: Internal Turmoil at the U.S. Agency for Global Media during the Last Year of the Trump Administration." Mar. 10, 2022. https://www.americanoversight.org/in-the-records-internal-turmoil-at-the-u-s-agency-for-global-media-during-the-last-year-of-the-trump-administration.

Anderson, Judith Icke. *William Howard Taft, an Intimate History.* New York: W. W. Norton, 1981.

Associated Press. "Anonymous Sources." https://www.ap.org/about/news-values-and-principles/telling-the-story/anonymous-sources.

———. "China's Virus Pandemic Epicenter Wuhan Ends 76-Day Lockdown." VOA News, Apr. 7, 2020. https://www.voanews.com/a/science-health_coronavirus-outbreak_chinas-virus-pandemic-epicenter-wuhan-ends-76-day-lockdown/6187130.html.

Athey, Amber. *The Snowflakes' Revolt: How Woke Millennials Hijacked American Media.* New York: Bombardier Books, 2023.

Baker, Peter, and Susan Glasser. *The Divider.* New York: Doubleday, 2022.

Banner, James. *Presidential Misconduct: From George Washington to Today.* New York: New Press, 2019.

Baragona, Justin. "Gadfly Reporter Throws White House Presser into Chaos with Over-the-Top Tantrum." *Daily Beast,* Mar. 20, 2023. https://www.the

dailybeast.com/gadfly-reporter-simon-ateba-throws-white-house-presser-into-chaos-with-over-the-top-tantrum.

Berg, Scott. *Wilson.* Waterville, ME: G. P. Putnam's Sons, 2013.

Berry, Joseph. *John F. Kennedy and the Media: The First Television President.* Lanham, MD: Univ. Press of America, 1987.

Bluey, Rob. "As White House Limits Access to Press Briefings, Daily Signal Reporter Loses Credentials." *Daily Signal,* July 18, 2023. https://www.dailysig nal.com/2023/07/18/biden-boots-daily-signal-reporter-from-white-house -press-briefings/.

Boburg, Shawn, Emma Brown, and Ann E. Marimow. "Influential Activist Leonard Leo Helped Fund Media Campaign Lionizing Clarence Thomas." *Washington Post,* July 20, 2023. https://www.washingtonpost.com/investiga tions/2023/07/20/leonard-leo-clarence-thomas-paoletta/.

Bolton, John. *The Room Where It Happened.* New York: Simon & Schuster, 2020.

Bornet, Vaughn Davis. *The Presidency of Lyndon B. Johnson.* Lawrence: Univ. Press of Kansas, 1984.

Brandeis, Louis D. *Other People's Money and How the Bankers Use It.* New York: Stokes, 1914.

Brayman, Harold. *The President Speaks Off-the-Record.* Princeton, NJ: Dow Jones Books, 1976.

Brody, Richard. *Assessing the President: The Media, Elite Opinion, and Public Support.* Stanford, CA: Stanford Univ. Press, 1992.

Bublé, Courtney. "Trump's Global Media CEO Abused Authority and Wasted Funds, Review Finds." *Government Executive,* May 15, 2023. https://www .govexec.com/oversight/2023/05/trumps-global-media-ceo-abused-auth ority-and-wasted-funds-review-finds/386361/.

Bulla, David, and Gregory Borchard. *Journalism in the Civil War Era (Mediating American History).* New York: Peter Lang Inc., International Academic Publishers, 2010.

Calderone, Michael. "Bezos Blackmail—Abramson Fallout—'Surreal Week' in Richmond." *Morning Media,* Politico, Feb. 8, 2019. https://www.politico.com/ media/newsletters/morning-media/2019/02/08/bezos-blackmail-abramson -fallout-surreal-week-in-richmond-001734/.

Callaghan, Peter. "What We Know about Trump's Time in Minnesota before Testing Positive for Coronavirus." MinnPost, Oct. 2, 2020. https://www.minn post.com/national/2020/10/what-we-know-about-trumps-time-in-minnesota -before-testing-positive-for-coronavirus/.

Caralle, Katelyn. "Sinkhole Forms on White House North Lawn." *Washington Examiner,* May 22, 2018. https://www.washingtonexaminer.com/news/sink hole-forms-on-white-house-north-lawn.

Caro, Robert. *The Passage of Power: The Years of Lyndon Johnson.* Vol. 4. New York: Vintage, 2013.

Cohen, Michael. *Disloyal—a Memoir: The True Story of the Former Personal Attorney to President Donald J. Trump.* New York: W. W. Norton, 2020.

Columbia Journalism Review. "The Reporters' Story: A Roundtable of Journalists at JFK's Assassination." *Columbia Journalism Review* (Winter 1963): 6–17.

Condon, George E., Jr. "When Presidents Play Golf." *Atlantic,* June 18, 2011. https://www.theatlantic.com/politics/archive/2011/06/when-presidents-play -golf/240645/.

Cox, Peter, Brian Bakst, and Mark Zdechlik. "Where Trump Went and Who He Met in Minnesota Ahead of Testing Positive for COVID-19." *MPR News,* Oct. 2, 2020. https://www.mprnews.org/story/2020/10/02/where-trump-went-and -who-he-met-in-minnesota-ahead-of-testing-positive-for-covid19.

Cull, Nicholas J. *The Cold War and the United States Information Agency: American Propaganda and Public Diplomacy, 1945–1989.* Cambridge: Cambridge Univ. Press, 2008.

Cumming, William. "'Keep Your Voice Down': Trump Has Another Confron- tation with a Reporter at Coronavirus Briefing." *USA Today,* Apr. 20, 2020. https://www.usatoday.com/story/news/politics/2020/04/20/trump-con fronts-reporter-weijia-jiang-coronavirus-briefing/5163639002/.

Dallek, Robert. *An Unfinished Life: John F. Kennedy, 1917–1963.* New York: Back Bay Books, 2004.

Darcy, Oliver, and Jim Acosta. "White House Correspondents Association Re- moves Far-Right Outlet from Briefing Room Rotation." CNN, Apr. 1, 2020. https://www.cnn.com/2020/04/01/media/oan-far-right-personality-corona virus-briefing/index.html.

Davidson, Jonathan R. T., Kathryn M. Connor, and Marvin Swartz. "Mental Illness in U.S. Presidents between 1776 and 1974: A Review of Biographical Sources." *Journal of Nervous and Mental Disease* 194, no. 1 (Jan. 2006): 47–51. https://journals.lww.com/jonmd/Abstract/2006/01000/Mental_Illness_In _U_S__Presidents_Between_1776_and.9.aspx.

Davis, Sid. Interview by the author, Feb. 24, 2023, Bethesda, MD.

De Luce, Dan. "Trump Pick to Run Voice of America, Other U.S. Global Media Accused of Carrying out 'Purge.'" *NBC News,* Aug. 13, 2020. https://www .nbcnews.com/news/world/trump-pick-run-voice-america-other-u-s-global -media-n1236669.

Dickson, EJ. "Journalist Yamiche Alcindor on 'Bringing the Hard Truth to Amer- ica.'" *Rolling Stone,* Feb. 22, 2021. https://www.rollingstone.com/culture/cul ture-features/yamiche-alcindor-pbs-donald-trump-1127664/.

Donaldson, Sam. *Hold on, Mr. President.* New York: Ballantine, 1988.

Dutt, Ela. "Oddball NRI in Bush Media Team." IANS via *Hindustan Times,* Mar. 1, 2006. https://www.hindustantimes.com/india/oddball-nri-in-bush-media -team/story-GokdEMypfCVekmTpkFLm90.html.

Easdale, Roderick. "When a Gunman Took Hostages at Augusta National." *Golf Monthly,* Mar. 6, 2016. https://www.golfmonthly.com/features/the-game/ when-a-gunman-took-hostages-at-augusta-national-88200.

Editorial Board. "How a Trump Appointee Tried to Destroy Voice of America." *Washington Post,* June 7, 2023. https://www.washingtonpost.com/opinions /2023/06/07/voa-agm-whistleblowers-michael-pack/.

Edwards, Erika, and Vaughn Hillyard. "Man Dies after Taking Chloroquine in an Attempt to Prevent Coronavirus." *NBC News,* Mar. 23, 2020. https://

www.nbcnews.com/health/health-news/man-dies-after-ingesting-chloro
quine-attempt-prevent-coronavirus-n1167166.

Emery, Michael, and Edwin Emery. *The Press and America: An Interpretive History of the Mass Media.* Englewood Cliffs, NJ: Prentice-Hall, 1988.

Eveleth, Rose. "Peruse the Weird Medical History of Every Single U.S. President." *Smithsonian Magazine,* Dec. 12, 2013. https://www.smithsonianmag
.com/smart-news/peruse-the-weird-medical-history-of-every-single-us
-president-180948143/.

Farhi, Paul. "Judge Slaps down Trump Appointee Who Has Sought to Reshape Voice of America and Related Agencies." *Washington Post,* Nov. 21, 2020.
https://www.washingtonpost.com/lifestyle/media/judge-slaps-down-trump
-appointee-who-has-sought-to-reshape-voice-of-america-and-related
-agencies/2020/11/21/125d285a-2baa-11eb-92b7-6ef17b3fe3b4_story.html.

———. "A 'Strange and Eerie Time' for White House Reporters—and a Risky One, Too." *Washington Post,* Mar. 20, 2020. https://www.washingtonpost.
com/lifestyle/media/a-strange-and-eerie-time-for-white-house-reporters-
-and-a-risky-one-too/2020/03/19/fdc514e2-6990-11ea-abef-020f086a3fab_
story.html.

Farnsworth, Stephen J. *Presidential Communication and Character: White House News Management from Clinton and Cable to Twitter and Trump.* New York: Routledge, 2018.

The Federalist Staff. "How Michael Pack Is Draining the Swamp and Rooting out Bias in Taxpayer Journalism." *Federalist,* Aug. 27, 2020. https://thefederal
ist.com/2020/08/27/why-public-broadcasting-drifted-left-and-what-can-be
-done-to-fix-it/.

Feldstein, Mark. "The Nixon White House Plotted to Assassinate a Journalist 50 Years Ago." *Washington Post,* Mar. 25, 2022. https://www.washingtonpost
.com/history/2022/03/25/nixon-jack-anderson-assassination/.

Ferling, John. *Adams vs. Jefferson: The Tumultuous Election of 1800 (Pivotal Moments in American History).* New York: Oxford Univ. Press, 2005.

Fitzgerald, Brendan. "White House 'Skype Seats' Offer Fodder for Local Journalists." *Columbia Journalism Review,* Feb. 2, 2017. https://www.cjr.org/politics
/skype_seats_white_house_spicer.php.

Flegenheimer, Matt. "What Does Off the Record Really Mean?" *New York Times,* Aug. 2, 2018. https://www.nytimes.com/2018/08/02/reader-center/off-the-
record-meaning.html.

Fleischer, Ari. *Taking Heat: The President, the Press, and My Years in the White House.* New York: William Morrow, 2005.

Folkenflik, David. "Federal Inquiry Details Abuses of Power by Trump's CEO over Voice of America." NPR.org, May 21, 2023. https://www.npr.org/2023
/05/21/1177208862/usagm-michael-pack-voa-voice-of-america-investigation
-trump-abuse-of-power.

———. "VOA White House Reporter Investigated for Anti-Trump Bias by Political Appointees." NPR.org, Oct. 10, 2020. www.npr.org/2020/10/04
/919266194/political-aides-investigate-voa-white-house-reporter-for-anti
-trump-bias.

Friedman, Stanton T., and Don Berliner. *Crash at Corona: The Definitive Study of the Roswell Incident.* Boston: Da Capo Press, 1997.

Fuchs, James R. "Robert B. Landry Oral History Interview." Harry S. Truman Library, Feb. 28, 1974. https://www.trumanlibrary.gov/library/oral-histories/landryr.

Funabashi, Yōichi. *Meltdown: Inside the Fukushima Nuclear Crisis.* Washington, DC: Brookings Institution Press, 2021.

Garrett, Major. *Mr. Trump's Wild Ride: The Thrills, Chills, Screams and Occasional Blackouts of an Extraordinary Presidency.* New York: All Points Books, 2018.

Gibbs, Nancy, and Michael Duffy. *The Presidents Club: Inside the World's Most Exclusive Fraternity.* New York: Simon & Schuster, 2012.

Gold, Hadas. "Fox News Radio Correspondent Confronts Gateway Pundit Reporter in White House Briefing Room." Politico. https://www.politico.com/blogs/on-media/2017/03/fox-news-radio-correspondent-gateway-pundit-writer-235942.

Goldberg, Nicholas. "Column: One Last Opinion." *Los Angeles Times,* June 30, 2023. https://www.latimes.com/opinion/story/2023-06-30/final-column-nick-goldberg.

Good, Timothy. *Above Top Secret: The Worldwide UFO Coverup.* New York: William Morrow & Co., 1988.

Goodwin, Doris Kearns. *The Bully Pulpit: Theodore Roosevelt, William Howard Taft, and the Golden Age of Journalism.* New York: Simon & Schuster, 2013.

Gramer, Robbie. "Trump Taps Bannon Ally for Top Broadcasting Job." *Foreign Policy,* June 4, 2018. https://foreignpolicy.com/2018/06/04/trump-taps-bannon-ally-for-top-broadcasting-job-michael-pack-broadcasting-board-of-governors-voice-of-america-radio-free-europe-asia/.

Greene, John Robert. *The Presidency of George W. Bush.* American Presidency Series. Lawrence: Univ. Press of Kansas, 2021.

Grisar, P. J. "Bernie Sanders Made a Documentary on Socialist Leader Eugene V. Debs and It's the Most Bernie Sanders Thing Ever." *Forward,* Feb. 27, 2020. https://forward.com/culture/440601/bernie-sanders-made-a-documentary-on-socialist-leader-eugene-v-debs-and/.

Grisham, Stephanie. *I'll Take Your Questions Now: What I Saw at the Trump White House.* New York: Harper, 2021.

Grossman, Michael Baruch. *Portraying the President: The White House and the News Media.* Baltimore: Johns Hopkins Univ. Press, 1981.

Group W (the Westinghouse Broadcasting Co.) audio tapes, 0492-MMC. Special Collections and University Archives. https://hdl.handle.net/1903.1/43884.

Gude, Gilbert. "Presidents and the Potomac." *White House History* no. 2 (June 1997): 86.

Haberman, Maggie. *Confidence Man: The Making of Donald Trump and the Breaking of America.* New York: Penguin Press, 2022.

Hansler, Jennifer. "Former Talk Radio Host Who Pushed Conspiracy Theories Hired by US Global Media Agency." *CNN Business,* Aug. 14, 2020. https://www.cnn.com/2020/08/14/media/frank-wuco-usagm/index.html.

Harper, Robert. *Lincoln and the Press.* New York: McGraw-Hill, 1951.

Hayden, Craig. "Scope, Mechanism, and Outcome: Arguing Soft Power in the Context of Public Diplomacy." *Journal of International Relations and Development* 20 (2017): 331–57. https://doi.org/10.1057/jird.2015.8.

Heil, Alan, Jr. *Voice of America.* New York: Columbia Univ. Press, 2003.

Herman, Steve. "COVID-19 Diaries: Where Have All the White House Reporters Gone?" *VOA,* Apr. 22, 2020. https://www.voanews.com/a/covid-19-pandemic_covid-19-diaries_covid-19-diaries-where-have-all-white-house -reporters-gone/6187996.html.

———. "Little Time to Relax for Reporters on Air Force One." *VOA,* May 1, 2017. https://www.voanews.com/a/little-time-to-relax-for-reporters-on-air -force-one/3832655.html.

———. "The Many Challenges of Questioning President Trump." *VOA,* Mar. 15, 2020. https://www.voanews.com/a/usa_us-politics_many-challenges -questioning-president-trump/6185821.html.

———. "Reporters Surprised When Another Plane Spotted Close to Air Force One." *VOA,* Apr. 10, 2017. https://www.voanews.com/a/reporters-suprised -when-another-plane-spotted-near-air-force-one/3803639.html.

———. "Spicer: White House Press Briefings 'Absolutely' Should Resume." *VOA,* June 17, 2019. www.voanews.com/a/usa_us-politics_spicer-white -house-press-briefings-absolutely-should-resume/6170189.html.

———. "Trump Escalates Culture War." *VOA,* July 7, 2020. https://www.voanews .com/a/usa_us-politics_trump-escalates-culture-war/6192323.html.

———. "Trump Lectures NATO Leaders on Insufficient Defense Spending." *VOA,* May 25, 2017. https://www.voanews.com/a/trump-lectures-nato-leaders-on-insufficient-defense-spending/3870893.html.

———. "Trump, Saudi King Sign Defense Deals Worth Hundreds of Billions of Dollars." *VOA,* May 19, 2017. https://www.voanews.com/a/trump-to-meet -dozens-of-muslim-leaders-leaders-during-saudi-visit/3862443.html.

———. "Trump to Sign New Coronavirus Aid Package Friday." *VOA,* Apr. 23, 2020. https://www.voanews.com/a/covid-19-pandemic_trump-sign-new -coronavirus-aid-package-friday/6188115.html.

———. "White House Condemns Judge's Decision Halting Travel Ban." *VOA,* Oct. 19, 2017. https://www.voanews.com/a/whtie-house-travel-ban-/4075742 .html.

———. "White House Reporters Prefer Sunlight to Spotlight." *VOA,* Mar. 14, 2017. www.voanews.com/a/white-house-reporters-sunlight-/3765865.html.

Herman, Steven L. "Alien Visitation: The Ultimate Trip." *Tokyo Weekender,* Apr. 16, 1999.

Hill, Clint, and Lisa McCubbin. *Five Days in November.* New York: Gallery Books, 2013.

Hill, Fiona. *There Is Nothing for You Here: Finding Opportunity in the 21st Century.* Boston: Mariner Books, 2022.

Hoffman, Gil, and Ariel Whitman. "Netanyahu Orders Reluctant Israeli Ministers to Greet Trump at Airport." *Jerusalem Post,* May 21, 2017. https://www .jpost.com/Israel-News/Politics-And-Diplomacy/Netanyahu-orders-reluc tant-ministers-to-greet-Trump-upon-arrival-in-Israel-492402.

Holzer, Harold. *The Presidents vs. the Press: The Endless Battle between the White House and the Media—from the Founding Fathers to Fake News.* New York: Dutton, 2020.

Hornshaw, Phil. "'SNL': Watch Melissa McCarthy's Sean Spicer Hit White House Press with Podium (Video)." *Wrap,* Feb. 4, 2017. https://www.thewrap.com/snl-watch-melissa-mccarthy-sean-spicer-podium/.

Iskikoff, Michael. *Uncovering Clinton: A Reporter's Story.* New York: Three Rivers Press, 1999.

Itkowitz, Colby. "Pelosi Treated Trump Like a Misbehaving Teenager Last Night. Just Ask Her Daughter." *Washington Post,* Feb. 6, 2019. https://www.washingtonpost.com/politics/2019/02/06/pelosi-treated-trump-like-misbehaving-teenager-last-night-just-ask-her-daughter/.

Jacobs, James. "The President, the Press and Proximity." *White House History* no. 37 (Spring 2015): 4–22.

Johns, Larry C., and Alan R. Johns. *The Baneberry Disaster: A Generation of Atomic Fallout.* Reno: Univ. of Nevada Press, 2017.

Johnson, Ted. "New White House Briefing Room Seating Chart Unveiled: Who's in and Who's Out." *Deadline,* Dec. 17, 2021. https://deadline.com/2021/12/new-white-house-briefing-room-seating-chart-unveiled-1234898893/.

Jurey, Philomena. *A Basement Seat to History: Tales of Covering Presidents Nixon, Ford, Carter and Reagan for the Voice of America.* Washington, DC: Linus Press, 1995.

Kakutani, Michiko. *The Death of Truth: Notes on Falsehood in the Age of Trump.* New York: Tim Duggan Books, 2018.

Kalb, Marvin. *One Scandalous Story: Clinton, Lewinsky and Thirteen Days That Tarnished American Journalism.* New York: Free Press, 2001.

Kallina, Edward, Jr. *Kennedy V. Nixon: The Presidential Election of 1960.* Gainesville: Univ. Press of Florida, 2010.

Kaplan, Fred. "Obama's Other Secret War." *Slate,* May 20, 2013. https://slate.com/news-and-politics/2013/05/james-rosen-named-a-co-conspirator-why-is-barack-obamas-justice-department-going-after-a-national-security-reporter.html.

Karanth, Sanjana. "Trump Won't Answer CNN Reporter's Question about His False Coronavirus Comments." *HuffPost,* Mar. 12, 2020. https://www.huffpost.com/entry/trump-coronavirus-cnn-jim-acosta_n_5e695b4fc5b6dda30fc2b55c.

Karl, Jonathan. *Betrayal: The Final Act of the Trump Show.* New York: Dutton, 2022.

Kelly, John. "In the 1880s, D.C.'s Doctors Argued about Malaria and Its Cause." *Washington Post,* Aug. 6, 2022. https://www.washingtonpost.com/dc-md-va/2022/08/06/history-of-malaria/.

Kinsley, Michael. "The Decline of the Racist Insult." *Atlantic,* Jan. 2010. https://www.theatlantic.com/magazine/archive/2010/01/the-decline-of-the-racist-insult/307871/.

Klein, Woody. *All the Presidents' Spokesmen: Spinning the News—White House Press Secretaries from Franklin D. Roosevelt to George W. Bush.* Westport, CT: Praeger, 2008.

Knappen, Theodore M. "Baruch Finds Prosperity Is Here to Stay." *New York Tribune,* Nov. 15, 1918. https://www.loc.gov/resource/sn83030214/1918-11-15/ed-1/?r=-0.055,-0.033,0.821,0.644,0.

Knudson, Jerry. *Jefferson and the Press: Crucible of Liberty.* Columbia: Univ. of South Carolina Press, 2006.

Kumar, Martha Joynt. "The Kennedy White House and the Press." Heritage Lecture Series. Washington, DC: US State Department, May 16, 2011. https://www.whitehousehistory.org/presidential-press-conferences.

Lajka, Arijeta. "Video of Biden with Reporters Was Not Digitally Altered." Associated Press, Mar. 17, 2021. https://apnews.com/article/fact-checking-afs:Content:9982884730.

Lambre, Jerry. "Political Appointees Conducted 'Confidential' Investigation into Top Voice of America Journalist over Alleged Anti-Trump Bias." *Law & Crime,* Oct. 5, 2020. https://lawandcrime.com/high-profile/political-appointees-conducted-confidential-investigation-into-top-voice-of-america-journalist-over-alleged-anti-trump-bias/.

Lee, Matthew. "Trump Global Broadcasting Chief Quits amid Voice of America Staff Revolt." Associated Press (via *Baltimore Sun*), Jan. 20, 2021. https://www.baltimoresun.com/news/nation-world/ct-nw-voice-of-america-chief-resigns-20210120-6xq6zwk5d5drplphladelvqo6y-story.html.

Leibovich, Mark. *Thank You for Your Servitude: Donald Trump's Washington and the Price of Submission.* New York: Penguin Press, 2022.

Lelyveld, Joseph. *His Final Battle: The Last Months of Franklin Roosevelt.* New York: Knopf, 2016.

Leonnig, Carol, and Philip Rucker. *I Alone Can Fix It: Donald J. Trump's Catastrophic Final Year.* New York: Penguin Press, 2021.

Levin, Linda Lotridge. *The Making of FDR: The Story of Stephen T. Early, America's First Modern Press Secretary.* Amherst, NY: Prometheus Books, 2008.

Liebovich, Louis. *The Press and the Modern Presidency: Myths and Mindsets from Kennedy to Election 2000.* Westport, CT: Praeger, 2001.

Light, Larry. "The Long Feud between Trump and an Arrested Saudi Prince." *CBS News,* Nov. 7, 2017. https://www.cbsnews.com/news/trump-prince-alwaleed-long-feud/.

Long, Colleen. "President Biden Has Started Using a CPAP Machine at Night to Deal with Sleep Apnea." Associated Press, June 28, 2023. https://apnews.com/article/biden-cpap-sleep-apnea-66a3af21b1410e72e0ad74b2b146db63.

Loughran, Trish. *The Republic in Print: Print Culture in the Age of U.S. Nation Building, 1770–1870.* New York: Columbia Univ. Press, 2009.

Lyman, Brianna. "Exclusive: WHCA Advised Biden Admin on New Rules Governing Press Passes." *Daily Caller,* May 11, 2023. https://dailycaller.com/2023/05/11/whca-advised-biden-admin-new-rules-potentially-ban-journalists/.

Mackey, Robert. "Republican Operative in Press Corps Helps Trump Use Briefing on Pandemic to Attack Critics." *The Intercept,* Mar. 19, 2020. https://theintercept.com/2020/03/19/republican-operative-press-corps-helps-trump-use-briefing-pandemic-attack-critics/.

Mahdawi Arwa. "Michael Pack: The Bannon Ally Critics Fear Will Become Trump's Global Propagandist." *Guardian,* June 6, 2018. https://www.theguard ian.com/media/2018/jun/06/michael-pack-steve-bannon-ally-broadcasting -board-of-governors.

Mailer, Norman. "The Search for Carter." *New York Times,* Sept. 26, 1976, SM15.

Marcus, Josh. "White House Warns Reporter Who Yells over Colleagues about His Behaviour." *Independent,* July 13, 2023. https://www.independent.co.uk /news/world/americas/us-politics/white-house-simon-ateba-warning-b237 4334.html.

Marimow, Ann E. "A Rare Peek into a Justice Department Leak Probe." *Washington Post,* May 19, 2013. https://www.washingtonpost.com/local/a-rare -peek-into-a-justice-department-leak-probe/2013/05/19/0bc473de-be5e -11e2-97d4-a479289a31f9_story.html.

Martin, Jeffrey. "Pence Demands Apology from Reporter Who Tweeted VP's Requirements for Journalists to Wear Surgical Masks to Mayo Clinic." *Newsweek,* Apr. 30, 2020. https://www.newsweek.com/pence-demands-apology -reporter-who-tweeted-vps-requirement-journalists-wear-surgical-masks -1501353.

McAdoo, Eleanor Wilson. *The Woodrow Wilson.* New York: Macmillan, 1937.

McClellan, Scott. *What Happened: Inside the Bush White House and Washington's Culture of Deception.* New York: Public Affairs, 2008.

McClendon, Sarah. *Mr. President, Mr. President! My Fifty Years of Covering the White House.* Los Angeles: General Publishing Group, 1996.

Meadows, Mark. *The Chief's Chief.* St. Petersburg, FL: All Season's Press, 2021.

Milbank, Dana. "Wrapping up Tough Questions with Foil." *Washington Post,* Jan. 22, 2002, A13. https://www.washingtonpost.com/wp-dyn/articles/ A15642-2002Jan21.html.

Miller, Michael. "Nixon Had an Enemies List. Now So Does Trump." *Washington Post,* Aug. 19, 2018. https://www.washingtonpost.com/news/retropolis/ wp/2018/08/17/nixon-had-an-enemies-list-now-so-does-trump/.

Morrissey, Brian. "Media's Less Glamorous Future: Bobbing on an Ocean of Crap." *The Rebooting,* June 8, 2023. https://www.therebooting.com/p/medias -less-glamorous-future.

Myers, Dee Dee. *Why Women Should Rule the World.* New York: Harper Perennial, 2009.

Nelson, Steven. "White House Unveils New Press Badge Restrictions, Rules for Access." *New York Post,* May 5, 2023. https://nypost.com/2023/05/05/ white-house-unveils-new-press-badge-restrictions-rules-for-access/.

Nelson, W. Dale. *Who Speaks for the President? The White House Press Secretary from Cleveland to Clinton.* Syracuse, NY: Syracuse Univ. Press, 1998.

Nieman Report. "President Trump, Michael Pack, and the Future of Voice of America." Oct. 19, 2020. https://niemanreports.org/articles/president -trump-michael-pack-and-the-future-of-voice-of-america/.

Noah, Timothy. "Earl Butz: History's Victim: How the Gears of Racial Progress Tore up Nixon's Agriculture Secretary." *Slate,* Feb. 4, 2008. https://slate.com /news-and-politics/2008/02/earl-butz-history-s-victim.html.

Noonan, Peggy. *What I Saw at the Revolution: A Political Life in the Reagan Era.* New York: Random House, 1990.

Obama, Barack. *A Promised Land.* New York: Crown, 2020.

Papenfuss, Mary "Reporter Who Tweeted about Face-Mask Fiasco Says He Was Banned from Future Pence Trips." *HuffPost,* May 1, 2020. www.huffpost .com/entry/mike-pence-steve-herman-voa-face-mask_n_5eab9795c5b62da 419efoa2d.

Pasley, Jeffrey. *The Tyranny of Printers: Newspaper Politics in the Early American Republic.* Charlottesville: Univ. of Virginia Press, 2002.

Perino, Dana. *And the Good News Is . . . : Lessons and Advice from the Bright Side.* New York: Twelve, 2015.

Pollard, James. *The Presidents and the Press: Truman to Johnson.* Washington, DC: Public Affairs, 1964.

Pomar, Mark. *Cold War Radio: The Russian Broadcasts of the Voice of America and Radio Free Europe/Radio Liberty.* Lincoln, NE: Potomac Books, 2022.

Pompeo, Mike. *Never Give an Inch: Fighting for the America I Love.* New York: Broadside Books, 2023.

Powell, Jody. *The Other Side of the Story: Why the News Is Often Wrong, Unsupportable, and Unfair—an Insider's View by a Former Presidential Press Secretary.* New York: William Morrow, 1986.

Ramspott, Larry. *The Baneberry Vent: A Geologist Remembers.* Discovery Bay, CA: Actaea Press, 2010.

Robinson, Eugene S. "The Earl Butz End of a 'Joke.'" *Ozy,* Feb. 11, 2018. https:// www.ozy.com/true-and-stories/the-earl-butz-end-of-a-joke/83773/.

Rosenwald, Michael S. "A President Has Never Been Indicted Before. But One Was Arrested." *Washington Post,* Mar. 30, 2023. https://www.washington post.com/history/2023/03/21/president-arrested-ulysses-grant-speeding/.

Ross, Irwin. *The Loneliest Campaign: The Truman Victory of 1948.* New York: New American Library, 1968.

Rubin, Richard L. *Press, Party and the Presidency.* New York: W. W. Norton, 1981.

Rubino, Kathryn. "Biglaw Firm's Work for the Trump Administration." *Above the Law,* Mar. 5, 2021. https://abovethelaw.com/2021/03/biglaw-firms-work -for-the-trump-administration/.

Rumsfeld, Donald. *Rumsfeld's Rules: Leadership Lessons in Business, Politics, War and Life.* New York: Broadside Books, 2013.

Samuels, Brett. "WHCA Rearranges Seats in Briefing Room to Increase Social Distancing." *Hill,* Mar. 16, 2020. https://thehill.com/homenews/media/487 754-whca-rearranges-seats-in-briefing-room-to-increase-social-distancing/.

Sanders, Sarah Huckabee. *Speaking for Myself: Faith, Freedom, and the Fight of Our Lives inside the Trump White House.* New York: St. Martin's Press, 2020.

Savage, Charlie. "Appeals Court Blocks White House from Suspending Reporter's Press Pass." *New York Times,* June 5, 2020. https://www.nytimes .com/2020/06/05/us/politics/brian-karem-press-pass-white-house.html.

Saxbe, William B. *I've Seen the Elephant: An Autobiography.* Kent, OH: Kent State Univ. Press, 2000.

Schmidt, Michael. *Donald Trump v. the United States: Inside the Struggle to Stop a President.* New York: Random House, 2020.

Simon, John Y. *The Papers of Ulysses S. Grant.* https://scholarsjunction.msstate.edu/usg-volumes/28/.

Sims, Cliff. *Team of Vipers: My 500 Extraordinary Days in the Trump White House.* New York: Thomas Dunne Books, 2019.

Smith, Curt. *The Presidents and the Pastime: The History of Baseball and the White House.* Lincoln: Univ. of Nebraska Press, 2018.

Smith, Richard Norton. *An Uncommon Man: The Triumph of Herbert Hoover.* New York: Simon & Schuster, 1984.

Sommer, Will. "Gateway Pundit Drops White House Reporter after He Went on White Nationalist Podcast. *Daily Beast.* https://www.thedailybeast.com/gateway-pundit-dumps-lucian-wintrich-after-he-went-on-white-nationalist-podcast.

Spicer, Sean. *The Briefing: Politics, the Press, and the President.* Washington, DC: Regnery Publishing, 2018.

Stengel, Richard. *Information Wars: How We Lost the Global Battle against Disinformation and What We Can Do about It.* New York: Atlantic Monthly Press, 2019.

Stevens, Elisabeth. "1918 Flu Killed Millions." *Washington Post,* Oct. 24, 1965, M6.

Tangel, Andrew. "Delays in Boeing's New Air Force One Causes Costs to Pile up for Shareholders, Taxpayers." *Wall Street Journal,* Nov. 3, 2022. https://www.wsj.com/articles/delays-in-boeings-new-air-force-one-cause-costs-to-pile-up-for-shareholders-taxpayers-11667475082.

Tebbel, John, and Sarah Miles Watts. *The Press and the Presidency: From George Washington to Ronald Reagan.* New York: Oxford Univ. Press, 1985.

Tomlin, Gregory M. *Murrow's Cold War: Public Diplomacy for the Kennedy Administration.* Lincoln, NE: Potomac Books, 2016.

Tracy, Phil. "The Shame of Being Left off Nixon's Enemies List." *Village Voice,* July 5, 1973. https://www.villagevoice.com/2019/03/25/the-shame-of-being-left-off-nixons-enemies-list/.

Tur, Katy. *Unbelievable: My Front-Row Sea to the Craziest Campaign in American History.* New York: Dey St., 2017.

US Agency for Global Media. "VOA Charter." www.usagm.gov/who-we-are/oversight/legislation/voa-charter/.

US House of Representatives Select Committee to Investigate the January 6th Attack on the US Capitol. Deposition of Judson P. Deere. https://january6th.house.gov/sites/democrats.january6th.house.gov/files/20220303_Judson%20P.%20Deere.pdf.

Verma, Pranshu. "How an AI-Written Star Wars Story Created Chaos at Gizmodo." *Washington Post,* July 8, 2023. https://www.washingtonpost.com/technology/2023/07/08/gizmodo-ai-errors-star-wars/.

———. "Trump Appointee Is Turning Voice of America into Partisan Outlet, Lawsuit Says." *New York Times,* Oct. 8, 2020. https://www.nytimes.com/2020/10/08/us/politics/trump-voice-of-america.html.

Viguerie, Richard A., and David Franke. *America's Right Turn: How Conservatives Used New and Alternative Media to Take Power.* Chicago: Bonus Books, 2004.

Wead, Doug. *Game of Thorns: The Inside Story of Hillary Clinton's Failed Campaign and Donald Trump's Winning Strategy.* London: Biteback Publishing, 2017.

White House Historical Association. "The Press at the White House: 1933–1941." Washington, DC: WHHA. www.whitehousehistory.org/the-press-at-the -white-house-1933-1941.

Wicker, Tom. "Johnson Won't Run." *New York Times,* Apr. 1, 1968, 1.

William, Elliot. "The Forgotten Epidemic: A Century Ago, DC Lost Nearly 3,000 Residents to Influenza." *Washingtonian,* Oct. 31, 2018. https://www.washing tonian.com/2018/10/31/the-forgotten-epidemic-a-century-ago-dc-lost-nearly -3000-residents-to-influenza/.

Williamson, Elizabeth. "White House Mounts Heated Attack on U.S. Government Media Voice." *New York Times,* Apr. 10, 2020. https://www.nytimes .com/2020/04/10/us/politics/white-house-voice-of-america.html/.

Wolfe, Michael. *Fire and Fury: Inside the Trump White House.* New York: Henry Holt, 2018.

Woodward, Bob. *Rage.* New York: Simon & Schuster, 2020.

Woodward, Bob, and Robert Costa. *Peril.* New York: Simon & Schuster, 2021.

Wright, Kate, Martin Scott, and Mel Bunce. *Capturing News, Capturing Democracy: Trump and the Voice of America.* Oxford: Oxford Univ. Press, 2023.

———. "Soft Power, Hard News: How Journalists at State-Funded Transnational Media Legitimize Their Work." *The International Journal of Press/Politics* 25, no. 4 (May 2020). https://journals.sagepub.com/doi/full/10.1177/194 0161220922832.

INDEX

Page numbers in *italics* refer to photographs.

ABC (American Broadcasting Company): on Clinton-Lewinsky scandal, 130; presidential press relations, 126, 132; Stephanopoulos's career with, 131; Trump's criticism of, 81; Trump's golf photos tweeted by, 100; White House press corps rank of, 23

Access Hollywood audio recording, 26, 143

Acheson, Dean, 117

Acosta, Jim, 42, 197

Adams, John, 134, 158–59

Adams, John Quincy, 159

Affordable Care Act, 134

Agence France Presse (AFP), 82, 95, 96

Agency for Global Media. *See* US Agency for Global Media (USAGM)

Air Force (US) and Roswell incident, 59–63

Air Force One: on day of Kennedy's assassination, 92; Israel–Saudi Arabia travel, first trips by, 36, 37; press corps travel by, 27–34; recording prohibitions, 18; tweeted locations of, 194

Air Force Two, 28, 30, 165, 167–70

Akerson, George, 112–13

Alcindor, Yamiche, 42

Alhurra TV, 169

Alien and Sedition Acts (1798), 158–60

Alwaleed bin-Talal (prince of Saudi Arabia), 35

American Daily Advertiser (gazette), 158

American Press Institute, 207

American Society of Newspaper Editors, 119

Ananias Club, 109

Anderson, Jack, 189

Angelo, Bonnie, 123–24

appointment pass, 105

The Apprentice (TV show), 102

Area 51, 57

Arthur, Chester, 151

al-Assad, Bashar, 17

Associated Press (AP): Associated Press Television, 168; on Biden conspiracy theory, 203; and Daniszewski, 176; and health reports about presidents, 151; Herman's work for, 46; NORC Center for Public Affairs Research, 207; and off-the-record statements, 139; presidential press relations, 108, 115, 122; press briefings, 9, 12; on reporters' clothing, 144; VOA's subscription to, 96; and VOA/USAGM controversy, 185; White House press corps rank of, 23, 29

Ateba, Simon, 156–57

Atomic Energy Commission (AEC), 52–53

AT&T, 25

Aurora (newspaper), 158, 159

Axios (website), 102

Bache, Benjamin, 159

background vs. off-the-record comments, 25–26

Baker, Frank, 48

Baker, Peter, 134

Baldwin, Hanson, 118

balloon story and Roswell incident, 60–63

Baneberry nuclear test, 54–55

Bannon, Steve, 171

"barber's hour," 109

Barrett, Amy Coney, 149

Bartlett, Dan, 100

Baruch, Bernard, 139

A Basement Seat to History (Jurey), 5

BBC (British Broadcasting Corporation), 26, 115, 203
Beebe, Florence, 51
Bennett, Amanda, 169, 173, 187
Bennett, Charles, 48
Berger, J. M., 82
Bergman, Ingrid, 54
Bernstein, Carl, 123
Berra, Yogi, 145
Biberaj, Elez, 176, 177, 179, 186
bicycles, Secret Service training on, 87
Biden, Joe: on Capitol insurrection (Jan. 6, 2021), 162; conspiracy theory about, 203; on Electoral Count Reform Act (2022), 163; first official trip abroad, 35; flight from Israel to Saudi Arabia by, 37; golfing by, 97; health of, 154-55; inauguration of, 196, 197; Pompeo on, 187; presidential campaign (2020), 150, 154; presidential press relations, 8, 9, 11-12, 131, 132; and Secret Service on ground transportation, 88; Trump on, 40; on trust fund for nuclear testing victims, 55-56; on USAGM, 181, 184
Bierbauer, Charles, 43
Bierman, Noah, 43, 44
Birx, Deborah, 39
Blanchard, William, 60
Bloomberg, 20, 23, 100, 140, 149
BlueSky (social media site), 21
Boeing, 29-32
Boghosian, Joyce, 100
Boone, Pat, 142
Bornstein, Harold, 153
Boston Globe, 138
Boutrous, Ted, Jr., 9
Boyer, Charles, 54
Brack, Dennis, 100
Brady, James, 126
Brandeis, Louis, 12
Brayman, Harold, 139
Brazell, Mac, 60, 61
Breckinridge, John, 162
Breitbart radio, 82
Brennan, John, 179
Briskman, Juli, 95-96
Broadcasting Board of Governors (BBG), 170, 187. See also US Agency for Global Media (USAGM)
Bruen, Brett, 168
Bryan, William Jennings, 110
Buckmaster, Bill, 50, 53, 54, 190

Bunce, Mel, 188
Bush, Billy, 26
Bush, George H. W.: first official trip abroad, 35; golfing by, 98-99; health of, 153; presidential press relations, 127-28, 137; as vice president, Las Vegas visit, 50
Bush, George W.: first official trip abroad, 35; golfing by, 98-99; management style, 103; presidential press relations, 100, 105, 132-33; on UFOs, 58
Bush, Mia, 96
Butt, Archie, 109
Butz, Earl, 142-43

Caddell, Pat, 82
Cadillac One (The Beast), 86
Callender, Thomas, 159-60
Capitol insurrection (Jan. 6, 2021), 101, 162-64, 184
Capturing News, Capturing Democracy (Wright, Scott, and Bunce), 178-79, 188
Cardin, Ben, 193-94
Carney, Jay, 135
Caro, Robert, 92
Carter, Billy, 124
Carter, Jimmy: first official trip abroad, 35; golfing by, 97; New York Times Magazine interview, 26; presidential election of, 49; presidential press relations, 5, 124-25; on UFOs, 58
Carville, James, 129
CBS (Columbia Broadcasting System): on Clinton-Lewinsky scandal, 130; Evening News, 45; presidential press relations, 137; and Schorr, 81; and White House photo releases, 100; White House press corps rank of, 23
Celebrity Apprentice (TV show), 193
Centers for Disease Control and Prevention (CDC), 38, 169
Central Press Bureau plans, 115
Chao, Kelu, 179, 187
Chase, Chevy, 124
ChatGPT, 206
Cheney, Dick, 132
Chicago Tribune, 116
China: and Falun Gong, 105-6; Xi's Mar-a-Lago visit, 17
Christian, George, 121
Churchill, Winston, 118
CIA (Central Intelligence Agency), 138, 176

Civil Rights Act (1964), 98
Claypoole, David, 158
Cleveland, Grover, 107, 139, 151, 198
climate change, Trump on, 18–19
Clinton, Bill: first official trip abroad, 35; golfing by, 98; management style, 103; presidential press relations, 124, 128–33; on UFOs, 58
The Closing of the Muslim Mind (Reilly), 186
Clymer, Adam, 132
CNET, 206
CNN (Cable News Network), 176; presidential criticism of media, 81; Trump's criticism of, 170; Trump's responses to questions by, 42, 43; White House press corps rank of, 23
Coast to Coast AM, 57
Collins, Susan, 163
Columbia Journalism Review, 100, 131, 134
Columbus Dispatch, 206
Comey, James, 15
Compuserve, 192
Condon, George, 43
Congressional Research Service, 169
Connolly, John, Jr., 89, 90
Connolly, Nellie, 90
The Conqueror (film), 53
Conway, Kellyanne, 102, 149
Coolidge, Calvin, 97, 111–12, 139
Cooper, Thomas, 159
Corona crash site, 62
Cortelyou, George, 107, 151
Coughlin, Charles, 116
courtroom reporting, 141
COVID-19 pandemic, 38–41, 148–50, 165–69
Cox, James, 200
Cronkite, Walter, 45
Crosswell, Harry ("Robert Rusticoat"), 160
Cruz, Ted, 164
C-SPAN (Cable-Satellite Public Affairs Network), 131, 134

Daily Signal (website), 9
Dale, Daniel, 140
Daniels, Stormy, 199
Daniszewski, John, 176
Davis, Elmer, 115
Davis, Martin, 148
Davis, Sid, 89–94
Debs, Eugene, 200
Decker, Jon, 106
Deere, Judd, 101

Defense Biometrics Identification System (DBIDS), 27
Defense Counterintelligence and Security Agency (US Defense Department), 176
DeFrank, Tom, 123
Dennis, Glenn, 61
Detroit News, 123
Dewey, Samuel, 179
Dewey, Thomas, 117
"dialing for dollars" (stringing/freelancing), 60
Digiday, 207
"Dirty Harry" bomb test, 52–53
Dole, Bob, 130
Donaldson, Sam, 126–27
Doocy, Peter, 12, 132
Duane, William, 159
DuBose, Thomas Jefferson, 63
Dukakis, Michael, 131
Duke University, 119
Dunn, Anita, 135

Early, Stephen, 113–14
Earnest, Josh, 135–36, 143
Edison, Thomas, 110, 113
Eisenhower, Dwight, 35, 46, 98, 117, 139, 152
Electoral Count Act (1887), 163
Electoral Count Reform Act (2022), 163
Eliot, Rory, 90
Emanuel, Rahm, 100
"enemies of the people," journalists as, 81–83, 122, 189
Enemy of the People (Kalb), 82
Energy Department, US, 52–54
Engel, Eliot, 172, 173, 187
Epoch Times (Falun Gong newspaper), 105–6
Epstein, Jeffrey, 156
Espionage Act, 200
ethics: of AI, 206; of gifts, 25, 144
Evening Star (Washington, DC), 107
Executive One Foxtrot, 28
"executive time" of presidents, 101–4
extraterrestrials, 57–58, 59–63

Facebook, 179, 192, 201, 204, 205
Face the Nation (CBS), 137
"fake news" (Trump's media criticism), 42–44, 81–84, 137–38, 170, 207
Falun Gong, 105–6
Fang, Bay, 174
Farhi, Paul, 38–39, 171
Farid, Hany, 203

Farrow, Mia, 170–71
Fauci, Anthony, 39
Fauver, Jiggs, 91
FBI (Federal Bureau of Investigation), 118, 122, 127, 189
Federal Communications Commission (FCC), 83
Federal Protective Service, 168
Feldstein, Mark, 189
Fernandez, Alberto, 174
Finland, Trump's and Putin's conference in, 106
1st Airlift Squadron, 29
Fitzwater, Marlin, 127, 128, 153
509th Composite Bomb Group, 59
Flegenheimer, Matt, 140–41
Fleischer, Ari, 132
"floaters," 11
Fly, Jamie, 174
Foley, Roger, 55
Folkenflik, David, 180
Ford, Gerald: and Butz, 143; characterization of, 47, 49; first official trip abroad, 35; golfing by, 98; presidential press relations, 5, 123–24
Foreign Information Service, 115
Forth (social media site), 21
Fort Worth Star-Telegram, 63
Fosse, Ray, 48
Foster, Vince, 130
Fox News: Pence and mask controversy, 166; presidential press relations, 106, 132, 133, 135, 137; Trump's preference for, 44, 84, 102; White House press briefings, 12; White House press corps rank of, 23
Franklin, Benjamin, 159
Frazin, Rachel, 100
freelancing by journalists (stringing, "dialing for dollars"), 60
Friedman, Stanton, 62–63
Front Row at the White House (Thomas), 129
Frost, Robert, 94
Fukushima earthquake: deaths, damage, and hardships from, 67–74, 77–80; earthquake events, 64–66; financial cost of, 66; Fukushima Nuclear Power Plant, 67–70, 71–76, 78–80, 102; Japanese government response to, 69, 72, 80; radiation exposure from, 74–77; VOA exhibit of, 76

"gaggles," 18, 29
"gaslighting," 54
Gergen, David, 131
Gibbs, Robert, 135
Gibson Dunn (law firm), 156, 179
Gidley, Hogan, 145–46, 147
"giggle chorus," 114
Gizmodo Bot, 206
Glass, Jackie, 53
Glenn, John, 47
Glionna, John, 79
Goldberg, Nicholas, 208
Goldwater, Barry, 89, 154–55
golfing by presidents, 97–100
Gorka, Sebastian, 156
Government Accountability Project (GAP), 181, 186
Goyal, Raghubir, 143
Grant, Ulysses, 151, 199
Grayson, Cary, 151
Gray TV, presidential press relations, 106
Greer, Bill, 90
Gridiron Club, 139
Grisham, Stephanie, 10, 37, 103, 141, 153–54, 156
Groom Lake facility, 57
Ground Force One, 87
ground transportation: for presidents, 85–88; for vice president, 90
Guelzo, Allen, 161, 162

Hagedorn, Jim, 166
Hahn, Stephen, 166
Halberstam, David, 118
Halfback (Queen Mary), 90
Hamilton, Alexander, 40, 157, 160
Hanks, Tom, 103
Harding, Warren, 97, 111, 112, 151–52, 200
"hard pass," 5, 9
Haut, Walter, 59–60, 61
health of presidents: concealment of, 150–54; and COVID pandemic, 38–41, 148–50; mental health of presidents, 119, 154–55
Hearst, William Randolph, 116
Hearst News Services, 115, 129
Heinlein, Peter, 5, 184
Hemings, Sally, 160
Hendler, Clint, 100
Heritage Foundation, 9
Herman, Steven L, *5, 28, 76, 146, 191; Air Force Two* travel ban of, 167–70; early

Herman, Steven L (*cont.*)
    career of, 46, 51–53; early interest in
    presidents, 45–49; freelance work by,
    60, 64; Japan assignment of, 64–80;
    Seoul assignment of, 15, 64–67; Twitter
    use and *Air Force One* incident, 145–47;
    Twitter use/suspension, 190–95; and
    USAGM controversy, 2, 3, 169, 178–79;
    VOA hiring of, 64; White House as-
    signment of, 3–4
Hicks, Hope, 149, 150
The Hill (Washington, DC), 100
Holland, Steve, 23, 197
Holzer, Harold, 134, 161, 162, 163
Hoover, Herbert, 97, 112–13, 114
House Foreign Affairs Committee (US
    Congress), 186
Houseman, John, 115
Howell, Beryl, 179–80
Huber, Oscar, 91
Huff, Aubrey, 203
Hughes, Howard, 53
Hughes, Sarah, 92
Hu Jintao, 105–6
Humphrey, Hubert, 46
Hussein, Saddam, 132
Husseini, Sam, 106

I'll Take Your Questions Now (Grisham), 10
India: Taj Mahal, *191;* terror attack (2008),
    192
India Globe, 143–44
Ingraham, Laura, 166
Institute for Public Accuracy, 106
Intercept news organization, 178
Internal Revenue Service (IRS), 189
International Broadcasting Act (1994), 182
International News Service, 118, 121
International UFO Museum and Research
    Center, 59
iPhone, 204
Israel: Saudi Arabia trips by *Air Force One,*
    36, 37; Trump's official visit to (2017), 37

Jackson, Andrew, 159
Jackson, David, 54
Jackson, Ronny, 153
Jacobs, Jennifer, 23, 149
Japan, earthquake in. *See* Fukushima
    earthquake
Japan Meteorological Agency, 65
Jean-Pierre, Karine, 9, 12, 131

Jefferson, Thomas, 40, 157–60
Jerreat, Jessica, 176
Johnson, Boris, 44
Johnson, Lady Bird, 90, 93, 119
Johnson, Lyndon: *Air Force One* and press
    corps, 29; characterization of, 47, 48,
    119, 147; first official trip abroad, 35;
    golfing by, 98; and Kennedy's assassi-
    nation, 90–93; off-the-record remarks
    by, 25, 26; presidential press relations,
    83, 118, 119–21, 126, 134; and Secret Ser-
    vice on ground transportation, 87
Johnson, Walter, 48
Joint Base Andrews (Maryland), 27
Jones, Alex, 204
journalism business: and artificial intelli-
    gence (AI), 205–6; changing nature of,
    204–5; and confirmation bias, 203–4;
    digital environment of, 201; as "ene-
    mies of the people," 81–83, 122, 189;
    and ethics of gifts, 25, 144; "fake news"
    accusations against, 42–44, 81–84,
    137–38, 170, 207; as gatekeepers of
    information, 204, 208; journalistic in-
    tegrity, 206–8; media/news literacy of
    audience, 202, 205; and social media
    influence, 20–22, 201–3; spy accusa-
    tions against, 176; stringing ("dialing
    for dollars"), 60. *See also* media tech-
    nology; pool reporting; presidential
    press relations; White House press
    corps; *and individual names of journal-
    ists; individual names of media outlets*
Jurey, Philomena, 5
Justice Department, US, 134, 180, 181

Kalb, Marvin, 82, 189
Kan, Naoto, 69, 72
Kansas City Star, 116
Karem, Brian, 156–57
Kellerman, Roy, 90
Kelly, John, 103, 140
Kennedy, Jacqueline, 89–93
Kennedy, Joe, 118
Kennedy, John Fitzgerald: assassina-
    tion of, 87, 89–94; characterization
    of, 46–47; Clinton in audience of, 128;
    first official trip abroad, 35; golfing by,
    98; health of, 152; and off-the-record
    statements, 139; presidential press re-
    lations, 117–19; *Profiles in Courage,* 118;
    and Salinger, 118–20

Kennedy, Robert, 92, 121
Kerry, John, 5, 26, 132
Kilduff, Malcolm, 91, 92
Kim Jong Un, 10, 34, 84, 106, 145
Kimmel, Jimmy, 166
Kirby, John, 12, 131
KLAS-TV (Las Vegas), 57
Kligerman, David, 174
Knapp, George, 57
Knappen, Theodore M., 139
Knox, Olivier, 85, 100
Koizumi, Junichiro, 80
Kono, Taro, 69
Koriyama Municipal Gymnasium, 74
KORK AM (Las Vegas), 53–55
KTBC AM/FM/TV (Austin), 119
Kumar, Martha Joynt, 139

Lahey, Frank, 152
Lamont, Daniel, 151
Landry, Robert B., 61
Lanier, Cathy, 199
Lansing, John, 175
Las Vegas: author's early career in, 51–53; Nevada Test Site, 51–56, 57, 68
Leno, Jay, 88
Letterman, David, 193
Lewinsky, Monica, 129, 130, 131
Life (magazine), 152
Limbaugh, Rush, 99
Lincoln, Abraham, 134, 151, 161
Llamas, Lloyd, 87
Lockhart, Joe, 40, 131–32
Lopez, Yolanda, 187
Los Angeles Times, 43, 79, 116, 208
Lucas, Fred, 9

Madison, James, 158
Mailer, Norman, 26
Making Gay Okay (Reilly), 186
Malinowski, Tom, 81
Manchin, Joe, 171
Mao Zedong, 82
Mar-a-Lago, 17, 81
Marine One helicopter, 7, 13–14, 21–22
Marion Star (OH), 111
Marković, Dūsko, 35
mask controversy, and Pence, 165–68
Mastodon (social media site), 21, 194, 195
Mayo Clinic, 165–68
McCarthy, Joseph, 117
McCarthy, Melissa, 11

McClellan, Scott, 132–33
McClurkin, Brenda, 63
McCurry, Mike, 131–32
McEnany, Kayleigh, 149–50, 166
McGuire Woods law firm, 181
McKinley, William, 97, 107, 151
McLaughlin, Ann, 127
McMurray, Julia, 86
Meadows, Mark, 149, 150
media criticism by presidents. *See* presidential press relations
Media Insight Project, 207
media technology: *Air Force One* recording prohibitions, 18; digital environment of, 201; vs. "pen-and-pad" sessions, 141–42; recording of audio, 13–19; recording protocol for still photographers, 13–15; reporters' evolving use of, 108, 109-13, 117
Menendez, Robert, 171, 174
mental health of presidents, 119, 154-55
Merkley, Jeff, 175
Metzenbaum, Howard, 47
Meyer, Jane, 144
Middle East Broadcasting Networks, 169, 174
Miller, Katie, 167
Miller, Stephen, 167
Miller, Zeke, 23, 185–86
Mills, Doug, 23–24
mimeograph, 113
Minneapolis Tribune, 112
Mitchell, Andrea, 170
Miyazawa, Kiichi, 128
Mogul project, 60
Moon Jae-in, 15
Morley, Michael, 163
Morrissey, Brian, 207
motorcycles, Secret Service training on, 87
Moyers, Bill, 121
MSNBC, 12
MTV, 129
Mulvaney, Mick, 145, 146
Munakata, Takeshi, 71–72
Murach, Thomas, 86, 88
Murdoch, Rupert, 137
Musk, Elon, 21, 193–94, 195
Myers, Dee Dee, 124, 129, 130–31

The Nation (magazine), 106
National Christmas Tree lighting event (2018), 85

National Journal, 43
National Park Service, 21
National Press Club, 139
National Task Force on Election Crises, 163
Naughton, James, 122
Navy, US, 111
NBC (National Broadcasting Company): *NBC News,* 81, 170, 189; presidential press relations, 123, 124, 130, 135; *Saturday Night Live,* 11, 124; and White House photo releases, 100; White House press corps rank of, 23
Nessen, Ron, 123–24
Netanyahu, Benjamin, 37
Nevada Test Site, 52–56, 57, 68
Newhouse, Barry, 33
Newsmax cable channel, 44
newsreels, 112–13
Newsweek (magazine), 121–23
New York Sun, 108
New York Times: on Briskman's (middle) finger gesture to Trump, 95; and health reports about presidents, 154; and Nixon, 189; and off-the-record statements, 140; presidential press relations, 118, 122, 132, 134, 135, 137; still photography by, 23–24; Trump's "fake news" accusation against, 81; and White House photo releases, 100
New York Times Magazine, 26
New York Tribune, 139
NHK (Japan Broadcasting Corporation), 66
Nixon, Richard: characterization of, 47, 48–49; "enemies list" of, 83, 122, 189; first official trip abroad, 35; golfing by, 98; presidential press relations, 5, 121–23, 124, 126
Nogar, August, 54
North Korea: and Fox News correspondent, 135; Kim Jong Un, 10, 34, 84, 106, 145
NPR (National Public Radio): digital adaptation of, 201; on Fukushima earthquake, 70; and pool reporting, 18; presidential press relations, 129; and Schorr, 83; on USAGM controversy, 178, 180
nuclear reactor. *See* Fukushima earthquake
nuclear testing, Las Vegas area, 51–56, 57, 68
Nunamaker, William, 55

Obama, Barack: conspiracy theories about, 179; first official trip abroad, 35;

golfing by, 99; management style, 103; off-the-record remarks by, 25; presidential press relations, 42, 108, 132–36, 137, 138; press conference tone of, 143; press staff of, 11; and Secret Service on ground transportation, 85, 87; on UFOs, 58; and White House photo releases, 100
Office of Censorship, US, 115
Office of Cuba Broadcasting, 169
Office of the Inspector General (OIG), 174, 175, 181–82, 186
Office of Personnel Management, US (OPM), 176
Office of Special Counsel, US (OSC), 180–83, 186
Office of War Information (OWI), 115
off the record: vs. background comments, 25–26; vs. "on the record," 139–44
One America News Network (OANN), 39
Open Technology Fund, 181, 182
Operation Cresset, 54
Operation Upshot-Knothole, 52
Orenstein, Mitchell, 81, 82
Ortiz, Tito, 203
Oval Office: pool reporting in, 13–19; reporters' access to, 5, 108, 121–22; and White House layout, 7. *See also* White House layout

Pack, Michael, 170, 171–72, 173–77, 178–83, 186–87
Palmer, Arnold, 98
Pan American World Airways, 94
Panetta, Leon, 130, 131
Paramount Newsreel Company, 113
"partial lid," 17
PBS Newshour, 42
"Pebble Beach," 7
Pelosi, Christine, 24
Pelosi, Nancy, 23–24, 179, 184
"pen-and-pad" sessions, 141–42
Pence, Karen, 165, 166
Pence, Mike: *Air Force Two* and press corps, 30; and Biden's inauguration, 197; and Capitol insurrection, 163, 184, 198; and COVID mask controversy, 165–68; and COVID press briefings, 39; and presidential press relations, 137; and Trump's health, 154
Perino, Dana, 133
Pew Charitable Trust, 207

phonographic recordings, 109-10
Pierpoint, Robert, 90
Playboy (magazine), 156
Player, Gary, 98
Poe, Edgar Allen, 208
Political Breakdown (podcast), 131
Pompeo, Mike, 184-86
pool reporting: camaraderie of, 20; earliest use of, 114; "gaggles," 18, 29; media
accompaniment to presidential motorcade, 85-88; in Oval Office, 13-19;
"partial lid," 17; pool duty, 7-8; pool
sprays, 43-44; social media component of, 20-22; traveling with president, 24-26, 148-50
post.news (social media site), 21, 194
Powell, Jody, 113, 124-25
Powers, Shawn, 175
presidential press relations, 105-36; Carter, 124-25, 126; Clinton, 124, 128-32;
Coolidge, 111-12; "enemies of the people," journalists as, 81-83, 122, 189; and
evolving media technology, 108, 109-
10, 111, 112, 117; "fake news" (Trump's
media criticism), 42-44, 81-84, 137-38,
170, 207; Ford, 123-24; Franklin Roosevelt, 113-16; George H. W. Bush, 127-
28; George W. Bush, 132-33; Harding,
111; Hoover, 112-13; incidents involving, 105-6; Johnson, 119-21; Kennedy,
117-19, 128; Nixon, 121-23, 124; Obama,
133-36; press questions about controversial issues, 156-60; Reagan, 125-27;
Taft, 109-10; Theodore Roosevelt, 108-
9; Truman, 116-17; White House access
to president, 5, 5-12, 105-8, 121-22;
Wilson, 110-11. *See also individual names
of US presidents*
Presidential Protective Division of the US
Secret Service (PPD), 15, 27
presidents: "executive time" of, 101-4;
golfing by, 97-100; health of, 38-41,
148-55. *See also* presidential press relations; transportation of presidents;
and individual names of US presidents
The President Speaks Off-the-Record (Bray-
men), 139
"President Trump Criticizes VOA Coverage of China's COVID-19 Response"
(Congressional Research Service), 169
press relations. *See* presidential press relations

press secretaries: Biden administration,
8, 11-12; first female press secretary,
123-24, 130-31; Trump administra-
tion, 8-12. *See also* presidential press
relations; *and individual names of press
secretaries*
Price, Ned, 102
Price, William "Fatty," 107, 108
Proctor, Loretta, 60
Profiles in Courage (Kennedy), 118
Psaki, Jen, 11-12
Public Broadcasting Service (PBS), 38, 42
Public Law 94-350 (1976), 2
Pulliam, Eugene, 119
Putin, Vladimir, 15, 84, 106
Putzel, Michael, 144

Queen Mary (*Halfback*), 90

Radiation Exposure Compensation Act
(1990), 55
radio: *Air Force One* recordings by radio
pool, 29; Harding's use of, 111; recording of audio, 13-19; World War Two
use by government, 115. *See also* Her-
man, Steven L
Radio Free Asia (RFA), 169, 174, 176, 177,
187-88
Radio Free Europe/Radio Liberty (RFE/
RL), 169, 170, 174, 176, 187-88
Radio Sawa, 169
Radio and TV Marti, 169
Ramey, Roger, 63
Randle, Kevin, 63
Rather, Dan, 189
Reagan, Nancy, 127, 144
Reagan, Ronald: assassination attempt, 8;
first official trip abroad, 35; golfing by,
98; health of, 153; presidential press
relations, 5, 43, 83, 125-27, 128; on re-
porters' clothing, 144
The Rebooting (Morrissey), 207
Reedy, George, 120-21
Regan, Don, 127
Reilly, Robert, 184-87
Reporters Committee for the Freedom of
the Press, 180
Reuters, 20, 23, 96, 100, 203
Richmond Examiner, 159
Richmond Recorder, 160
Rion, Chanel, 39
Risen, James, 134

Robbins, Elizabeth, 185, 186
Roberts, Charles, 121
Roberts, Chuck, 91–92, 93
Roberts, Harley, 55
Roberts, John, 166–67
Rolling Stone (magazine), 130
Romney, Mitt, 87
Roosevelt, Franklin: golfing by, 97; health of, 152; and off-the-record statements, 141; presidential press relations, 83, 113–16; and Secret Service on ground transportation, 87
Roosevelt, Theodore, 42, 108–9, 110, 119
Rose, Pete, 48
Rosen, James, 135
Roswell incident (1947), 58, 59–63
Rowan & Martin's Laugh-In, 124
Rumsfeld, Donald, 139
Rusk, Dean, 119
"Rusticoat, Robert" (Harry Crosswell), 160
Ryack, Paul, 76

Safer, Morley, 83
Salinger, Pierre, 118–20
Salman (king of Saudi Arabia), 36
Sanders, Bernie, 200
Sanders, Sarah Huckabee, 10, 102–3, 143, 144, 145, 146
Saturday Night Live (NBC), 11, 124
Saudi Arabia, Israel trips by *Air Force One,* 35–37
Sawyer, Charles, 151–52
Saxbe, Bill, 47
Scavino, Dan, 168–69
Schiller, Keith, 15
Schmidt, Michael, 154
Schorr, Daniel, 83, 189
Schultz, George, 98
Scott, Martin, 188
Scott, Winfield, 162
Secret Service, 7, 9, 15, 27, 85–88
Sedition Act (1798), 158–60
Seide, David, 181
Sensitive Compartmented Information Facility (SCIF), 142
Sherwood, Robert, 115
Short, Marc, 166, 167
al-Sisi, Abdel Fattah, 17
Sites, Kevin, 202
"1600 Daily" newsletter, 169
Skype seats, press briefings, 10–11

Smialowski, Brendan, 96
Smith, Al, 46
Smith, Merriman, 91–92, 115, 121–22
Snow, Tony, 133
Snyder, Jim, 93
social media reporting, 20–22, 201–3. *See also individual names of social media sites*
Society of Newspaper Editors, 115
Sophocles, 82
Sorensen, Ted, 118
Sorkin, Aaron, 103
South Korea: author's assignment to, 15, 64–67; Moon's White House visit, 15
Speakes, Larry, 113, 126
Spicer, Sean, 10, 11, 34, 138, 143
Spilotro, Tony "the Ant," 141
Spoutible (social media site), 21, 194
Springer, Steve, 180, 182
Stalin, Josef, 81
Stanton, Frank, 83
State Department, US, 72, 117, 173–75, 181–82, 186
State of the Union: evolution of, 112; 2019, 23–24
stenographers, and press coverage, 107, 108
Stephanopoulos, George, 129, 131
Sterling, Jeffrey, 134
Stevenson, Adlai Ewing, 151
St. George (Utah), nuclear testing near, 62–63
still photographers: *Air Force One* protocol, 29; and Franklin Roosevelt's health, 152; recording protocol, 13–15; State of the Union (2019) photo of Pelosi, 23–24; and Theodore Roosevelt's press relations, 108; White House photographer's role, 100
St. Louis Post-Dispatch, 189
stringing ("dialing for dollars"), 60
Substack Notes (social media site), 21, 202
Sugawara, Sandy, 173
Sulzberger, A. G., 140
Sunbury and Northumberland Gazette (PA), 159
Supreme Court, US, Barrett's nomination, 149
Swindal, Jim, 92
Syria, Trump on military action in, 17–18

Taft, Robert, 45, 46
Taft, William Howard, 45, 48, 97, 109–10
Taj Mahal, *191*

Tanaka, Keiko, 77–78
Tate, Sheila, 127
Ted Lasso (TV show), 157
Telegram, 201
television, Kennedy's use of, 117–18
TEPCO (Tokyo Electric Power Company), 67–68, 69, 73, 76, 80
terHorst, Jerald, 123
Thomas, Clarence, 172
Thomas, Ginni, 172
Thomas, Helen, 123, 128–29, 144
Thomas Jefferson Foundation, 160
Thompson, Lexi, 99
Threads (social media site), 21
Thunberg, Greta, 18–19
TikTok, 201
Tillerson, Rex, 5
Tillman, Mark, 31
Time (magazine), 19, 122, 123, 135
Tokyo Stock Exchange, 66
Toronto Star, 140
Tracey, Bree, 85
Transaero, 32
Transom nuclear test, 54
transportation of first ladies (by air), 28
transportation of presidents: *Air Force One,* 18, 27–34, 36, 37, 92, 194; ground transportation, 85–88; *Marine One* helicopter, 7, 13–14, 21–22
transportation of vice presidents: *Air Force Two,* 28, 30, 165, 167–70; ground transportation, 90
traveling press. See *Air Force One;* pool reporting
Truman, Harry, 58, 60–61, 97, 116–17
Trump, Donald, Jr., 58
Trump, Donald J.: *Access Hollywood* video, 143; author on coverage of, 154, 188; Briskman's (middle) finger gesture to, 95–96; and Capitol insurrection (Jan. 6, 2021), 101, 161–64, 184, 198; controversial legacy of, 196–98; and COVID press briefings, 38–41; "executive time" of, 101–4; first official trip abroad, 35–37; golfing by, 97, 99; green screen controversy about, 203; health of, 148–50, 153–55; legal troubles of, 198–200; North Korea summit of, 145; off-the-record remarks by, 25–26, 140–41; Oval Office coverage of, 15–19; on Pence and mask controversy, 166; and

Pompeo, 185; presidential campaign (2020), 150, 154; presidential press relations of, 5, 9–12, 42–44, 81–84, 105–6, 115, 120, 126, 137–38, 170, 207; press corps questions of, about controversial issues, 156; press corps remarks by, on *Air Force One,* 29, 32; and Secret Service on ground transportation, 86; "seven-word rule" of, 16, 18; State of the Union (2019), 23–24; Twitter use of, 193; on UFOs, 57–58; vice president running mate choice, 165; on VOA and USAGM, 2, 23, 168–72, 173–77, 178, 183
Trump, Ivanka, 165
Trump, Melania, 28, 36, 37, 196
Tucker, Lem, 189
Turner, Grant, 174–75, 180, 181
Turner v. US Agency for Global Media, 179–80
Twitter, 21, 75, 100, 145–47, 190–95

UFOs, 57–58, 59–63
United Kingdom, "deep background" comments in, 26
United Press International (UPI): and Kennedy's assassination, 91, 92; presidential press relations, 9, 108, 115, 121, 123, 129; White House press briefings, 9. *See also* Thomas, Helen
US Agency for Global Media (USAGM): entities run by, 169; and OIG whistle-blower complaints, 180–83; Pack, Biden's replacement of, 184, 187; Pack, Trump's nomination of, 170–72; Pack's investigation of author (Herman), 2, 3, 169, 178–79; Pack's "Wednesday Night Massacre," 173–77; and Reilly, 184–87; *Turner v. US Agency for Global Media* (2020), 179–80; and Widakuswara's demotion, 184–86
UseNet, 192

Vanocur, Sander, 189
Van Susteren, Greta, 44
Vietnam War, 83
Virginia and Kentucky resolutions, 158–59
Voice of America (VOA): author's hiring by, 64; author's standards-and-practices unit assignment, 188–89; as external media entity, 190; Herman's *Air Force Two* travel ban, 167–70; inception of, 115; as microcosm of global media,

Voice of America (*cont.*)
202; operation and staff of, 3–4; Pack's
(USAGM) investigation of author
(Herman), 2, 3, 169, 178–79; and press
room protocol, 38; principles of, 2;
and White House photo releases, 100;
White House press coverage by, 5, 8,
9, 12; wire services used by, 96. *See
also* Herman, Steven L; US Agency for
Global Media (USAGM)
Voices from America ("Stimmen aus
Amerika"), presidential press relations, 115

Wackenhut Corporation, 55
Wall Street Journal, 130, 144
Walz, Tim, 166
Washington, DC, media presence in, 1. *See
also individual names of media outlets*
Washington, George, 151, 157–58
Washingtonian (magazine), 118
Washington Post: Farhi and COVID press
briefings, 38–39; and Nixon, 189;
Pence and mask controversy, 166;
presidential press relations, 122, 123,
126; on Trump's VOA criticism, 169,
171; on USAGE controversy, 182; and
VOA/USAGM controversy, 187
The Wasp (Hudson, NY), 160
Watergate scandal, 122–24
Wayne, John, 53
West, William, 199
Westerhout, Madeleine, 101
Westinghouse Broadcasting, 89
The West Wing (TV show), 103
What Happened (McClellan), 132–33
WhatsApp, 201
White House Coronavirus Task Force,
39–41
White House Correspondents' Associa-
tion (WHCA): COVID pandemic, 39;
Pence and mask controversy, 167; on
presidential press relations, 122, 137;
and Reagan on media criticism, 83;
and Secret Service on ground trans-
portation, 85; on VOA/USAGM con-
troversy, 185; and White House photo
releases, 99–100; White House press
briefings, 9
White House layout: family kitchen, 22;
media on grounds ("campus") of, 24;

North Lawn sinkhole story (2018), 21;
press access, 5, 5–12, 105–8, 121–22. *See
also* Oval Office
White House News Photographers' Association (WHNPA), 100
White House press conferences: James
Brady Press Briefing Room, 38; protocol and operation of, 5–12, 38, 107–8,
125–26, 134; protocol and ranking, 23;
protocol for seating, 9–11, 38; White
House Press Office, 91–92, 105 (*see also*
presidential press relations); "wranglers," 13, 147. See also *Air Force One;*
pool reporting; press secretaries;
White House press corps
White House press corps: *Air Force One*
travel by, 27–34, 145–47; clothing of,
126, 144; and COVID coverage, 38–41,
148–50, 165–69; first White House
correspondent, 107; "hard pass" of, 5,
9; nature of work, 1–4, 5–12; on presidents' first official trips abroad, 35–37;
press conferences, questions asked by,
5–12, 38, 42–44, 107–8, 125–26, 134. *See
also* pool reporting
Widakuswara, Patsy, 39, 148, 184–86
Will, George, 128
Wilson, Edith, 151
Wilson, Woodrow, 97, 110–11, 134, 151
"wire calls," from *Air Force One,* 33
wire services, reporting by, 20, 23. *See also*
Associated Press (AP); Bloomberg; Reuters; United Press International (UPI)
Wolfson, Paula, 6, 8
Woodward, Bob, 123
working relationships of presidents and
press. *See* presidential press relations
World Economic Forum (Jan. 2020), 18–19
Worldnet, 171
World War Two, radio use by government,
115
"wranglers," 13, 147
Wright, Kate, 188
Wuco, Frank, 179

X. *See* Twitter
Xaykaothao, Doualy, 70, 75
Xi Jinping, 17

Yahoo, 202
Yahoo News, 100

Yamaguchi, Akihiko, 78
Yarborough, Ralph, 89
Yoho, Ted, 82
YouTube, 201
Yucca Flat, 55

Zappa, Frank, 208
Zero Hedge, 202
Ziegler, Ronald, 121, 122

ABOUT THE AUTHOR

Steven L Herman is the chief national correspondent of the Voice of America. He covered the White House for VOA during the Trump administration and the first eight months of the Biden administration. In 2022 Steve was named a Kiplinger Fellow, an Oxford Climate Journalism Network First Cohort, and the JURIST journalist-in-residence at the University of Pittsburgh School of Law. He is also an adjunct assistant professor at Shenandoah University and an adjunct journalism lecturer at the University of Richmond.

Steve previously was posted as a regional bureau chief for VOA in New Delhi, Seoul, and Bangkok before returning to the United States in 2016 as chief diplomatic correspondent. He has traveled to more than 75 countries and territories, including reporting assignments in Afghanistan, Argentina, Bhutan, Burma, China, the Gaza Strip, North Korea, Peru, and Vietnam.

The veteran broadcast journalist, before joining VOA, was a reporter for the Associated Press and a media executive in Asia for the Discovery Channel. He is a former president of the Foreign Correspondents' Club of Japan and the Seoul Foreign Correspondents' Club. The Ohio native began his media career in Las Vegas and currently resides close to the Potomac River on a secluded peninsula in Virginia.